PORTUGAL IN AFRIC

PORTUGAL IN AFRICA

The Last Hundred Years

by
Malyn Newitt

C. HURST & CO., LONDON

First published in the United Kingdom by
C. Hurst & Co. (Publishers) Ltd.,
38 King Street, London WC2E 8JT

© 1981 by Malyn Newitt

ISBN: 978-0-90583-849-6

HURST & COMPANY, LONDON
www.hurstpub.co.uk

Printed and bound in Great Britain by
Marston Book Services Limited, Oxford

CONTENTS

Preface   *page* viii

1. The Portuguese in Africa before 1870   1
   West Africa   1
   Eastern Africa   7
   Did the Portuguese underdevelop Africa?   11
   The abolition of the slave trade   13
   Forward policy of the government 1840–1870   20

2. The International Dimension   24
   The stimulus of the 'Scramble for Africa'   24
   The attempt at bilateral settlements   25
   The aftermath of the Ultimatum   31
   Railways and labour recruitment   33
   The Republic   40
   The New State   43
   Keeping the United Nations at bay   46

3. Resistance and Pacification   49
   What policy options did the Portuguese possess?   49
   African collaboration in the era of pacification   51
   The politics of pacification   54
   Why was unrest endemic in Mozambique?   57
   Why was resistance endemic in Angola?   64
   The pacification of Guiné   68
   Conclusion   70

4. The Rule of the Concession Companies   72
   *The economic relations of Portugal and Africa at the end
   of the nineteenth century*   72
   A modern feudalism   76
   The Mozambique Company   79
   The Niassa Company   83
   The Zambesi prazos   85
   The Moçamedes Company   88
   The development of specialised capital enterprise   89
   Sena Sugar estates   91

		Diamang	92
		Conclusion	93
5.		The African Population under Portuguese Rule, I	94
		The autonomous development of African economies	94
		The re-orientation African trade and production	95
		Portuguese 'native' policy	100
		Land policy	102
		Chiefs	104
		Labour	106
		South African mine labour	112
		Labour within the colonies	115
6.		The African Population under Portuguese Rule, II	121
		The régime of the crop-marketing companies	121
		Mission and mission influence	124
		Syncretist religions and messianism	129
		Wage-earning, towns and the survival of the peasant farmer after 1945	134
		The road to assimilation	138
		The mestiços and the world	142
7.		The White Community in the Portuguese Colonies	148
		Convicts	150
		Free white immigration up to 1940	152
		The whites of Southern Angola	155
		The independent planter class	156
		The white official	160
		White immigration under the New State	163
		Race relations	167
		Representative institutions for the whites	171
8.		Salazar, Africa and the New State	175
		Colonial policies of the Monarchy and the Republic	175
		The rule of the high commissioners	177
		The New State—fact and fiction	180
		The New State in Africa—continuity and change	184
		Economic policy	188
		The colonies after the war	193
		Political adaptation	198
9.		Portugal's Islands	201
		The characteristics of island culture	201
		São Tomé and Principe	204
		The Cape Verde Islands	211

10.	Portugal and the Wars of Independence	219
	Was 1961 the decisive year?	219
	Economic change	220
	The crisis of the New State 1958–1962	221
	The nationalist revolt	225
	The Portuguese military response	228
	The diplomatic struggle	232
	Portuguese policies to develop the colonies during the 1960s	237
	The limits of success	240
	The collapse of the régime	242
	The end in Africa	245
Glossary		248
Bibliographical Guide for English Readers		250
Select Bibliography		254
Index		264

MAPS

Portugal and her African colonies	ix
Angola	ix
Mozambique	x
Portuguese Guiné	x
Mozambique: areas of operation of the concession companies	80
Cape Verde Islands	202

PREFACE

This book is an account of how the Portuguese obtained their African empire, pacified, occupied and attempted to develop it. The issues dealt with include colonial ideology, native policy, administration, contract labour, international relations and the economic links between Portugal and Africa. Although the amount of research done on Portuguese Africa was limited, such a survey seemed possible and appropriate in 1980. The ideological dust of the wars of liberation had begun to settle, making the view of the historical landscape rather clearer, while the publication of a number of excellent monographs, notably those of Clarence-Smith, Pélissier, and Vail and White, to all of whom I am greatly indebted, made a general study a realistic enterprise. Many readers may feel that not enough allowance has been made for the extreme complexity of many of the issues, but I can only say that, while fully aware of this complexity, I feel that there is some virtue in pausing to make a broad survey of the empire before the next generation of research exposes fresh layers of interpretation.

This book was written at the suggestion of Christopher Hurst and owes a very great deal to his help and encouragement. I am also particularly grateful for the help I received from my wife, Joan, and my sister, Hilary, who read and corrected the manuscript, and from Seàn Goddard who drew the maps.

Exeter M.N.
November 1980

PORTUGAL AND HER AFRICAN COLONIES

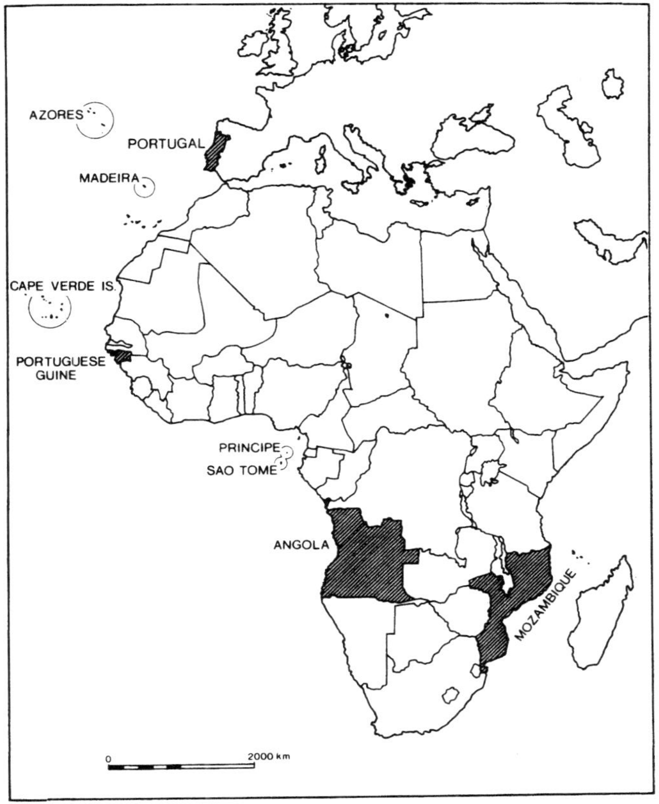

ANGOLA

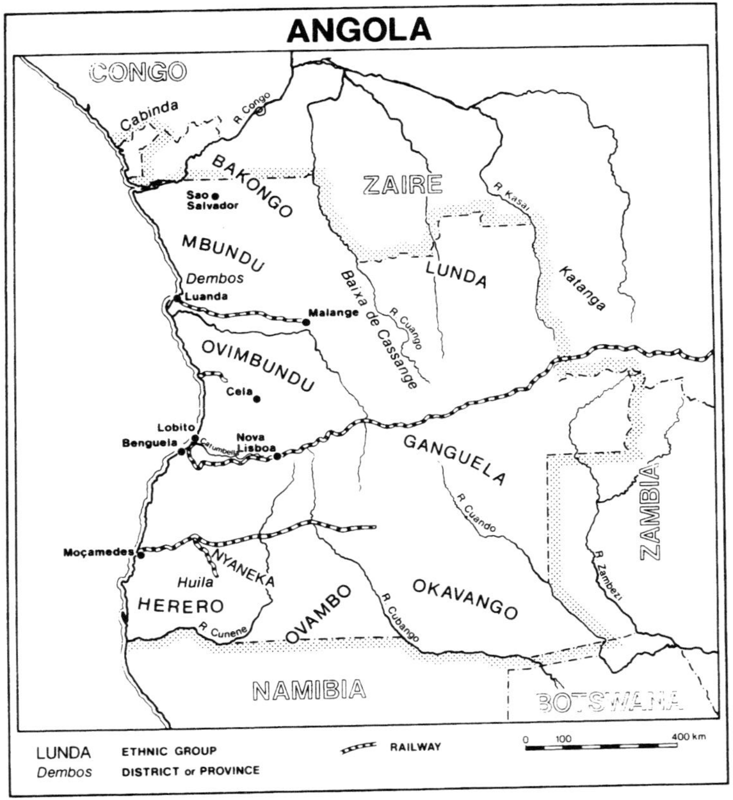

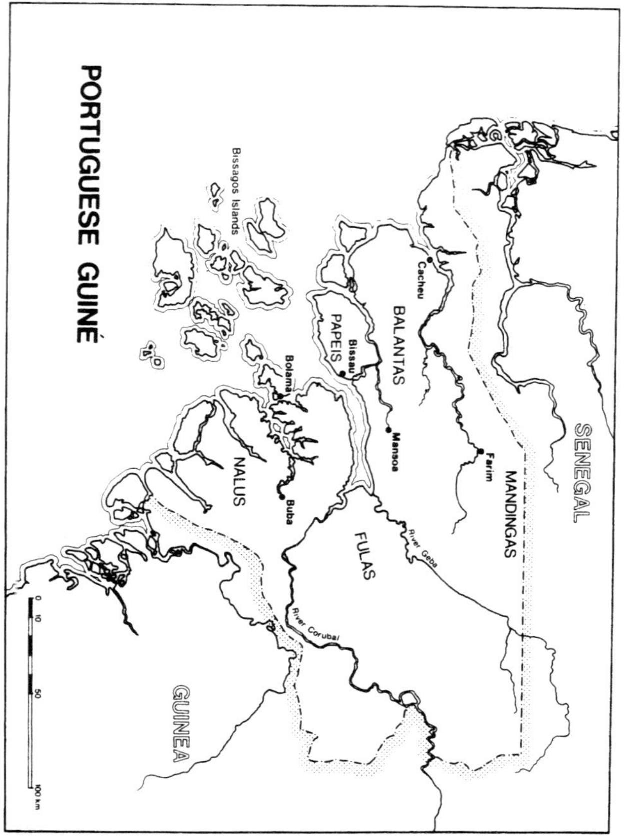
PORTUGUESE GUINÉ
SENEGAL
MANDINGAS
Farim
Cacheu
BALANTAS
Mansoa
River Geba
FULAS
Bissau
PAPEIS
Bolama
Buba
River Corubal
Bissagos Islands
NALUS
GUINEA
0
10
50
100 km

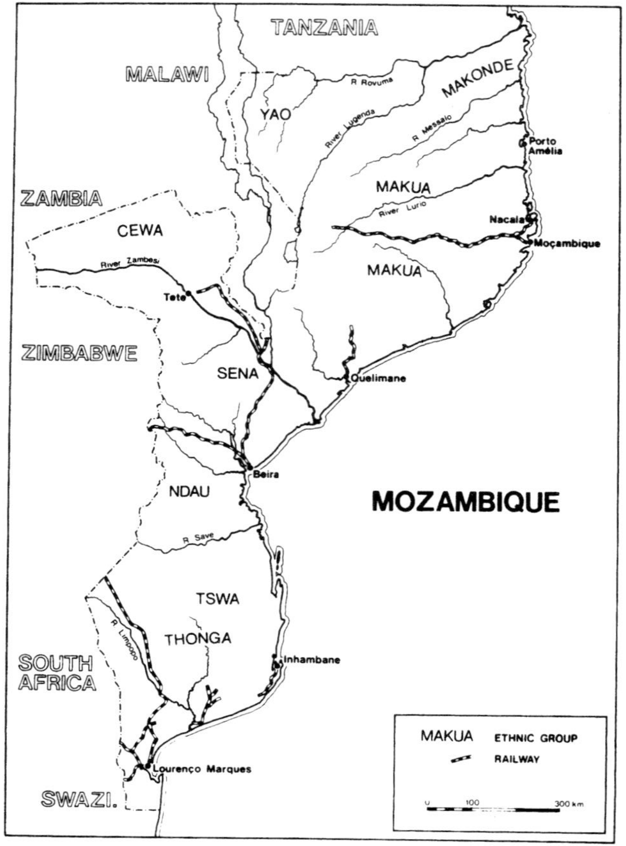
TANZANIA
MALAWI
YAO
R Rovuma
MAKONDE
River Lugenda
R Messalo
Porto Amélia
MAKUA
River Lurio
Nacala
Moçambique
MAKUA
ZAMBIA
CEWA
River Zambesi
Tete
ZIMBABWE
SENA
Quelimane
Beira
NDAU
MOZAMBIQUE
R Save
TSWA
R Limpopo
THONGA
Inhambane
SOUTH AFRICA
Lourenço Marques
SWAZI.
MAKUA ETHNIC GROUP
RAILWAY
0
100
300 km

1
THE PORTUGUESE IN AFRICA BEFORE 1870

West Africa

The Portuguese first made contact with the peoples of sub-Saharan West Africa in 1443. Their principal object was to obtain slaves, gold and other valuable commodities to trade in European markets. After a few initial expeditions in which they raided coastal communities for slaves, they learned to establish relations with coastal chiefs with whose permission and co-operation they traded. This commerce was, from the start, treated as a crown monopoly, even though it was sometimes granted out to others, and the Portuguese monarchs devised a series of policies for maintaining their rights. Treaties were made with accessible African sovereigns like the king of the BaKongo; trading factories were established under the control of a royal factor; an array of legislation controlled the terms under which individuals could participate in West African commerce; and treaties were made with other European states, notably with Castile in 1479, to secure their recognition of Portugal's rights.[1]

However, at the same time that they were establishing a monopolistic trading organisation, the Portuguese were also planting settler colonies. In the 1460s they began the settlement of the Cape Verde Islands and after 1480 the islands of the Gulf of Guinea were also colonised. Various attempts were made to encourage agriculture in the islands and to repeat the success that had been achieved with sugar, wheat and wine in Madeira and the Azores. Sugar did briefly become a profitable crop in São Tomé in the sixteenth century, and cotton was produced in the Cape Verde Islands. The Cape Verdians, indeed, were able to develop a modest industry manufacturing cloth for the West African markets. However, climatic conditions in the islands were extremely hard and from the earliest days of the settlement it was found to be more profitable to trade with mainland Africa. The Cape Verdians crossed to trade in the rivers of upper Guinea, while the men from São Tomé, early in the sixteenth century, founded a trading base on an island off the mainland which was later to be the site of the city of Luanda.[2]

1. Diffie and Winius (see Select Bibliography).
2. Bentley Duncan (1972), chap. 2.

The islanders threatened to destroy the whole concept of the royal trade monopoly. From bases conveniently near to the African coast they were able to evade the royal officials and to penetrate coastal communities, making themselves indispensable to rulers who had no previous experience of European commerce. Initially they may have invested trading capital and provided shipping, but this function was soon taken from them by the extension of the royal monopoly, and they themselves were outlawed by fierce-sounding royal laws decreeing the death penalty for any convicted illicit traders. This in no way inhibited their activities, and during the sixteenth and seventeenth centuries they came to form a class of brokers who organised trading relations between African chiefs and visiting European ships. Their language became the trade language of West Africa and their methods of doing business came to predominate.[3]

These backwoods traders were never a class subservient to the interests of Lisbon's imperialism. The earliest island settlers had sometimes been convicts or exiles and few of them had any expectation of returning to Portugal. They had married African wives and over the generations their families became increasingly Africanised, though they often retained their Portuguese names and other trappings of their European origin which helped to maintain their identity as a group. For the most part these Afro-Portuguese dynasties became separated from their island origins, establishing themselves on the West African mainland and sometimes successfully setting themselves up as chiefs. The São Tomé islanders who had settled at Luanda broke their connections with the island and found their numbers swollen by fresh arrivals from Europe. However, in upper Guinea the Cape Verdians continued active in the mainland trade.

At first Portuguese trade with West Africa was very varied. Gold, pepper, ivory, civet and slaves were taken to Europe, and metalware, some cloth, wheat and horses were brought back.[4] However, the Portuguese also stimulated seaborne commerce between different parts of West Africa, for instance carrying the bark cloth of the Congo for sale in Benin. As late as the end of the sixteenth century Portuguese traders appear to have been as eager to obtain access to local supplies of salt, copper and silver as to indulge in the slave trade. However, by the early seventeenth century slave trading was proving so profitable that few traders bothered to concern themselves with other commodities. The profitability of the slave trade led on the one hand to vigorous attempts by the crown to enforce its monopoly and on the other to the rapid dismantling of this mono-

3. Rodney (1970), chap. 3.
4. Crone (1937).

poly along much of the coast by European rivals.[5]

The moves made by the crown to strengthen its monopoly and establish a formal empire in west central Africa are well known. Military expeditions were sent to dominate the Congo and Angola so that the whole trade of the area would be channelled through Portuguese ports where it could be taxed. However, sixteenth-century administrative resources were not adequate to achieve this goal, and in the seventeenth century the governors of Angola were given the privilege of administering the monopoly in their own interests. They quickly reached an understanding with the Afro-Portuguese backwoods traders and the chiefs of the interior fairs and created the lucrative slave trading system which made Luanda, until the nineteenth century, the greatest slaving port in Africa.[6]

North of the Congo the Portuguese lost most of their slave trading ports to European rivals during the Dutch wars in the seventeenth century and it was only in upper Guinea that they retained control of some coastal factories. Here royal control of the trade proved equally elusive. At first slaves were concentrated at Santiago in the Cape Verde Islands for sale and tax, but the islands were too open to attack by British and Dutch pirates and the trade of Guinea was then granted to a series of monopolistic companies — the two Cacheu Companies in 1676 and 1690 and the Company of Para and Maranhão in 1755. The story of the Cacheu Companies, as indeed the story of Portuguese Guinea as a whole, shows how firm was the control of local traders over the conduct of commerce in Guiné, and it was they who provided the principal share capital. Only in the case of the Maranhão Company was there any significant injection of outside capital and outside control.[7]

From early times the local Afro-Portuguese mulatto community was the dominant force in Portuguese West Africa. Trade was conducted in their interests and they only maintained the royal monopoly when this suited them. Increasingly after 1600 it proved more profitable for them to trade with Dutch, English or French and directly with Brazilians. After the Dutch wars Luanda and Benguella, their islands and the settlement of Cacheu remained on paper the only official Portuguese trading establishments in West Africa, but this grossly under-represents the true nature of the Portuguese presence. Afro-Portuguese brokers continued active in almost every part of the Guinea coast, trading with Dutch or English where there were no Portuguese. Indeed, far into the nineteenth

5. Birmingham (1970).
6. Birmingham (1966); Curtin (1969).
7. Rodney (1970).

century Dutch, English and French trading houses used Portuguese and Afro-Portuguese personnel to conduct trade for them in West Africa.[8]

In spite of strict mercantilist legislation, the Portuguese Atlantic empire never formed a closed 'triangular' system. At every stage it was permeated by other economic interests. Trade goods sent from Europe were, by the end of the eighteenth century, almost entirely non-Portuguese, and much of the shipping too was English or Dutch. Portuguese traders on the coast sold readily to outsiders, while the demands for slaves in Brazil had to be met by importing from other than Portuguese sources. Indeed, early in the eighteenth century the traders of Bahia opened their own slaving establishment at Whydah (Ajuda) on the Dahomey coast and exported their tobacco directly to African markets. By the end of the eighteenth century most of the capital invested in the 'Portuguese' Atlantic slave trade was probably Brazilian or non-Portuguese.[9]

The Portuguese crown was very sensitive to this situation and under the inspiration of the Marques de Pombal made serious moves to nationalise the trade of the colonies. The founding in 1755 of the Company of Para and Maranhão was the most significant move as far as west Africa was concerned, and was aimed at trying to supply Brazil's needs from wholly 'Portuguese' sources and in Portuguese ships.[10] The crown was also aware of the danger that the dominance of foreign capital would lead eventually to direct foreign political control. In the late eighteenth century there were moves to secure Portugal's rights in two of the threatened areas — Bolama, where the British were periodic visitors, and Cabinda.[11] There were also moves to try to establish the economy of Angola on a different footing. A policy, particularly associated with the governor Sousa Coutinho, was actively pursued to encourage plantation crops and a metal industry, while it was hoped that the establishment of a regular administration would increase royal revenues through direct taxation. All these moves were resisted by the traders of the *sertão* (hinterland) who were determined that nothing would interfere with their lucrative commerce in slaves.

In 1800 Portuguese or Cape Verdian trading establishments existed up a number of the Guinea rivers. On the Casamance was Ziguinchor, on the Cacheu they had a port at Farim, and they traded also on the Buba and Geba rivers. These were served by coastal ports

8. Mouser (1973).
9. Verger (1964).
10. Maxwell.
11. Lavradio, pp.35–53; Hammond, pp.47, 54–5.

at Cacheu, Bolama and Bissau among the islands. The trading stations were sited at the highest tidal point of the rivers and slaves were bought there from African traders, the most important of whom were Mandinga. Already, however, Fula chiefs were beginning to bring slaves to the coast, and in the upper Guinea region the slave trade appears to have played a large part in the spread of Islam westward into the forest zone. It also encouraged the westward movement of the peoples of the savannah, who were pressing the original inhabitants of the coastal forests into an ever narrower belt of territory.

In the Bight of Benin 'Portuguese' interests were still represented at the fort of Ajuda (Whydah), although in practice this remained a Brazilian factory, run by local trading families.[12] The islands of São Tomé and Principe were also Portuguese, but at this stage they played no role in the trade of West Africa.

Further south the Portuguese had a station at Cabinda whence they participated, alongside English, Dutch and French, in the trade of the Loango coast. To the ports on this stretch of coast, long-distance caravans manned by the Vili brought up to 20,000 slaves a year. Vili caravans frequently crossed the Congo river and tapped the hinterland of Angola, undercutting the Portuguese trade from Luanda, in particular by bringing firearms which the Luanda authorities would not allow to be traded. By 1800 the value of long-distance trade had seriously undermined the institutions of African government in this region. Slave trading allowed powerful individuals to build up armed followings with which they could defy traditional authorities and levy tolls on commerce. This in turn increased their wealth, while the difficult terrain of the Loango hinterland also favoured a fragmentation of the political systems.[13]

In 1800 the Congo estuary and the area immediately to the south formed a dangerous no man's land. The ancient kingdom of the Manicongo had disintegrated totally during the eighteenth century leaving many centres of power, some little larger than villages. The endless feuding was encouraged by the ready sale which war captives found on the coast. At the same time there had been a notable increase in commercial activity along the coast and in the Congo estuary. Vili traders and Afro-Portuguese found the journey to the Congo coast from the principal slave market at Kasanje shorter, and there was the possibility also of avoiding tolls along the route to Loango and the customs dues levied at Luanda. As the importance of this stretch of coastline grew, it was inevitable that the Portuguese

12. Hammond, pp. 68–71.
13. Martin.

— mindful of their historic connections with the Congo kingdom — would claim the region as their own and attempt to establish permanent stations there.[14]

In 1800, however, Portugal's principal slaving and trading ports were Luanda and Benguela. Dependent on Luanda were the lower reaches of the Cuanza valley whose Mbundu inhabitants owed tribute and carrier service to the Portuguese. Ambitious governors had sought to extend this domain ever since the sixteenth century, believing that prosperity could be found by bringing more chiefdoms under tribute. The interests of the slavers had always prevented such an extension of formal Portuguese control. From settlements on the Cuanza, notably Ambaca, the mulatto traders (*ambaquistas*) organised their caravans for Kasanje, the Imbangala kingdom situated west of the Cuango. The collection of slaves had been concentrated here for many decades, the Imbangala king successfully maintaining a monopolistic barrier between the coast and the Lunda empire of the far interior. Before the nineteenth century the Portuguese did not seriously challenge this system and were content to cultivate relations of mutual advantage with the Imbangala. However, the slave trade was too valuable for it to be confined in this way, and there was always a tendency for Kasanje to be outflanked either to the south or the north; there was also a tendency for unofficial traders to undercut the established caravan system, by-pass the official fair at Kasanje, and conduct trade directly with the lineage heads in the localities. To the north the Portuguese backwoodsmen traded through Matamba into the Kasai region, and to the south traders penetrated the plateau behind Benguela, sometimes attacking, and sometimes trading with the Ovimbundu kingdoms. On the coast the monopoly of Luanda was challenged, as we have seen, by French, British and Dutch buying from the Vili caravans along the Loango coast, and increasingly at ports south of the Congo itself.[15]

In the eighteenth century this trading system seemed to possess a kind of stability contrasting strongly with the disorder and radical political change of the seventeenth and nineteenth centuries. The slave trade, clearly, could have either a strengthening or a weakening effect on African political systems. If a chief could retain control of the trade, tax it to his advantage and impose his authority on caravan leaders, then he could use it to build a stable government with a greater degree of centralisation than was common among central African Bantu states. On the other hand, there was the equal possibility that caravan leaders and minor chiefs would assert their power

14. Martin, p.137.
15. Martin; Miller (1973).

and use slaves bought for trade to swell their own followings. There was no inevitability about either process, and both can be seen affecting the peoples of west-central Africa in the eighteenth century, with the fragmentation and decline of the Loango and Kongo kingdoms on the one hand and the continued strength of Kasanje, Matamba and the Lunda states on the other. In the light of events in the nineteenth century, it is also probable that Portugal's embargo on the trade in firearms was a stabilising factor. It is true that firearms could be imported from Dutch or French traders on the Loango coast and that their availability helped to promote trade in that region, but the embargo at Luanda limited the flow of firearms to central Africa and prevented the sort of anarchy and destruction which was to occur in the nineteenth century when all effective restraints ceased.

The early nineteenth century was a glorious Indian summer for the slavers and the slave trading states. The war in Europe limited access to the coast by Dutch and French traders and after the war the abolition of the trade restricted the British also. The field was left to the Portuguese and Brazilians, aided and partly financed by Cubans and American southerners. For the Portuguese traders it was a period of great prosperity. It was also a period of minimum government interference. From 1807 to 1852 Portugal was torn by civil strife and was unable to produce an effective government. The colonies were left largely to their own devices.[16]

Eastern Africa

Portuguese activity in eastern Africa was initiated early in the sixteenth century by the crown which wished to control the trade in gold between central Africa and Asia. The gold trade dwindled in importance, largely because of the heavy-handed Portuguese disruption of the trading network, but ivory soon took its place, and Mozambique Island continued to be of great importance as a stopping-place for Portuguese Indiamen. Periodically in the late sixteenth century and throughout the seventeenth, the Portuguese crown tried to conquer the 'mines' of central Africa, dispatching forces many times larger than those with which Pizarro had conquered Peru. It was defeated in its objectives, partly by disease and partly by the fact that there were no mines which could be developed by the sort of intensive operations which the Spaniards applied in America. It proved impossible to 'conquer' innumerable scattered riverside washings.[17]

16. Martin, chap. 7.
17. Axelson (1973); Newitt (1980).

However, a major factor in thwarting the crown's ambitions to found an economically successful colony was the rise to power of the local Portuguese backwoodsmen. In 1584 the crown had been forced finally to surrender its ivory monopoly to the captains of Mozambique in return for a large annual payment. The captains were then able to use their influence to obtain the maximum profit from importing trade goods and exporting ivory. Their sphere of influence extended from Inhambane in the south up to, but not including, Mozambique Island. They openly discouraged the settlement of more European Portuguese, and operated this monopoly through a handful of collaborating local mulattos and Portuguese traders. With the captain's connivance, these established their political and judicial authority over the Tonga of the Zambesi valley and then used recruits and food supplies obtained from these chiefdoms to conquer the plateau. In spite of resistance by the Karanga aristocracy, this was substantially achieved by 1634 and the whole of Manica and the (later) Rhodesian plateau as far south as Hartley was partitioned among Portuguese warlords and their bands of armed retainers.

Mozambique Island and the coast to the north was open to the trade of the Portuguese *moradores* (settlers). As far north as Cape Delgado they were subject to the administrative authority of the captains of Mozambique but beyond this began the territory of the captains of Mombasa. South of Inhambane the Portuguese traded in the bay of Lourenço Marques to which the royal factor sent an annual trading ship.[18] During the seventeenth century ivory remained the most important export from eastern Africa, although gold continued to come from Zambesia. Slaves too were traded, through Arab and Swahili middlemen based in the Comoro Islands and western Madagascar, with the ports of the Red Sea, Persian Gulf and India.

In the 1690s the Portuguese suffered a series of humiliating setbacks. In 1694 the *sertanejos* on the Rhodesian plateau were defeated and expelled from their strongholds, and in 1698 the Arabs of Oman captured Mombasa. The reasons for these defeats can be found partly in the successful military organisation of the Arabs and the southern Karanga chiefs, but also in the extremely small numbers of the Portuguese who had ceased to confine themselves to trade and had tried to maintain political domination over large parts of Africa.[19]

During the eighteenth century the Afro-Portuguese of mixed race

18. Axelson (1960).
19. Axelson (1960); Newitt (1973).

retained their hold over much of the lower Zambesi valley and exacted from their Tonga peasants tribute in the form of foodstuffs, cotton cloths, ivory and gold dust; some of them even began to embark on new conquests north of the Zambesi as gold discoveries were made in the escarpment north of Tete, but increasingly their orientation became one of trade. They dispatched trading expeditions to the fairs in the Manica highlands and to Zumbo at the confluence of the Zambesi and the Luangwa, using mostly professional African traders whom they called *mossambazes*. Late in the eighteenth century these began to open up new territory north of the Zambesi, making contact with the Lunda kingdom of Kazembe and trading through much of the intervening country.[20]

On the coast opposite Mozambique Island the Portuguese never successfully established settlements, trading instead through the medium of Muslim sheikhs whose towns were scattered along the coast to the north and south. The relationship with these chiefs was never easy; the Portuguese tried repeatedly to exert some kind of control over them and were strongly resisted, the sheikhs having no desire to lose their profitable control of the trade with the interior. Most of the ivory they traded was brought from the interior by Yao caravans, whose leaders also had a strong interest in maintaining the trading system. The coastal Makua did not participate to any great extent in ivory hunting or in supplying the trade.[21]

In the bay of Lourenço Marques the Portuguese had European rivals as Dutch and Austrians tried at different times to control the trade. However no permanent European station proved successful, and the trade of the bay continued to be carried on by visiting trading ships. The markets were in the hands of the chiefs round the bay who in turn were supplied by caravans coming principally from the southwest, as far away as Zululand.[22]

Late in the eighteenth century significant changes began to occur. The French establishments in the Indian Ocean steadily increased their demands for plantation slaves. The traditional markets in Madagascar and the Comoros were no longer adequate to supply their needs, and they tried to open trading relations with coastal rulers in eastern Africa. They approached the Swahili of Kilwa and increasingly sent ships to trade clandestinely with the mixed-race Portuguese of the Querimba archipelago.[23] The Portuguese responded by strengthening their presence in the north, building a fort and

20. Newitt (1973), chap. 5.
21. Hafkin; Alpers (1975).
22. Hedges.
23. Alpers (1970).

customs house at Ibo in the 1790s. Increasingly, however, the French bought directly from the ports under Portuguese jurisdiction, and slave exports from Mozambique ports rose sharply at the end of the century. The importance of the slave trade increased steadily in the early nineteenth century when Brazilian, Cuban and American buyers joined the French, encouraged to attempt the longer haul to East Africa by the systematic closure of slaving ports in West Africa. By the 1830s Mozambique was exporting as many slaves as Angola.[24]

There is a strong probability that the profitability of slave trading in the early nineteenth century drove away the ivory traders. Ivory exports from Portuguese ports north of the Zambesi fell off and were diverted to Zanzibar. This has usually been attributed to Mozambique's high tariff policy, which made trade at Zanzibar more attractive, but the rise of the slave trade must have played its part. The Muslim sheikhs of the coastal ports adapted quickly to the new situation; the Yao did so less quickly, and their caravans were increasingly displaced by the Makua of the Mozambique lowlands who came to the fore in supplying slaves and held their position throughout the nineteenth century, so that the term 'Makua' came to be used generally in the French Indian Ocean colonies for all black slaves.[25]

The slave trade never became important south of the Zambesi, although some slaves were exported from Sofala and Inhambane; the trade in ivory retained its prominence. The reason for this is not entirely clear since events later in the century were to show that in the south there was a large surplus of manpower in relation to the needs of the subsistence economy.

Very little of the profit of the east African trade accrued in any way to the Portuguese or to metropolitan Portugal. From the late seventeenth century onwards, Indians from Gujerat and Goa had played an important part in financing Mozambique's commerce and their influence increased also among the *senhors* of the great Zambesi *prazos*. The profits of trade and the quasi-feudal tribute exacted from the *prazos* were remitted to Goa, to which individuals who made their money in Africa increasingly retired. As Portuguese formal control receded, until it had become little more than vestigial early in the nineteenth century, it was inevitable that there would be a struggle for power between the local warlords. The growth of the slave trade only encouraged this process. The great Zambesi *senhors* had, for a long time, maintained retinues of 'slaves', called *chicunda*, who had been used to hunt ivory, guard trading caravans

24. Vail and White, chap. 1.
25. Alpers (1975).

and obtain tribute from the Tonga peasants.[26] Slave trading gave these *chicunda* a new role, and the nineteenth century saw a rapid breakdown of the African states north of the Zambesi which were subjected to the attentions of these Afro-Portuguese and Afro-Indian warlords. By the 1840s the rival armies of *chicunda* were engaged on a struggle to dominate the Zambesi valley and to establish political and economic control over the routes leading to central Africa.[27]

Did the Portuguese underdevelop Africa?

For three centuries, between 1500 and 1800, the Portuguese had provided the principal means whereby the peoples of central Africa had been able to trade and communicate with the outside world. In western Africa they initiated a maritime trading system; in eastern Africa they merely took over one that had already existed for centuries. The most widely-held view is that the trade carried on by the Portuguese (and other outsiders) with Africa was of a kind which stunted and retarded the productive capacity of the African people. Slave trading, ivory hunting or gold washing involved the expenditure of many working hours and the diversion of manpower which could have been devoted to production. Moreover, these exports were used to pay for the importing of such items as cloth and metalware which Africans could have provided for themselves. From this, it is argued, much of the present underdevelopment of Africa and also much of its dependence on the rest of the world has arisen. A further consequence of international trade was the concentration of economic and political power in the hands of an élite of chiefs, brokers or caravan leaders, whereas, had African peoples increased their own production, wealth would have been much better distributed throughout the population.[28]

Before assessing this argument, it is worth observing that, like their Muslim predecessors, the Portuguese were prepared to indigenise themselves and operate within the conventions and bounds of African society. Although the captains of Mozambique or Angola might try to impose monopolies on the coast, the backwoods traders had to come to terms with African kings in the interior and conform to the practice of the country. In some areas they may have been able to play off one chief against another, but the studies that have been made of the fairs at which the Mozambique traders bought gold and

26. Isaacman (1972).
27. Newitt (1973), chap. 13.
28. Alpers (1975), chap. 1.

ivory show how completely the markets were controlled by their African overlords and how completely these determined the terms of trade.[29] Nor did the Portuguese presence involve any cultural dominance. Indeed it has often been held against Portugal that after three centuries she had altogether failed to create a Christian population or to alter the cultural, spiritual or material condition of Africa in any discernible way. Far more striking was the degree to which the Portuguese themselves came to accept African values, African institutions and African means of production.

Has international trade, therefore, been the principal cause of an underdevelopment which apparently affected not only the Africans but the Portuguese who settled in Africa? There is at least a *prima facie* case for thinking that the importance of trade for many African societies has been exaggerated. Whereas some African societies which were most closely associated with the caravan trade or with the hunting for slaves and ivory may have had to adjust their societies to its demands, for many of the peoples of Africa international commerce, together with the procurement of the commodities to supply it, was of minor importance. Yet the underdevelopment of Africa, in the sense of low levels of production and relative backwardness in technical skills, is widespread and varies little whether one is considering societies which had a long tradition of trade with the outside world or those which had little or no such contact.

The failure to adopt new technologies of production can be seen as both cause and effect of this underdevelopment. During the period when the Industrial Revolution was taking shape in Europe, there were few if any significant technological advances in sub-Saharan Africa. It might fairly be objected that since she herself was economically and technologically backward, Portugal was scarcely the country to introduce technical change, but she failed to transmit even the technologies of the European Middle Ages based on wind, water and ox-power, which metropolitan Portugal did possess. Instead the Portuguese, like their Muslim predecessors, abandoned their own technologies and adopted those in use in Africa.

An explanation of these phenomena may lie in the sparseness of Africa's population. This has enabled 'slash and burn' agriculture to remain the dominant form throughout almost the whole continent. As is well-known, this requires the minimum input of labour and the very simplest of technology, but it produces by far the greatest yield per unit of labour of any known agricultural system.[30] Most African societies have therefore been able to satisfy their needs while at the

29. Bhila; Mudenge.
30. Boserup.

same time having abundance of surplus labour. Labour expended on caravan trading or ivory hunting was not necessarily labour taken from production, but was that which would otherwise not have been utilised at all. This basic labour surplus explains how great numbers of able-bodied slaves could be exported over many centuries without damaging the structure of a society. It also may explain why technologies were never adopted simply to replace human labour. There was always surplus labour to act as carriers or to pound millet or carry water for miles in a water-pot, so that the technologies of the wheel, of the mill or of water supply were not required.

In one respect the Portuguese may indeed have accentuated this underdevelopment but it had nothing to do with their trade. The Portuguese were responsible for the introduction of a large number of new food crops. Of these maize and cassava were of great significance, for they were both crops with a high yield but which could be grown using a minimum of labour. In the conditions of African 'slash and burn' agriculture the introduction of maize and cassava would have increased food yields while, if anything, decreasing the amount of labour required.

It is not suggested that these factors alone explain Africa's failure to adopt the new technologies introduced between 1500 and 1800. There are almost certainly other factors, among them the clearly marked and often ritualised divisions of labour which must have militated against innovation, and the prevalence of a system of value, status and exchange based on cattle, a form of wealth which required little in the way of technology to accumulate.

Three centuries of trade with Africa may, however, have done much to leave Portugal underdeveloped . Unlike other nations that traded with Africa, the Portuguese were not, on the whole, selling their own products. They started as entrepreneurs supplying Africa with the shipping services to enable it to trade with Europe and America. By the eighteenth century most of the shipping and capital in the trade was no longer Portuguese, but had been taken over by English, Brazilians or Indians. Of the Portuguese in Africa some had become an indigenous trading class, while others lived off feudal rents or taxes as colonial officials and *senhors* on the Cuanza or the Zambesi. By 1800 Portugal herself gained nothing from her empire and contributed almost nothing to do it.

The abolition of the slave trade

In the nineteenth century the commonest epithet used by outsiders to describe the Portuguese empire was 'decadent'. The implications of this epithet are many, but they include the idea that the effects of tropical climate, together with intermarriage with African women and the subsequent dilution of European culture, prevented the Portuguese from applying themselves with Anglo-Saxon vigour to the exploitation of the region's resources, while instead they allowed their enterprises to die though inanition and lack of enterprise. Rather than speak of decadence it would be more relevant to see the Portuguese African settlements as having become increasingly Africanised and specialised in their economic activity. The trade in slaves and ivory required sophisticated organisation and the development of a network of contacts throughout central Africa. The interests of many different groups of chiefs, caravan leaders, suppliers and middlemen had all to be reconciled and a system maintained, as far as possible, to the mutual advantage of all. The Portuguese governors on the coast and the Afro-Portuguese backwoods traders were a part of this system, but only a part. They did not always have a decisive say in how it operated. These relationships between the dominant élites of the different communities of central Africa were very specialised and could not always be easily adapted to other forms of economic enterprise. For this reason the international moves to abolish the slave trade had a serious and lasting impact.

The Portuguese officially abolished the slave trade in 1836. By that time those involved in the trade should have had a whole generation in which to adapt to the change, for Britain had taken the first steps towards abolishing the trade in 1807, and in 1815 had signed a treaty with Portugal limiting it to south of the Equator. This had had the inevitable effect of increasing the trade of Angola and of promoting greatly the export of slaves from Mozambique. Attention was fully concentrated on profiting from this great increase in the trade, now a virtual monopoly of Portuguese-controlled ports, with little thought being given to developing an alternative economy. During the 1820s and 1830s, when civil war at home had reduced metropolitan authority to a minimum, almost every official in the colonies from the governor downwards was deeply involved in the trade, a necessity in order to survive in office. When the trade was finally declared illegal, it was not British pressure alone that was responsible; a large part was played by liberal politicians in Portugal determined to impose a liberal juridical façade on the country regardless of the pre-capitalist condition of its society and economy.[31]

The abolition of the slave trade threatened the Portuguese colonies, and many of the chiefs and peoples of central Africa, with

31. Hammond, chap. 2.

the fate of any society which has come to depend on a single export and then finds the market for this commodity suddenly disappear. The position of the dominant élites was at once endangered, and in the economic reorientation that followed there were important shifts in political power. The effects were least felt at village level, where the routines of subsistence agriculture continued much as before.

In Angola 'abolition' was neither as complete nor as drastic as the term might imply. The export of slaves to America did indeed become risky and quickly dwindled away, particularly after Portugal signed a convention with Britain in 1842 which allowed for mutual search and established a prize court at Luanda. However there remained a market for slaves within Africa itself and, even when the institution of slavery was finally banned in 1875, the trade continued under the guise of engaging contract labourers until well into the twentieth century. Even so, the abolition in 1836 quickly suppressed probably as much as 80 per cent of the traffic and totally destroyed slave trading as the mainstay of the wealth of the African and Afro-Portuguese élites.

In eastern Africa the abolition took longer to implement, and the effects were less immediate. This was due to the resistance put up by the Sultan of Zanzibar, which was not overcome until 1873, and to the fact that the markets in Arabia were independent of Europe and could not effectively be closed. Moreover, Portugal did not control much of the coastline which was nominally under her influence, and slaves continued to be exported from the smaller harbours, creeks and estuaries of the coast long after the trade had been suppressed within range of the Portuguese forts. Often traders only had to make the short dash across to the cover of Madagascar waters, and this particular route remained in use for the export of slaves until early in the twentieth century. East Africa also had a local market for slaves and a limited one for 'contract labour' in the various French Indian Ocean islands.[32] However, the labour which was engaged in the southern parts of the country for work in South Africa was not connected with the slave trade and came from areas which the trade had not touched.

The abolition was of crucial importance for all the societies of central Africa. In its early stages, when the trade still remained profitable but had to be conducted with great secrecy, there was a development of new ports; there was a tendency for slaves to be assembled in large numbers and held in readiness for the arrival of ships, all the commercial dealings having been completed in advance by agents; shippers kept larger stocks of trade goods ashore and

32. Hafkin; Dubins; Graham.

hence had to increase the capital tied up in the business. Many of the traditional trading ports declined, but others grew and flourished almost overnight.[33] However, this shift of the trade to new ports was soon overtaken by the general suppression of the trade. Throughout central Africa caravan leaders and chiefs, who had lived on the profits of the trade and the tolls on the caravans, were threatened with ruin. The main source of the wealth so essential for the maintenance of their authority threatened to disappear. At the same time, supplies of slaves began to accumulate in the hands of the dealers who could find no outlet for them and who increasingly enlisted them into private armies. Before long this set in motion a major political revolution throughout the savannah states. The large segmentary monarchies were savagely attacked by newly-emergent groups both from west and east, which had frequently been involved in slave trading and now turned their organisation and their slaves to the plundering of the established central African societies and to the seeking of wealth through political dominance. In west central Africa, the rise of the Cokwe led to the overthrow of the ancient Lunda kingdoms, while further east men who had been involved in the slave trade like Msiri and Tippu Tib increasingly turned to territorial conquest and the spoils of chieftainship.[34]

Many of these trends can be seen in microcosm in the history of the sultanate of Angoche on the Mozambique coast. The port of Angoche had maintained a modest role in local coasting trade in the seventeenth and eighteenth centuries and had exported a certain amount of ivory; with the suppression of the slave trade at the Portuguese-controlled ports of Mozambique and Quelimane in the early 1840s, it rose rapidly to prominence. American, Cuban and French vessels called, its trade boomed and large quantities of arms were imported. By the 1850s the Portuguese were beginning to put pressure on the Angoche sultans. The port was bombarded in 1847, in 1854 the Portuguese tried to install a garrison, and in 1855 they blockaded the port for ninety days. At the same time they tried to exert their influence in what was for them a more traditional manner, namely by interfering in the endless quarrels among Angoche's leading families.[35] The increasing restrictions placed on the slave trade led the Angoche ruling clans to turn to territorial conquest inland. Under the leadership of Muhammad Musa Sahib (Musa Quanto) they raided extensively the lands to the south as far as the Shire and the Zambesi, and built up a political dominance

33. Martin, chap. 7.
34. Vansina.
35. Lupi.

which survived the successful Portuguese occupation of Angoche Island itself in 1861.[36]

Other groups reacted differently to the changed circumstances, and tried to find a commercial substitute for slaves which would enable them to continue to trade with the Portuguese on the coast. Eventually this was done with success in all the regions under Portuguese influence. Of course, it is impossible to say that this economic diversification would not have occurred even if the slave trade had continued. The demands of international capitalism were changing, and it was this rather than political abolitionism that ultimately killed the trade and established alternative economic enterprises in its place. Nevertheless, politically-inspired abolition was a direct incentive for the development of alternative forms of economic enterprise. The most striking success achieved by any central African people in reorientating its economic activity must be that of the Ovimbundu. The Portuguese had traded slaves on the plateau behind Benguela and had had a working relationship with the kings of Bihe and Bailundu. When the trade in slaves began to dry up, the Ovimbundu responded by intensifying their competition with the Portuguese backwoods traders until the latter could no longer maintain their position in the interior. At the same time the Ovimbundu expanded their trading network deeper into the interior in order to tap new exportable commodities. They revived the trade in ivory and built up a market for wax and honey. They were also quick to appreciate the value of wild rubber and to pioneer its collection and exportation.[37]

By the 1870s the caravan trade from the Angolan plateau was in a flourishing condition and the caravan leaders were more powerful and better organised than ever before, collecting round themselves large followings and revolutionising the old social structures with their scattered lineage villages. It appears that it was the Ovimbundu traders who supplied the Cokwe with the firearms which made them such a formidable military force in central Africa, and whose example encouraged them to embark on their predatory migrations.

In eastern Africa the trading caravans also began to deal in wax and rubber, although here the decline in the slave trade was a more gradual process. However, there appears to have been no social and economic transformation comparable to that affecting the Ovimbundu. Instead there was a return, particularly in the northern regions, to peasant farming with surpluses being marketed by Indian commercial houses. While the slave trade flourished, most Indian

36. For Angoche's history see: Hafkin; Newitt (1972); Mello Machado.
37. Pössinger (1973).

trading houses had remained on the coast, financing and supplying the trade but leaving to others the rough and tough business of obtaining slaves and marching them to the coast. As the slave trade declined, Indian traders began to penetrate inland. Slaves had been objects of high value and, as they were able to move of their own accord, did not require inland points of collection. Agricultural surpluses, however, tended to be high in bulk and low in value, and required many points of collection. Indian traders were prepared to purchase groundnuts, sesame, coconut products, *mafura* (seeds of the Cape mahogany) and surplus grain, and did so through a network of stores throughout the more settled areas of the interior. When significant quantities had been collected, they would be brought to the coast and shipped, the Indians frequently making use of the old slave-trading ports like Ibo and Angoche.[38]

The abolition of the slave trade produced a crisis also for the Portuguese community, a crisis which was political as well as economic. Initially the settlers had tried to resist abolition, and there had been talk in both Angola and Mozambique of breaking ties with Portugal and joining independent Brazil. Considerable capital had been invested in trade goods and shipping, and although some of this was able to continue earning profits exporting palm oil and forest products, nothing could disguise the severe recession that was caused in the colonies by abolition. In 1844 Angola's foreign trade was reduced to 30 per cent of its 1825 level, and there was to be no significant recovery until the 1870s.[39] Capital which had been deployed by the Afro-Portuguese traders in the interior was also endangered since many of these were driven by African competition to abandon their commercial activities. It is against this background that one must see the ambitious attempts by the government to promote plantation agriculture and to build an infrastructure of services to support it.

With slaves a glut on the market but slavery still legal within the colonies, investment in plantations seemed an obvious course of action. Land grants were made in the Cazengo region inland from Luanda from about 1850, and experiments were carried out in growing coffee, cocoa, sugar and cotton.[40] Plantations, to be successful, needed a system of government in the colony wholly different from that which had sufficed in the days of the slave trade; they required direct rule rather than informal arrangements with chiefs, and it was the attempt to impose direct rule which accounts

38. Vail and White, pp.62-7.
39. Hammond, p.51.
40. Birmingham (1978); Jill Dias.

for the 'forward' policies pursued by Angolan governors up to the 1860s. The plantation experiments, however, were tried before an adequate administrative or transport infrastructure had been created. It proved expensive and difficult to carry goods from the plateau to the coast; land could only be obtained by methods little short of requisitioning from local chiefs, who resented the pressure and resisted; labour was recruited through the old slaving networks and suffered severe haemorrhage as slaves found it easy to escape in the unsettled conditions of the interior; world coffee prices were always unstable, and at the end of the century underwent a severe slump. These factors prevented the plantations from ever becoming fully established, although they were successful enough for coffee plants to become indigenised and for their cultivation to spread among the African farmers of the region.[41]

Cocoa provided quite a different story. It was soon discovered that the fertile volcanic soils of São Tomé and Principe were ideally suited to its growth. The plant was introduced in the 1820s, and after a slow start the islands started to attract major investment from Lisbon banks, Portuguese aristocrats and others. The Portuguese had done nothing to develop any infrastructure on the islands, but the sea provided adequate transport and labour, once imported, was captive and could not desert. For a glorious thirty years after 1870 the industry was able to expand without any awkward questions being asked about the means employed to produce such dazzling economic success.

There had been little Portuguese capital involved in the Mozambique slave trade and Europeans showed great reluctance to invest in the colony — not surprisingly, in view of its chronic state of disorder. Some surveying was carried out by French and British concerns, and after 1875 a limited number of enterprises became established on the lower Zambesi producing copra, sugar and opium and operating steamers.[42] The economy of southern Mozambique, however, began to feel the magnetic pull of South Africa as early as the 1850s. The sugar plantations of Natal attracted many migrant workers from the region south of the Sabi which suffered from naturally dry and sterile conditions. The opening of the diamond mines of Kimberley in the 1870s, far away as they were, increased the emigration which became a flood with the development of the Rand after 1886. Long before there was any Portuguese administration in the area to profit from migrant labour, individual Portuguese were pioneering the liquor traffic which would strip the returning workers

41. Birmingham (1978).
42. Vail and White, chap.2.

of his wages. The Portuguese proved adept at distilling the juice of cashew, sugar cane, coconut and almost anything else they could lay their hands on. Miners returning from the reef were encouraged to forget their weariness in the grog shops which were the vanguard of Portugal's civilising mission in the south.

On the whole, therefore, it was the African peoples of central Africa and the Indian traders of the east coast who made the most flexible response to the economic changes brought about by the suppression of the slave trade. However, if individual Portuguese contributed little to this economic diversification, the Portuguese colonial government did embark on policies which it considered favourable to the development of the colonies. In part the 'forward' policies which they pursued were designed to convince sceptics at home and abroad of the reality of Portugal's presence in Africa, but they were also a conscious attempt to have done with all the feudal relations of tribute and the monopolistic system of trade conducted between rulers, and to replace it with a modern capitalist economy.[43]

Forward policy of the government 1840–1870

Portugal's attempts to extend and consolidate her African territory clearly ante-date the general European 'scramble' for Africa by some decades. Although they were later to be affected by the 'scramble', they were essentially a separate and autonomous development. An active colonial policy was forced on the colonial governments by the breakdown in the system which for two centuries had governed the relations between the Portuguese of the coastal colonies and the inland African states. The system had been one which the ruling élites, the contractors and the middlemen had operated to their mutual advantage. Abolition destroyed this community of interests, for the Portuguese governors were inevitably closely associated in African minds with the abolition policy, reluctant as many of them may have been. From being valued allies and the dispensers of the much-prized European imports, they suddenly became a hostile and antagonistic force. The old structures of interest and influence rapidly broke down, and resistance and rebellion became widespread. It became unsafe for Portuguese to travel in the interior. Many of the Afro-Portuguese deserted the government entirely, and in some areas like Guiné the Portuguese, confronted by increasing hostility, were more or less confined within the walls of their forts.

43. Capela, pp.40–50.

Other factors besides abolitionism contributed to this loss of influence and control. In Guiné, Muslim Fulas pressed towards the coast, the vanguard of the general advance westwards of Fula pastoralists. In Mozambique the dispersal of the Ngoni led to most of the area south of the Zambesi being overrun by rival Ngoni armies who were at first little concerned to preserve the old trading relationships, and looked on the Portuguese as just another group to be plundered and reduced to tribute. Elsewhere in Mozambique resistance to the government crystallised around those who were most damaged by the abolition, namely the Swahili sheikhs of the coast and the Afro-Portuguese of the Zambesi *prazos* (the *muzungos*), whose open defiance of the abolition laws was tempered only by the hatred and jealousy they felt for each other.

Faced with what it saw as unprecedented resistance and opposition, the colonial government sought to assert its authority. However, the liberal statesmen in Portugal were not concerned merely to pacify unruly colonies and do away with slave trading; they were determined also to dispense with the feudalistic relations which existed between the authorities and the African peasants. Premature attempts were made as early as 1832 by Mouzinho de Silveira to end the hereditary leases under which the Zambesi *prazos* were held, but it was not until the liberals were firmly in power in the 1850s, and the principal battles over abolition had been won, that significant legislation was attempted. In 1854 the *prazos*, with their *senhorial* jurisdiction and rights over tribute and labour services, were abolished, to be replaced by rented property;[44] in 1856 the tribute of carrier service in Angola was abolished (not for the first time),[45] and in 1856 it was announced that slavery itself was to come to an end. In place of these older relationships were to be established new ones based on the payment of taxes to the state and on the growth of a free labour market. The Marquês de Sá da Bandeira, the colonial minister, instructed the Mozambique authorities to create 'a love of agricultural and industrial labour, creating among individuals the necessities of a civilised life which will bring them to acquire through their own labour the means to satisfy these new necessities'.[46]

However a new system of economic and social relations could not develop without administrative control and settled conditions. Certainly they could not arise in areas where the chronic disorder favoured the continuation of feudal protection by warlords. In Angola major military expeditions were launched against the

44. Newitt (1973), chap. 19.
45. Capela, p.43.
46. Capela, p.42.

Mbundu states inland from Luanda between 1838 and 1851. New stations (*presídios*) were founded in the interior, and in the Cazengo highlands plantations were established. In 1855 the Portuguese occupied the port of Ambriz on the coast south of the Congo estuary and made a major drive inland against the disorganised Kongo chiefs; in 1840 Moçamedes in the far south was founded, and in 1845 the plateau station of Huila was set up to be the nucleus of a white colonisation scheme which began operations in 1849. The expense of these projects proved crippling, and there was widespread African opposition to the payment of taxes in place of the old tributes and labour services. By 1861 the expansion of Angola had temporarily come to a halt, and as the caravan trade was now rapidly reviving there was a possibility that a commercial relationship along the lines of the old slave-trading system might re-emerge.[47]

In Mozambique the situation should have been more controllable. The rivalries of the *prazo senhors* and the hostility between many of the Makua chiefs and the coastal Swahili gave the Portuguese an ideal opportunity to divide and rule. This they achieved with some success — for example, in 1858 when the powerful slaver Paul Marianno Vas dos Anjos was defeated by a successful combination of local forces organised against him by the governor, and in 1861 when another Zambesi *senhor* was persuaded to attack the sultanate of Angoche and occupy it in the name of Portugal. The dangers of this policy, however, were obvious. Dissident chiefs could be crushed in this way but only by elevating others in the process, and trouble was bound to occur when these in their turn decided to defy the government. However, this was not the cause of the series of disasters which struck the colonial government in the 1860s — indeed it almost seems as if the governors fatally willed catastrophe upon themselves. Since the 1840s the middle Zambesi had been torn by the rivalries of the Pereira and da Cruz families, each seeking to control the commerce of the river. In this savage contest the Portuguese authorities wisely played a waiting game, but in 1863 they foolishly decided upon an attempt to crush the da Cruz in their stronghold of Massangano which lay between the towns of Sena and Tete. The result was four disastrous campaigns, each ending in humiliating defeat for the Portuguese, defeats brought about by the folly of trying to mount immensely costly European-style military campaigns in country where nature, the pattern of settlement and the arts of fortification all combined to favour the defence. By 1869 the government admitted defeat and sought to

47. Wheeler and Pélissier, chap. 3.
48. Newitt (1973), chap. 16.

rebuild its traditional alliances with collaborating *prazo* chiefs.[49]

Needless to say, these military catastrophes snuffed out any hope of a new colonial economy. The *prazos*, nominally abolished in 1854, continued to flourish unreformed, and many *prazo* chiefs, now unable to export slaves, turned their attention to territorial expansion, leading their armed retainers (*chicunda*) on forays deep into central Africa, thereby initiating a new phase, albeit an unofficial one, of Portuguese expansion.

49. Almeida de Eça; Newitt (1973), chap. 15.

2
THE INTERNATIONAL DIMENSION

The stimulus of the 'Scramble for Africa'

By 1870 the adventurous policies which the governors of Angola and Mozambique had undertaken in order to assert their authority and stimulate revenue and economic growth had been halted by military disaster and shortage of funds. The economies of central Africa had proved slow to recover from the disruption caused by the abolition of the slave trade, and the Portuguese in Europe and Africa were at a loss for a viable policy. At this stage, external pressures unceremoniously began to push Portugal once again into action. These pressures, which might loosely be described as the events of the 'scramble for Africa', took three forms.

First, there was the growth among a variety of educated groups in Europe of interest in, and knowledge about, Africa. David Livingstone was by no means the first non-Portuguese European to travel in Mozambique and Angola, but it was his books, published in 1857 and 1865, which most vividly described these long-established Afro-Portuguese communities for the outside world. Livingstone also inspired, directly and indirectly, a number of missionary societies in Britain to begin work in the areas he had explored. Between 1861 and 1878 missions were sent to Barotseland, the Shire Highlands and the Kongo region of northern Angola. The missionaries were uncomfortable bedfellows for the Afro-Portuguese traders and warlords of the interior, and in missionary correspondence the Portuguese were represented as being guilty of every conceivable form of vice and depravity. Criticism, flavoured with contempt, became the stock-in-trade of every British traveller who made it his business to write about Portuguese Africa. Such criticism worked on the Portuguese consciousness of their economic backwardness to produce something resembling a national inferiority complex. This in turn led Portuguese statesmen to adopt truculent and defiant attitudes and sometimes into that blatant non-cooperation which became the despair of other European diplomats.

The second stimulus was provided by the activities of speculators from Europe. Few of these were men of substance, for at this stage Africa's economic prospects were not such as to attract long-term investors. However Portugal's spheres of interest were so ill-defined that there was no possibility of preventing the activities of these men if, as so often happened, they were able to find some chief to sign land, mineral or trade concessions. The Portuguese authorities saw no option open to them but to initiate schemes for the 'opening up' of Africa under their own auspices.

The third form of external pressure was that applied by foreign governments. In 1842 Portugal had had to submit to an ultimatum from Britain over the right to stop and search suspected slavers. In 1855 she had to give way to a French ultimatum following the detention of just such a slaver, the *Charles et Georges*. What she now had to fear, however, was not a revival of international concern over slaving so much as the consequence which the geographical position of her African colonies gave her in international affairs. In the Atlantic, Portuguese islands spanned the shipping lanes; in western Africa her ports dominated the coast from Gabon to the Namib desert; in eastern Africa approximately one-third of the whole coastline lay in Portugal's traditional sphere of influence. She controlled all the points of access to the central African plateau including the mouth of the Zambesi, while in Delagoa Bay she also held the strategic key to the Transvaal.[1]

The attempt at bilateral settlements

Since the seventeenth century the alliance between Britain and Portugal had increasingly turned into a relationship which allowed Britain to dominate Portugal and her empire, first economically and later politically. Portugal occupied many places considered to be of great strategic or economic value to the informal, free-trade empire which the British had established after the Napoleonic wars. Britain was, on the whole, content for Portugal to occupy these areas as her proxy, provided she was amenable where British interests were at stake. If it suited Britain that Brazil should become independent of Portugal or that the slave trade should be abolished, Portugal had to give way. Although their position was often one of humiliating subordination, there were certain advantages for Portuguese statesmen in this relationship, especially during the civil wars when the liberals had received considerable aid from Britain.

Nevertheless it was always an objective of Portuguese foreign ministers to increase their country's independence and to obtain what leverage they could by courting other powers which might have an interest in the areas of Portuguese influence. Anglo-French rivalry in the Indian Ocean, for example, had enabled Portugal to resist British pressure for the abolition of the slave trade more

1. A general view of the period of the 'Scramble' can be had from Lavradio; Silva Rego; Hammond; Axelson (1967).

effectively than had been possible in the Atlantic. By the 1860s, however, this rivalry was largely played out, France having lost control of Zanzibar and Mauritius and retaining only the unimportant Réunion, Nossi Bé and Mayotte. Portugal could still benefit, however, from the hostility between the Boers and the British Cape authorities. Delagoa Bay lay close to the Transvaal high veldt and offered the Boers the opportunity to develop a route to the sea free from British control. The British were unreasonably sensitive to this supposed threat to their imperial interests, but they only made moves to secure the Bay themselves when Portugal and the Boers reached a formal boundary treaty in 1869. In 1870 Portugal had outmanoeuvred Britain by successfully referring the long-standing dispute over Bolama in Guiné to the arbitration of the President of the United States. The President had found in favour of Portugal and this encouraged her to refer the Delagoa Bay dispute to arbitration as well. In 1875 Marshal MacMahon, President of France, declared that Portugal's rights to the Bay were superior to those of Britain. Already in 1872, in anticipation of a favourable outcome, negotiations had begun for the construction of a railway from the high veldt to Lourenço Marques, and it was this, coupled with the final failure of her own claims, which helped to persuade Britain that the seizure of the Transvaal, a risky policy at the best of times, was a risk worth taking. In 1877 the Transvaal was annexed, and Portugal had once again lost her position of comparative strength in Indian Ocean diplomacy.[2]

In the same year, the complacency with which Britain and Portugal had regarded the *status quo* in western Africa was rudely broken by the much publicised explorations of the Congo by Stanley and de Brazza. Britain and Portugal had been the European states with the most important economic stake in Congo trade, and it was in both their interests to reach an agreement which would restore their supremacy in this vital region. A third problem had also arisen — this time on the Zambesi. In 1875 Scottish missions had been established in the Shire Highlands of what was later to become Nyasaland. The mission lobby pressed strongly for these infant religious colonies to be granted free access to the sea via the Zambesi and across Portuguese-held territory to Quelimane.

In 1878 Portugal and Britain began negotiations in an attempt to reach bilateral agreements which would cover the future control of the Congo and the Zambesi, and which would provide for a railway from Lourenço Marques to the Transvaal. Had these agreements been successful, it is probable that the frantic events of the scramble

2. The most recent study of these events is Katzenellenbogen (1981).

for central Africa might have been substantially avoided. Indeed, this part of Africa might never have been formally partitioned at all or, failing that, partitioned without creating the anomaly of modern Mozambique, a coastal state with no hinterland. In these negotiations Britain and Portugal were not seeking to partition central Africa at all; they merely wanted to make arrangements to secure their economic interests and to secure priority for themselves in any economic penetration that was to take place. In other words, even at this late date, they were attempting to prolong the informal trading empires of the past.

The bilateral agreements were opposed by France and ultimately, for his own Macchiavellian purposes, by Bismarck, but the real reason for their failure was the opposition to them within Portugal and Britain themselves. The Portuguese parliament was reluctant to ratify any agreement which appeared to limit Portuguese sovereignty, while in Britain commercial and missionary interests opposed any extension of Portugal's claims in the interior. Failure was based on deep mutual suspicion and on the total inability of politicians on both sides to appreciate the radical nature of the scramble for African territory that was about to begin.[3]

So the agreements were abandoned in 1884, all except for that concerned with Zambesi tariffs and transit dues, and Portugal and Britain were forced to accept the arrangements reached in 1885 at the Berlin Congress. The partition of the Congo basin drastically limited Portuguese rights in the Congo region, created the anomaly of the Cabinda enclave, and robbed her of territory over which she had far stronger claims than any other European power. The Portuguese parliament and public, which had been so reluctant to make voluntary concessions to Britain, showed themselves willing enough to accept the *force majeure* of the Berlin Congress. In defending the integrity of her African claims, Portugal was prepared to submit to rape but not to compromise her reputation with an arrangement.

That she was likely to get little comfort from any show of willingness to compromise was demonstrated in 1886. In that year Portugal made two frontier arrangements with Germany and France, in both of which she made tangible concessions in return for intangible promises. To Germany she ceded the Cunene-Okavango frontier between South West Africa and Angola. This frontier corresponded roughly to the commercial hinterlands of Walvis Bay and Moçamedes, but it cut through the Ovambo homeland and denied Portugal the frontier she had claimed on the 18th parallel.[4] To

3. Anstey; Axelson (1967), chaps. 2-4; Hammond, chap. 3.
4. Clarence-Smith (1975), p.154.

France the Portuguese ceded their trading stations on the Casamance river in Guiné, receiving in exchange land of no commercial value in the south of the colony.[5] Both these agreements were made in exchange for the supposed endorsement by Germany and France of Portugal's claims in central Africa. However, neither of the powers had any interests in the country of the Congo and Zambesi watersheds, and when the confrontation with Britain occurred, they lent Portugal no diplomatic support.

Portugal's claims to central Africa were published to the world in the 'rose-coloured map' in 1887, but already by then the Portuguese were taking measures to establish effective occupation. In general terms, their objectives were to secure control of the commercial hinterland of their Angolan and east African ports, a hinterland with which they had not only traded for several centuries but which had been frequently visited by Afro-Portuguese traders from the coast. Three regions were involved: those parts of the modern state of Zambia which are made up of the basins of the Kafue, the Luangwa and the upper Zambesi; the valley of the Shire; and the Mashonaland high veldt. These were all areas where there had been considerable Portuguese commercial penetration, and the problem was to turn them into internationally respectable political claims. The push to occupy Mashonaland was the work of Joaquim Paiva de Andrada, whose efforts to found a viable company to exploit the Zambesi lowlands had attracted the sympathetic support of the most powerful of the warlords of the lower Zambesi, the Indian Manuel António de Sousa. Together they mounted their first invasion of the high veldt in 1886, some two years ahead of Cecil Rhodes. Unfortunately for them, their forces were defeated in Mtoko, and in 1887 and 1888 all available men were diverted for the war against the da Cruz clan near Tete. When Andrada and Sousa renewed their attempt with an advance into Manica in 1890, they were confronted by Rhodes' men already in possession. African societies often played a decisive part in determining the outcome of the partition. Had it not been for the resistance of Mtoko and the da Cruz, Mashonaland and Manica would almost certainly have become Portuguese.[6]

On the upper reaches of the Zambesi, occupation was mostly the work of the local Afro-Portuguese warlords, José do Rosario Andrade and his son-in-law, José de Araujo Lobo. As a result of their raids, land on both banks of the Zambesi as far as Kariba and for some hundreds of miles up the Luangwa was annexed to Portugal. In 1889 two official missions were sent an attempt to add

5. Lavradio, p.146.
6. Newitt (1973), chap. 18.

respectability to the somewhat unorthodox proceedings of these backwoodsmen. An embassy went north to treat with Mpeseni, whose Ngoni state was centred on the Fort Jameson area of Zambia, and Victor Cordon was sent to Zumbo with troops to try to advance southwards into Matabele territory.[7]

On the Shire the position was still more tense. Since the establishment of the Scottish missions, an unofficial frontier had developed on the Ruo river. As this frontier became increasingly real, the frustrations of the Portuguese mounted. Two expeditions were sent to explore the Lake Nyasa region, and in 1889 Serpa Pinto was sent with specific instructions to force the Ruo frontier and uphold Portugal's claims in the Shire highlands. It was this move which precipitated the ultimatum from Britain.[8]

Early in 1890, the British prime minister Lord Salisbury forced Portugal to halt all her expeditions pending a negotiated settlement. The first attempt at a treaty broke down when the Portuguese refused to accept the proposed boundary, and it was not until 1891 that a treaty was finally signed. As in the case of the Congo, Portugal had eventually to settle under compulsion for far less favourable terms than she could once have obtained voluntarily.[9]

The events of the 'scramble' leading up to the ultimatum pose a variety of problems. First, why did Portugal commit herself to seize what amounted to the whole of central Africa? It has been argued that her empire was wholly an object of political interest and was by nature entirely 'uneconomic'.[10] More recent studies have emphasised the rapid growth of Portuguese capitalism in the last years of the nineteenth century and the growing realisation among the Portuguese commercial community that African markets were important.[11] Unlike the more economically developed states of Europe, Portugal did not have spare capital to invest abroad, but this did not mean that she had no economic interest in Africa, for the colonies were seen as a means of generating the capital that Portugal herself required. These economic ambitions and objectives were frequently not very clearly articulated, and the public propaganda for imperial expansion was left to a narrow group of enthusiasts who, by the tightness of their organisation and the single-mindedness with which they pursued their propaganda, came to have an influence out of all proportion to their numbers. In 1876 a group in Lisbon

7. Newitt (1973), chap. 17: Wiese (1891-2).
8. Hanna.
9. Axelson (1967).
10. Hammond, p.72.
11. E.g. Castro.

founded the Geographical Society which, under the presidency of Luciano Cordeiro, extolled Portugal's role in Africa and helped to organise quasi-scientific expeditions into the interior. It was they who sponsored Serpa Pinto, Capelo and Henrique de Carvalho on their expeditions between 1877 and 1885, and it was they who organised the international reputation that these explorers acquired.

Whatever economic interests may have been active, the main motivation of Portuguese ministers was probably political. Portugal regarded herself as already in possession of central Africa. The activities of other powers were not viewed as legitimate at all, but simply as moves to deprive Portugal of what was hers by right. It was very difficult for any Portuguese government to compromise or negotiate, as any such discussions must inevitably appear in the light of Portugal being prepared to give away part of the country's patrimony. This explains the refusal to compromise in negotiations and the willingness to accept instead the results of compulsion. An ultimatum was easier to 'sell' to the Portuguese public than a compromise solution.

The second problem associated with the partition is to explain the different outcome in Angola and Mozambique. After the negotiations over the Congo were over, Portugal found few European rivals to her ambitions in Angola. The treaty with Germany settled the bounds of Angola to the south, and there were no other challengers. In 1886 Portugal began to build the Trans-African railway, which was to cross the continent from Luanda and be a practical assertion of the realities of her central African empire. As a result, much of the central African trading system fell within the frontiers of the colonial state. There were, of course, disappointments. Barotseland was lost, and much of the Kasai region went to the Congo Free State, but the new Angola had, relatively, an economic rationale. The same could hardly be said for Mozambique. Portugal lost not only much of the commercial hinterland of her east African ports, but even some of the territory which she had 'occupied' according to the accepted rules of the partition.

The reason, of course, was that in east central Africa the Portuguese faced an opponent in Cecil Rhodes, who for a short time was able to combine decisive political influence in London with the economic resources necessary to back his ambitions in Africa. Yet this combination came together successfully only in 1890. When Rhodes tried to extend his empire further at the expense of the Portuguese in 1891 he received no backing from the British government.[12] As a result, Mozambique was left as an elongated coastal

---

12. Warhurst.

colony (including the valley of the Zambesi as far as Zumbo), while its economic hinterland fell to the British. Rhodes for his part was cut off from the sea, and the mining and agricultural wealth of his central African empire had no easy outlet. It was an unfortunate outcome, and one which profoundly influenced the future development of all the colonies in the area.

Important as the economic motives of imperialists were, they seldom led to economically logical solutions. The map of central Africa reflects much more the political realities of the 1890s than the rational economic objectives of British and Portuguese capital or commerce.

The aftermath of the Ultimatum

Britain's ultimatum to Portugal was one of only two occasions when European powers nearly went to war over the partition of Africa. For Portugal it was a painful experience which for a long time rankled deeply, and struck a fatal blow at the prestige of the constitutional monarchy which had been remarkably stable since the 1850s. The effect of this was not to strengthen the right but to make the political nation turn increasingly to the as yet young and untried Republican leaders.[13] The Ultimatum was also accompanied by financial disaster. The government went off the gold standard and opened negotiations with its foreign bondholders.[14] Funds ceased to be available for imperial operations. In an atmosphere of impotent rage a public subscription was opened to buy a battleship to confront the British navy, and a patriotic expedition of volunteers was sent to Manica to confront Rhodes and his henchmen.

There were others who resented the 1891 settlement, but for other reasons. Rhodes saw his infant empire in central Africa deprived of access to the sea, and till his death he sought to overcome this by attempts to seize Portuguese territory with filibustering expeditions (firmly discountenanced by the British Government), by infiltration, by bribing chiefs still independent of effective Portuguese control, and finally by buying himself into companies with concessions in the Portuguese colonies. Rhodes' activities helped to create the impression that the partition agreement of 1891 might not be permanent.[15] Although Rhodes died in 1902, Portugal continued to fear, at least until the end of the First World War, that the great powers would repartition Africa and that in the new order she would find no place.

13. Wheeler (1978), p.41.
14. Clarence-Smith (1975), p.189
15. Warhurst; Drechsler.

There was some substance to these fears.

Great power politics is concerned with the maintenance of international stability in a system of relationships where the individual component parts are often highly volatile. The 'scramble' for Africa was a temporary, but potentially very serious, destabilisation of the international system. Europe's diplomats had long experience of dealing with and neutralising the petty quarrels of traders and missionaries and the bravado of rival explorers. By themselves these things were seldom allowed to destabilise the fabric of alliances and international relations, and certainly need not have led to a phenomenon as extraordinary as the 'scramble'. British, Germans and French were chiefly concerned to safeguard their rather modest commerce in Africa at a time of growing protectionism. They were prepared to do so through the well-established means of claiming protectorates and spheres of influence of a more or less limited nature. When Gladstone ordered the invasion of Egypt in September 1882 and Bismarck laid claim to South West Africa and Tanganyika in 1884 — the events which in retrospect can be seen to have set the 'scramble' in motion — they did not anticipate that they were entering into long-term colonial commitments. Both, however, miscalculated, for the protectorate system depended on there being a local political authority through which to operate — an authority able to exert control over wide stretches of territory and under whose auspices trade could develop and capital be reasonably safe. It was Africa's lack of such régimes, the fact that throughout most of the continent states did not exist which could be adapted by the great powers to a system of informal empire, coupled with spasmodic but often fierce resistance, that turned the protectorates almost overnight into unwanted and ill-understood colonial responsibilities.

Many of the events of the 'scramble', then, were not well-thought-out moves to further rational interests, but were attempts by the powers to re-establish an order and stability in international relations which they had themselves unwittingly destroyed; and they sought to do this with the minimum possible expense and involvement.

Portugal threatened to be a continuing source of instability. Her colonies were, until the 1920s, unruly and unpacified. In neither Mozambique nor Angola could law and order and the safety of property be guaranteed. Traders, investors and travellers were subjected to harassment and arbitrary bureaucratic procedures; no uniform legal or administrative system was seen to operate. Even the politics of metropolitan Portugal were a source of instability. However, it was the labour scandals in the Portuguese colonies which were potentially the most destabilising factor of all, for the humanitarian agitation that they occasioned threatened to become an issue even in

British domestic politics.[16]

In the aftermath of the Ultimatum, Britain and Germany were concerned that Portugal's financial weakness and the anarchy in her colonies might make a re-partition necessary. To anticipate this situation, and at the same time to impose some restraint on their respective nationals on the spot, the two powers signed a secret agreement in 1898 for the division of the colonies between them should Portugal be forced to give them up. Britain was to take the southern part of Mozambique and central Angola, Germany northern Mozambique and the rest of Angola. The terms of this agreement soon became known and caused acute anxiety and anger in Portugal. In spite of the close relations that subsequently grew up between Britain and Portugal, the 1898 treaty was not abrogated and was even renewed in 1913 when the foreign ministries of Germany and Britain were seeking areas of mutual interest in an effort to relax international tension. Until the First World War, therefore, Portugal viewed all her relations with other colonial powers through the distorting lenses of these agreements.[17]

Yet these secret treaties, far from threatening Portugal's African possessions, were in truth a guarantee of their survival. They limited, to a certain extent, the competition between British and German nationals and concessionaires for influence in the Portuguese colonies, and they reassured the two powers of each other's intentions at a time when their relations elsewhere were deteriorating. Both were happy enough to see Portugal in possession knowing that they were the heirs-apparent to her empire.

Railways and labour recruitment

In the decades after the Ultimatum, Portugal faced the same problems as many small and poor countries in their relations with the great powers. While she sought every opportunity to assert independence of action, she was only too well aware of the need to secure the tolerance of Germany and Britain and to co-operate with their interests. Her poverty and the desperate situation of the colonial economies persuaded her still further in this direction.

Germany and Britain looked to Angola and Mozambique to provide them with transit and port facilities and the right to recruit labour. Portuguese ports had for centuries been the principal outlets for central African trade with the world, and in this respect the colonial era represented continuity with the past. The provision of

16. Duffy (1967).
17. Willequet.

these services, so essential in assuring the complacency of the powers, was to be of decisive importance in the evolution of the modern states of Mozambique and Angola. Not only were their economies and their transport systems tied closely to those of their neighbours, but pretexts were provided for political interference and capital penetration which threatened at various times to reduce Mozambique to the status virtually of a British protectorate.

The 1891 settlement had made provision for the building of a railway to connect Southern Rhodesia to the sea. The line was completed at great speed by 1898, and near its terminus the sea-port of Beira grew up on the mud flats of the Pungue estuary. The line was not entirely useless to Mozambique as it ran through the Manica uplands and helped farmers, white and African, to market their surpluses. However, there was no disguising that this was a Rhodesian railway and that the *raison d'être* of Beira was as the port of Rhodesia. Beira became a town almost more British than Portuguese with an English-language press, a sterling currency and property and commercial development carried out by British capital.[18] After 1909 the Mozambique Company, which administered the area between the Zambesi and the Sabi, was itself taken over by British and South African capital.

The building of the line from Lourenço Marques to the Transvaal was a somewhat different story. It had first been seriously proposed in 1876 as a way for the Boers to achieve effective independence from British commercial control. The Portuguese had been happy to let the small coastal station of Lourenço Marques develop as the port of the Transvaal, and in 1868 had negotiated a free trade treaty and had fixed transit dues at a low level. When Britain took over the Transvaal in 1877, the railway question became linked to the Zambesi and Congo issues, and it was not till after the restoration of the Transvaal's independence in 1881 that significant progress was made. The line was surveyed in 1883, and most of it was constructed by 1887. It was finally connected to the mining towns of the reef in 1894, considerable delay having been caused by litigation between the Portuguese government and the principal concessionaire, McMurdo.[19] The line had been conceived as a sort of 'freedom railway' which would rid both Boers and Portuguese of undue British pressure, and it soon acquired a notoriety at the centre of South Africa's internal politics. The line was favoured by the Kruger régime and by the monopolist Netherlands Railway Company at the expense of the Cape and Durban lines, and even when the Kruger

18. PRO FO 371 9485 (1923) 'Memorandum on the port of Beira...'
19. Hammond, pp.224-44; Katzenellenbogen (1981).

regime in the Transvaal was overthrown in 1901 and a British governor installed, its supremacy remained virtually unassailable. The reason for this was that the Portuguese made it a condition of allowing labour recruitment in her territory that the line be used for at least 50 per cent of the Rand traffic. This condition was often challenged by the other southern African colonies, but in essence it was renewed in the Mozambique-Transvaal conventions of 1909 and 1928 and became a permanent feature of the political and economic orientation of both countries.[20]

To many observers it seemed that the Portuguese used their control of Lourenço Marques and the transit route to the Rand to obtain considerable leverage against Britain and the South African authorities. Time and again, the details of the negotiations show that Portuguese privileges were allowed to override the interests of the other British colonies so that the supply of mine labour might continue. However, this leverage proved dangerous for Mozambique, and in the end increased its dependence on South Africa, not its independence from it. The development of the whole colony became distorted. The administrative centre was sited at Lourenço Marques in the far south, where South African political and business influence was strong, and the needs of the capital were largely met by South African imports paid for by the sterling earned by the mine workers. Mozambique's finances came to depend on the taxes paid by returning miners, the fees paid by recruiters and the customs and transit dues paid by the port traffic. Finally the agreements encouraged South African political interference in Mozambique. It was the ambition, particularly of J.C. Smuts, to acquire control of Lourenço Marques and make it fully a South African port. After the Act of Union in 1910, Smuts formulated a variety of plans which included a filibustering expedition to seize the port,[21] the sending of a gunboat, plans for a federation which would include Mozambique, and a more modest scheme in 1922 to run the port and the railway through a South African board of control. None of these schemes was ever realised but, with their knowledge of the secret Anglo-German partition agreements, the Portuguese were naturally made very nervous.

Nyasaland was the other neighbour which had to be accommodated over transit and port facilities.[22] British influence in the Shire Highlands and on Lake Nyasa dated from the establishment of the Universities Mission in 1862 and the Church of Scotland missions in

20. Katzenellenbogen (1981); Duffy (1967).
21. Vincent Smith (1975).
22. Vail (1975).

1875-6. Reluctantly the Portuguese had agreed to low transit dues for goods landed at Quelimane *en route* for the Highlands; however, the arrangement was not a happy one, and in 1887 the Portuguese had to impose an arms embargo to prevent the fighting on Lake Nyasa from spreading to their territory. The same year, the British negotiated a concession to build a port at Chinde on one of the southern mouths of the Zambesi; this would give them free access to an international waterway, and it avoided the need for overland porterage. They were granted extra-territorial rights for their Chinde concession, but this proved no more than a temporary solution because the shifting sands of the Zambesi made navigation, even for flat-bottomed steamers drawing only a foot, extremely difficult, while the annual floods quickly dissolved the Chinde foreshore and washed the British concession away.

Their long experience of Zambesi navigation led the Portuguese to contemplate a railway as early as the 1880s, but the British opposed the idea of building a line linking the interior with the port of Quelimane, apparently because it would run along the north bank which was in the area allotted to Germany in any future partition. Instead, they persisted with river navigation as far as Port Herald on the Shire, and from there constructed a line to Blantyre. The situation changed when British interests took control of the chartered Mozambique Company. A plan then surfaced to connect the port of Beira to the Nyasaland protectorate. However, this was a scheme which still required river transport from the Shire to a railhead on the south bank of the Zambesi at Sena. The plan made no economic sense, but it went ahead because it was argued that this would be an all-British railway, the existence of which would strengthen British influence in Mozambique. By 1922 the line from Beira to Sena was complete and Mozambique had acquired her third British railway. The treacherous shoals of the Zambesi still cut Nyasaland off from its railhead, however. The rise and fall of the river, with its disconcerting habit of shifting its bed from year to year, was added to the falling level of the Shire to increase the woes of those seeking transport to the protectorate. The answer was the Zambesi bridge, built in 1935 at a cost to be born by the Nyasaland exchequer.[23]

Once again, here was a line not entirely useless to Mozambique. Branch-lines were constructed during the 1930s to the Moatize coalfields near Tete and to the Zambesi sugar plantations, but there is little doubt that the best interests of both Mozambique and Nyasaland would have been served by a line linking the protectorate either with Nacala, near Mozambique Island, or with Quelimane.

23. Vail (1975).

Railways were indeed begun inland from both these ports before the First World War, but without British capital or British official backing no resources were forthcoming to complete them.

In Angola Portugal also came under pressure to provide transit rights for mine owners on the copper belt; German enterprises in South West Africa also wanted to use Angolan ports. In Angola Portugal had no treaty obligations to fulfill, and stood to gain comparatively little from granting railway concessions. Moreover she feared that Germans were actively infiltrating the south of Angola, and that there was a real danger of her control over the colony being entirely lost. German pressure in the south was countered by Rhodes and Beit who bought control of the Moçamedes Company soon after it was founded in 1894. The Germans wanted a main line direct from an Angolan port to South West Africa; the Moçamedes Company suggested a line to Humbe with a spur only going to German territory. The Germans had informed Portugal that failure to build a railway would be seen as an unfriendly act, so the Portuguese authorities took the only way out and agreed to build a line themselves in 1903. The Germans then withdrew their pressure and also their business, laying plans to develop Swakopmund instead. In 1905 Portugal began to construct the Moçamedes railway having bought her freedom from German harassment by lumbering herself with a largely useless line.[24]

Further to the north, access to the sea was sought by various copper interests in Katanga and Northern Rhodesia. Copper could be moved out along the southern lines through Rhodesia or by developing rail and river transport through the Congo, but a third possibility obviously existed if a line was built across Angola. This idea attracted the attention of Robert Williams, a Scottish mining engineer and former associate of Cecil Rhodes. Williams had backers among the financiers of Union Minière and in aristocratic circles in London. In November 1902 he obtained from the Portuguese foreign minister, Teixeira de Sousa, a secret concession to build the line. Seeking to steer a course between the Scylla of Rhodes' Chartered Company and the Charybdis of King Leopold, the railway from the outset won for itself more controversy and notoriety than solid financial support. In Lisbon it was opposed by those who pointed out that it duplicated Portugal's own Trans-African line, while the land concessions on each side of the railway aroused fears of the alienation of Angola to foreigners. In the field of international relations it embroiled Portugal with those Rhodesian and South African interests which opposed the completion of the route to the

24. Drechsler.

Atlantic. As a result, for twenty years Williams failed to deliver a viable rail link across Angola which would have been of some use to the colony. The line did not reach the Copperbelt finally until the 1930s.[25]

Mozambique's railways and ports had been developed largely to suit the needs of the British colonies. The same was to be true of her reserves of labour. When the Kimberley diamond mines were opened in the 1870s, it was found that many Africans travelled all the way from southern Mozambique (not then under Portuguese control) to earn money and to buy firearms. Recruits could also be obtained for the Natal sugar plantations and, later, for the gold mines, and labour touts were active in the kraals of many of the southern chiefs. Once effective colonial government was established in the area, Portugal came under considerable pressure to continue to allow recruiting. This she did, striking a very favourable bargain with the British authorities in the *modus vivendi* of 1901. By this agreement she allowed the contracting of 80,000 labourers a year in exchange for 50 per cent of Rand rail traffic and a capitation fee on each labourer. Neither party was satisfied with this arrangement, and there were almost continuous negotiations for its revision up to 1928. The Portuguese wanted to control recruitment themselves and to have payment of mine wages deferred until the workers returned. On their side, the South Africans wanted less bureaucracy so that recruits could be moved more speedily to the Rand, and they wanted the right to recruit throughout Mozambique. Neither side wholly got its way, but the arrangement continued to operate until the independence of Mozambique in 1975.[26]

Mozambique labour was as vital for the gold mines as were the railway and port facilities of Lourenço Marques, and this gave Portugal considerable muscle in international diplomacy. Increasingly also, it proved an embarrassment. By making herself indispensable to the Transvaal economy Portugal had put herself in a position from which there was no escape. To have ended the agreements, and to have begun to turn the *Sul do Save* into something other than a labour reserve, would have incurred real enmity from South Africa and might have led to intervention. The agreements also aroused jealousy among others who wished to recruit Mozambican labour. Rhodesia wanted farm labour and greatly resented the recruiting monopoly held by the Witwateersrand Native Labour Association (W.N.L.A.). Eventually she got her own labour agreement in 1913. The São Tomé cocoa planters turned to Mozambique

25. Katzenellenbogen (1973); Hutchinson and Martelli.
26. Katzenellenbogen (1981).

when the contracting of labourers in Angola was temporarily banned in 1910; the French wanted to recruit, as did the mine owners of the Copperbelt, and before the First World War the whole struggle of the rival groups of shareholders to control the Niassa Company was due to the desire of competing interests to turn the north of Mozambique into a single massive labour reserve.

Angola never fitted this pattern at all. In the south many of the Ovambo migrated to seek work in South West Africa but this was never officially organised or controlled.[27] The W.N.L.A. at various times sought recruiting rights in Angola, but with no success, and the opposition of the local planters to the foreign recruitment of labour was sufficiently strong to interfere even with the export of workers to the Portuguese island of São Tomé. Robert Williams even had to import labour for the building of his railway.

Angola was never able to develop as an international recruiting ground for labour, partly because of the sparseness of the population but also because the areas of extensive settlement were in the interior and the communications with the coast were poor. Such labour as was available was employed in Angola, and the local opposition to its export was stronger and better organised than in Mozambique. However, the principal reason was the gradual ripening of a major international scandal over Portuguese methods of contracting labourers in Angola.

At the beginning of the twentieth century, some 3,000 to 4,000 labourers a year were being contracted to the São Tomé planters. This number was infinitesmal when compared with the numbers contracted to the South African mines, but it was suspected that these labourers had been bought as slaves in the interior and that few if any of them returned. Discreet reports from British consuls in Angola, added to press reports, attracted the attention of the British and Foreign Anti-Slavery Society which began to put pressure on the Foreign Office and to stir up public opinion. The affair assumed the dimensions of an international scandal when Henry Nevinson published his articles in *Harper's Magazine* in 1906. The revelations of Portuguese slaving occurred at the very time when the atrocities in King Leopold's Congo were forcing the international community to act. Herein lay the danger for Portugal, and strong pressures behind the scenes, coupled with the anger of the Angolan planters who did not want the export of scarce labour to continue, forced the Angolan authorities to take ameliorative measures. The journalistic battle continued throughout the First World War, but thereafter was put in

27. Clarence-Smith (1975), pp.388-9.

the shade by other issues.[28]

In Portuguese eyes the British had been acting as bullies and hypocrites. Content to see tens of thousands of labourers taken to the South African mines where, it was claimed, mortality could be as high as on São Tomé,[29] they conducted a self-righteous campaign about the small flow of workers to São Tomé. Portugal detected the self-interest of British cocoa growers behind the campaign and the machinations of those who would have liked to see Angola prised from her grasp as the Congo had been prised from that of King Leopold. Probably, however, the concern of the British Foreign Office was simply to prevent the scandal from reaching the point where international action might be a serious possibility. This it succeeded in doing, and another threat to the stability of the partition of Africa was avoided.

The Republic

The declaration of the Republic in 1910, whatever else it may have signified, created only difficulties for Portugal in international politics. The great powers wanted nothing more than stability at a time when peace was so fragile, and it seemed likely that the volatile Portuguese Republic might create some international incident difficult to control. The Republic was on bad terms with its immediate neighbour, Spain, which gave open encouragement to royalist plotters. A Spanish intervention seemed a possibility and Britain made it known privately that she would not intervene on Portugal's behalf.[30] In Britain the agitation against the abuses of contract labour in São Tomé was at its height, and soon the anti-clericalism of the Republicans and their treatment of royalist internees raised up for them more British opposition, this time from within the ruling establishment. The instability of Portuguese domestic politics, therefore, added to the problems of the colonies where the Portuguese were aware that South Africa was plotting to obtain Lourenço Marques and the Germans and British were reaffirming their secret partition agreement.[31]

At the outbreak of war in Europe, Portugal tried to remain neutral as her two powerful neighbours in Africa came to blows. In 1914 violence overflowed into southern Angola, and there was a bloody clash between Portuguese forces and a German raiding party at

28. Duffy (1967).
29. Freire de Andrade (1914), p.33.
30. Vincent Smith (1975).
31. Wheeler (1978), chaps. 5 and 6.

Naulila. Portuguese neutrality, however, survived until 1916 when the decision was taken to enter the war on the side of the Allies. Portugal's intention was certainly to try to underwrite the security of her African possessions by openly assisting the side which she anticipated would win. The most immediate consequence, however, was the German invasion of northern Mozambique in November 1917. Until July 1918 von Lettow Vorbeck's army advanced southwards, capturing supplies from the Portuguese garrisons and enlisting the support of local chiefs. British and South African troops had to be rushed to the area while Portuguese forces were diverted to deal with the rebellion which had broken out in Barue. In the end the Germans withdrew in September 1918 without crossing the Zambesi.[32] The invasion had been a great humiliation for Portugal and ruined any hope she might have had of profiting from the Allied victory by gaining German territory. At the Versailles peace conference the frontier of Mozambique was rectified slightly by the addition of the Kionga triangle in the north, but Portugal was firmly warned not to press any claims to additional territory. Indeed the experience of British officers who had fought in Mozambique and the findings of British intelligence were already focusing attention on the appalling conditions prevailing in the interior of the Niassa Company's territory. Lord Balfour even produced a memorandum in 1919 calling for an inquiry and suggesting that Portugal's colonies might, like Germany's, also be placed under a mandate.[33]

The war had certainly removed the German threat to Angola and Mozambique and had eliminated the neighbour whom Portugal held chiefly responsible for fomenting unrest in her colonies, but this had been at the expense of increasing British dominance in southern Africa. Portugal now had no other power whose interests could be invoked to counter British pressure, and at every turn she seemed wholly dependent on British and South African goodwill. While the Republic lasted, this was generally withheld. The British showed open contempt for the 'transient and embarrassed phantoms',[34] as Lord Curzon described the Republic governments. 'Sooner or later', a Foreign Office official minuted to the Foreign Secretary, Austen Chamberlain, in 1925, 'the civilised world will refuse to tolerate Portuguese corruption, inefficiency and cruelty any longer.'[35]

32. For the war in the colonies see Gomes da Costa.
33. Katzenellenbogen (1981), chap. 7; PRO FO 371 8374 (1922); Carnegie to FO, 13.12.1922.
34. PRO FO 371 11086 (1925), Long to FO.
35. PRO FO 371 11094 (1925), Villiers minute on *Diário de Notícias* to Austen Chamberlain, 16.11.1925.

With the war over, negotiations began on a whole range of outstanding issues. Smuts wanted a new railway and labour agreement; Robert Williams wanted to complete his railway in Angola; Portugal needed British goodwill for the raising of substantial colonial loans; Britain wanted to build the railway to Nyasaland and the Mozambique Company, now British controlled, was seeking an extension of its charter to 1971. These issues all became interdependent, and J.C. Smuts was particularly concerned that Portugal should get no satisfaction until she had given way to South Africa on the issue of control over the port of Lourenço Marques. The most contentious issue, however, was the future of the Niassa Company. At the beginning of the war German interests had a majority share in the Niassa Company. Britain insisted that these be transferred to safe British hands, and Owen Philipps, Lord Kylsant, of the Union-Castle Steamship Co. was persuaded to take them up. The Niassa Company's territory was totally undeveloped, and the administration there was so scandalous that questions were asked in Parliament. Philipps declared that nothing could be done as the Company's charter was due to expire in 1929, and no money for investment could be raised on such a short prospectus. Philipps sought British government backing for the extension of the charter.[36]

Although it might seem that Portugal and her colonies were wholly in Britain's control, with British and South African interests owning the railways, the two charter companies and the largest sugar plantations, yet Portuguese diplomacy was generally skillful enough to avoid having to give way to British demands. The Foreign Office files show Portugal using every kind of evasion and bureaucratic obstruction; no progress was made in settling the minor complaints of aggrieved individuals or firms, and in the end a whole dossier was compiled in 1926 called 'Portuguese Misfeances'.[37] One exasperated under-secretary wrote that 'the real solution would be British cruisers in the Tagus and off Lourenço Marques. But this will never be allowed.'[38]

Bureaucratic evasion and procrastination, however, are the protective wiles of the weak against the strong. In the case of the Niassa Company, Portugal intelligently pointed out that Britain could not at one and the same time complain of the maladministration of a British-owned company and in the next breath ask for an extension of its charter. The logic of this was irrefutable, and the charter was not renewed. Nor would Portugal give way to South African

36. Vail (1976); Neil Tomlinson (1977).
37. PRO FO 371 11934 (1926).
38. PRO FO 371 11934 (1926), Minute by Shone 10.3.1926.

demands for control of the port and railway of Lourenço Marques. She rightly guessed that South Africa was too dependent on Mozambique to sever relations entirely. For the rest, Portugal was able to play rival British interests off against one another. Against the financial and diplomatic pressure that Smuts sought to apply over Lourenço Marques, Portugal could enlist Robert Williams and his railway, and James Hornung of Sena Sugar who was willing to negotiate a loan for Mozambique to extricate her from the South African stranglehold. Smuts vented his anger and frustration in a secret cable to London: 'Hornung's loan . . . renders that province independent of the Union. This should be prevented. . . Portugal should not be allowed to flout Union government with help of British money. Mozambique should come to Union for money.'[39]

Until the end of its days in 1926, therefore, the Republic had uneasy relations with its neighbours and with the international community. The Portuguese colonies remained indispensable to British southern and central Africa, but Portugal was never the compliant, co-operative ally that business and government hoped for. Portugal for her part was not able to convince Britain of the soundness of her administration or the stability of her régime at home or in Africa. Relations were grudging and tense, and co-operation over the minor affairs of everyday life did not exist. Doubt continued to surround the long-term future of the empire.

The New State

The coup of 1926 ushered in a series of right-wing military governments which, after 1930, evolved into a régime modelled in part on Mussolini's Italy and firmly under the control of the prime minister, Salazar. The cards he had to play in international affairs were no stronger than those of his predecessors, for Portugal still faced the problems of being a small state whose territory was of economic and strategic importance to the great powers. One of these powers was soon to be Germany under the predatory and expansionist Nazi régime. Salazar and his ministers, however, handled their public relations with incomparably more skill than their Republican predecessors had done, and they steered Portugal through the storms of the Spanish Civil War and the Second World War with astonishing agility.

Salazar's principal objective in Africa was to impose a uniform administration, centrally controlled from Lisbon. After the disorders and extravagances of the previous decades, this was a wise

39. PRO FO 371 8375 (1922). Coded telegram Smuts to FO, 31.1.1922.

policy, but it involved challenging the privileges of foreign concession-holders, the most important of whom were British and South African. It was the first great achievement of the Salazar government that, while it systematically eliminated the rights of concession-holders and reduced the opportunities for foreign interference, it was able at the same time to increase its international standing and security.

Britain and Spain at once looked more favourably upon the new régime. It was a régime which promised continuity and stability, always important in the development of diplomatic contacts, and with which conservative property-owners could feel at ease. It was not likely, for example, to indulge in the radical excesses of Costa's anti-clericalism. At the same time, for all its strong right-wing orientation, the new government made few concessions to monarchists or ultra-Catholics. Meanwhile, censorship increasingly stifled comment and criticism, and the blanket of silence that settled over Portugal and her colonies had the effect of concealing colonial scandals from view. It now proved difficult for the humanitarian and radical press to get enough information to embarrass the Portuguese or British governments. Indeed, so effective was the censorship that it is difficult even for historians to discover much about the state of Portuguese Africa during the 1930s and 1940s.

Throughout the decade of the Spanish Civil War and the Second World War (1936-46) Salazar sought to maintain Portugal's official neutral stance.[40] It was a balancing act essential for her survival for it is ingenuous to assume that neutrality was an easy option and that none of the belligerents really cared to waste their powder in an attack on Portugal. In truth, Portugal was uncomfortably close to the heart of the conflict and her colonial possessions were of considerable strategic importance. During the Spanish war Salazar openly favoured Franco. The two leaders shared common attitudes to contemporary affairs, particularly an extreme anti-communism. In spite of Portugal's traditional fear of a strong Spain, Salazar seems to have considered her future more secure with a nationalist government in Madrid than with the Spanish Republicans whose régime seemed to threaten the Iberian peninsular with balkanisation. Almost certainly, however, Salazar's backing of Franco was ultimately conditioned by the expectation that he would win. Although Salazar made no secret of his support for the nationalists, he made a point of co-operating with the international community, going along with the policy of non-intervention and even allowing British

40. This is the case argued in depth in Kay; for a personal memoir of these events, see Vintras.

observers to be placed on the Portuguese-Spanish frontier. It is clear that already at this stage he had perceived the importance of maintaining a posture of extreme rectitude in international affairs. Scrupulously observing the letter of international agreements, when frequently ignoring the spirit, was to become a hallmark of Portuguese foreign policy.

Salazar was also always particular about maintaining close relations with Britain. He understood well that Britain's self-interest was the best insurance for the integrity of the Portuguese empire, although it was typical of Salazar's love of abstractions that he liked to discuss Portugal's relations with Britain in terms of the historic alliance rather than mutual contemporary interests. Insistence on the ancient alliance was an attempt to bolster Britain's self-interest with moral considerations. Salazar knew that Germany had pressed Britain hard for a new colonial settlement. (In conversations held during 1937-8 Hjalmar Schacht, head of Hitler's Reichsbank, had suggested that Germany might be satisfied with the transfer of the Portuguese colonies, and Britain had been prepared to discuss the issue.) Standing by the alliance also enabled Portugal to keep close to Britain in the European war which broke out in 1939 while maintaining a neutral stance.

Salazar sought throughout to preserve Portugal's territory intact, and to achieve this he committed himself to keeping the whole Iberian peninsula neutral. Whatever Franco may have wished, there is little doubt that Salazar wanted an allied victory but he did not side openly with Britain as this would have provided an occasion for German intervention. This was a point that the British fully appreciated. However, Salazar also sought to profit by the war by selling Portuguese wolfram to both sides and by allowing colonial re-exports to find their way to the belligerents.[41]

Once it became clear that the Axis powers would leave the Iberians alone, the main threat to Portugal came from the Allies who wanted to use the Azores as a base during the battle of the Atlantic. At one stage Winston Churchill and the Americans contemplated seizing the Azores, as much to overcome Salazar's intransigence as to anticipate the Germans. Faced with a barely disguised threat of force, Salazar yielded and allowed a British occupation in October 1943, invoking once again the historic alliance and firmly maintaining his neutrality in the still continuing war. However, as victory for the Allies looked increasingly likely, he was able to emerge with

---

41. Kay, chaps. 7 and 8; but see letter to *The Times*, 18.5.70 by Sir Dingle Foot for the contrary point of view.

the appearance of having throughout been their secret friend and collaborator.

The aftermath of the Axis defeat was crucial for Salazar. As in 1919, the victory of Portugal's allies brought renewed anxieties. Once the common enemy was defeated, her friends were less warm and accommodating and less willing to forget the colonial scandals. Fascism was now out of fashion and it was not inconceivable that with the ideological victory of liberal principles, pressure would be brought to bear on Portugal to dismantle its police state. To fend off this admittedly remote possibility, Salazar began to hold elections and to revive the forms of local democracy, dropping meanwhile some of the more offensive public manifestations of fascism. As in other one-party states, elections were solemnly held for the return of nominees of the sole legal political party, and every five years elections were held for the office of President. Through administrative control of the electoral process, the régime was always able to secure the return of its candidate, but these elections provided the occasion for opposition to build up and for its public expression.

The formation of NATO gave Portugal an opportunity to secure her future in the post-war world. She applied to join the alliance and made her territories available for the Americans to use as military bases. Through NATO Portugal was to obtain her arms, but she also received diplomatic support, particularly at the United Nations, which was to prove even more valuable. Salazar appeared to believe that by making himself indispensable to NATO he had done all that was required of him in adjusting to the post-war world. NATO would protect Portugal and her colonies, and no trimming of sails to the winds of change seemed necessary.

Keeping the United Nations at bay

Portugal had been excluded from the United Nations by the veto of the Soviet Union, but she was eventually admitted in 1955. She at once became a focus for the attentions of the anti-colonial lobby, at first chiefly because of the anomalous position of Goa, Damão and Diu after India had achieved its independence. Under Article 73 of Chapter II of the United Nations Charter, all member countries were to submit information on their non-selfgoverning territories, and a committee was established to consider the reports that were sent in. This Committee on Information from Non-Selfgoverning Territories was to prove one of the most important ever established by the United Nations, since it helped to focus world attention on the colonial issue and greatly promoted the cause of decolonisation.[42]

42. Kay, chaps. 8 and 9; Abshire and Samuel, chap. 16.

Portugal early observed its selectivity. It did not concern itself with the imperialism of the Soviet Union or of the states of the American continent. These had both annexed and were continuing to rule alien peoples, but because their conquered territories were physically contiguous and because they were constitutionally integrated with the metropolis, they were deemed not to be colonies. It became Portugal's stance to meet rising United Nations criticism of her colonial role by declaring that her colonies too were an integral part of the mother-country even though they were physically separate. As the Portuguese delegate said in 1959:

The Portuguese nation, by being scattered over various continents, is not committing a crime: this has to be stated clearly and be understood. We have seen that geography by itself does not imply any idea of colonialism. Many other nations have territories in more than one continent, and their independence and the independence of the various component parts is not questioned. Why should ours be questioned on these grounds? [. . .] Is the United Nations going to investigate how nations were formed and came into being five centuries ago? How was the Untied States of America built: through peaceful co-existence in the Far West with the population of the land? How was the Soviet Union built: was there any process but the war carried out by the Principality of Moscow?[43]

In 1951 the use of the term 'colony' had been dropped and the African territories had been made officially part of the mother-country, while racial integration was stated to be the social policy of the empire. It was typical of Salazar and his advisers to believe that such simple strokes of the pen could spirit away all Portugal's problems as a colonial power.

Portugal's refusal to report on her colonies singled her out for the attention of the United Nations, and a special Committee of Six was established to investigate. Their report led in 1960 to a special resolution of the General Assembly on the Portuguese colonies. Together with South Africa, however, Portugal was to deny the right of the United Nations to pry into what she described as her internal affairs. Like South Africa she appreciated that even if international approval could not be obtained for her régime, at least she was on strong moral grounds in standing by the principle of strict legality in her international dealings. This community of interest with South Africa and later with the settler regime in Rhodesia was, of course, based on the closed mutual dependence of their economies, but it was to expand into a political and military alliance once the pace of the colonial independence movements gathered momentum.

Salazar, therefore, believed that he had founded the security of his

43. Nogueira, p.173.

African territories on a threefold base: he had defeated the interference of the United Nations by the formal integration of the colonies with the mother-country; in international politics he could shelter under the skirts of NATO and in Africa he was closely linked with the interests of the white settler régimes. It was a policy that seemed totally successful in the 1950s. Portugal's hold on her five African colonies seemed scarcely to have weakened, and even the sustained campaign of India against Goa appeared to have been blunted. However, this success made the régime dangerously insensitive to the forces of change in Africa, insensitive and inflexible in a way which even the die-hard Afrikaner nationalists of South Africa were not.

3
RESISTANCE AND PACIFICATION

What policy options did the Portuguese possess?

Of the last century of their presence in Africa the Portuguese spent half in trying to pacify their various territories. Almost every year from 1875 to 1924 saw military expeditions undertaken in all three of their mainland colonies, and 'police' operations were still needed in the years that followed. This period of 'pacification' lasted longer than the comparable period in most other European colonies. There were, for example, no major military operations required in South Africa or the Rhodesias after 1906. The length of time taken to make its authority felt is basically a measure of Portugal's weakness in military, administrative and economic resources, and although many of the peoples of Angola, Mozambique and Guiné fought in a determined way against annexation, it is doubtful whether such prolonged resistance would have been possible against the better-organised Germans, British or French.

Yet were expensive campaigns of pacification really necessary? Could the objectives of colonial government not have been achieved with equal speed by adopting more subtle and indirect means to influence and mould African society? Did military action not, in fact, cause traditional African societies to survive longer than would otherwise have been the case, their cohesion strengthened by the demands of armed resistance? In short, faced with the task of effectively occupying and establishing a colonial régime in an area approximately the size of western Europe, did Portugal have any realistic options open to her other than attempts at military conquest?

One possibility was undoubtedly to refrain from stirring up all the potential opposition that existed, and to await the effects of the economic and social changes which had already begun to break down old tribal structures, a process that was accelerating in the final years of the nineteenth century. The rapid growth of the cash economy resulting from exports of rubber, wax and cattle from Angola and oil seed and migrant labour from Mozambique were weakening the traditional ties based on land, cattle, marriage and lineage. Missions had also made considerable inroads into African consciousness. By the end of the century alternative, mission-led societies had begun to appear in both the Kongo region and in southern Angola, and everywhere Christian doctrines were proving to be a solvent to the old certitudes of African life. Without extensive campaigns of conquest it is likely that economic penetration and missionary influence would have brought the peoples of Angola and Mozambique progressively under Portuguese influence. Indeed it was these forces rather than military ones that weakened African resistance and permitted the establishment of the colonial régime.

The other option was to embark on a military conquest which would enforce respect for Portuguese authority and would impose swiftly and forcibly the demands of the colonial state. The issue was discussed by Henrique de Paiva Couceiro, himself responsible for some of the more vigorous campaigns of pacification. He saw the conflict of the military and the commercial ideals of empire as far back as the history of the Phoenicians and Romans, and thought that it was implicit in the well-known quarrel between Almeida and Albuquerque, the first two governors of Portuguese India. *Não-intervencionismo* was all very well, but how in that case could Portugal fulfill her international obligations? The colonies were becoming a refuge for dissident and criminal elements from other territories, a 'theatre of operations', to quote the text of a decree of April 1909, 'for individuals, European and non-European, acting outside the law . . . in which extortion, arson and armed robbery are daily occurrences'.[1] The need to appear to be an active and responsible imperial power in the face of sceptical foreign critics was therefore clear, but domestic Portuguese politics also demanded firm and swift solutions. Colonial successes of the more obvious kind had to be paraded to stiffen the flagging potency of the monarchical régime, and the soldiers never ceased to offer to the civilian politicians the illusion that military solutions would be swift, clean and, in the end, cheap. They seldom were.

However, in Portugal's empire the military had a disproportionate influence. Most of the officials serving in Africa were military men for whom colonial wars were the greasy pole of professional advancement. Some were to use reputations flamboyantly established in African campaigns to build themselves political futures at home. There were also white settlers in the south of Angola who favoured military solutions as their livelihood was increasingly coming to depend on the government's military spending. In spite of Portugal's chronic shortage of funds, therefore, it was a policy of military conquest that was pursued in all three colonies.

African collaboration in the era of pacification

It is difficult to categorise resistance to the Portuguese in terms of

1. Paiva Couceiro, p.49-50. This whole work is an apology for the policy of military pacification.

primary and secondary resistance. In all three African colonies the greatest resistance came from those peoples who had had the longest contacts with the Portuguese. In Angola the wars of pacification were overwhelmingly concentrated in the regions occupied by the BaKongo, Mbundu and Ovambo; in Mozambique resistance was most prolonged in the Zambesi valley and among the semi-Islamised coastal Makua; in Guiné it was the Papel peoples of Bissau who were the chief opponents of colonial rule.

For these African communities the attempts of the Portuguese authorities at the end of the nineteenth century to impose taxation, forced labour and the other blessings of colonial rule were no new experience. For many centuries their societies and economies had been moulded and modified by contacts with Europeans, and there had grown up a shifting pattern of rivalry and collaboration. The campaigns of pacification were frequently seen merely as a continuation of conflicts already many centuries old. Those peoples who had had longest contact with the Portuguese resisted most strongly, principally because trade had brought them stocks of firearms, and experience had taught them the techniques of defensive warfare. For example, the resistance of the Ovambo and of the Makua of Mozambique was only successfully overcome when the Portuguese banned the trade in firearms during the First World War.[2] It is not true, however, that their resistance stemmed from a greater unity in the face of the known implications of Portuguese colonialism. Unable to apply decisive force in any permanent way, the Portuguese had long since learnt to gain their ends in these regions by cultivating friends, allies and collaborators, and at different times most of the chiefs and ethnic groups had seen their advantage to lie in collaborating with the Portuguese rather than opposing them.

In only a few of their pacification campaigns did white regular troops play a decisive role. After reorganisation during the 1870s the colonial military establishment consisted of 3,684 officers and men in Mozambique and Angola and a further 1,000 stationed in the islands.[3] However, these numbers were seldom achieved and many of the troops were convicts sentenced to service in Africa for military crimes. The reforms of 1901 increased the establishments to a minimum of 4,895 for Angola and Mozambique with 1,103 in Guiné and the islands.[4] Most of these troops were widely scattered in garrisons and it was seldom that as many as 100 European troops could

---

2. Pélissier (1977), p.183. Norton banned the arms trade in Angola in 1912.
3. Lobo Bulhões, p.34.
4. Pélissier (1977), p.171.

be assembled for any operation. From the start, therefore, the pacification campaigns were fought using black troops and irregulars recruited from peoples willing to collaborate with Portugal. The extent of this collaboration is striking and has to be stressed. In nearly every part of their vast territories the Portuguese found local rivalries which they were able to exploit. Indeed, in Mozambique there can almost be said to have been a tradition of collaboration ever since Tonga warriors were employed in large numbers in the seventeenth century for the conquest of the Karanga in Mashonaland. Although collaborating groups could be found among all sectors of the African population, it is significant that some of Portugal's most important allies were found among peoples with whom their contacts were of fairly recent date. For example, both the Ngoni of northern Mozambique, who played such a crucial role in the pacification of Zambesia,[5] and the Fula of the savannah hinterland of Guiné had had relatively little to do with the Portuguese before 1875.

The Portuguese dependence on African allies greatly influenced the nature and effectiveness of the pacification campaigns. Too often, expeditions intended to pacify turned into prolonged forays by bands of warriors armed by the Portuguese and let loose to kill and plunder at will. The incentive for the Ngoni to support the Portuguese in Mozambique throughout this period was almost certainly the license granted to them to prey on the areas being pacified. Likewise there were few illusions in the minds of contemporary observers about the motives of the *chicunda* chiefs who fought for the Portuguese on the middle Zambesi or in Barue. Writing of the former, Carlos Wiese, a German who carried out a diplomatic mission for Portugal in 1889, wrote:

In these bloody raids whole regions are devastated just as if a violent hurricane had passed over them. . . the men are killed or sold; all that cannot be eaten or taken away is destroyed and the villages are burnt. The women and children who escape death are exchanged with the Arabs for powder or trade goods, or go into productive slavery to cultivate the fields of the conqueror. . . Public authorities to their shame have made use of [the *chicunda* chiefs], conferring on them offices which place them in a better position to carry out their rapine. . . Rapine takes on the character of being authorised when they are called on by the government, with their forces, to crush some rebel chief who frequently has far better qualities than they and who was sometimes even incited by them to rebel.[6]

Another way in which African collaboration, albeit unwilling,

5. Vail and White, chap.2; Isaacman (1976) pp.169–71.
6. Wiese (1891-2); (1891) p.249.

could be obtained was by transferring troops from one colony to another. Angolans serving in Mozambique or Senegalese recruited for service in Guiné would often prove effective and loyal soldiers since they did not identify with the local population and were deprived of the opportunity of escaping.

In Angola the Portuguese were also able to use white irregulars. The Boers who had settled round Humpata in southern Angola after 1881 were willing to enter Portuguese service as irregulars and for largely the same reasons that the Africans were. They received captured cattle and other booty, and their wagons were employed in the government's transport service. Many of them came to depend on the pacification campaigns for their economic survival.[7]

So, with a few exceptions like the final campaign of Mouzinho de Albuquerque* against Gungunhana in 1895 which was fought by mounted white troops, every campaign depended for its success on the black troops who fought under the Portuguese flag. Although there were significant examples of African peoples achieving an unaccustomed unity in order to confront the colonial take-over, this was rare and disunity prevailed. There was simply no consciousness of a common struggle against a common foe. For many the coming of the colonial era was a unique opportunity to advance personal or group interests, and the opportunity was taken. Ultimately, therefore, Portuguese victory was achieved not by superior weapons so much as by superior unity and organisation and by the fact that they were able to recruit important sections of the African population to their side, so isolating the resisters. However, this process which turned so many of the pacification campaigns into African civil wars was responsible for prolonging resistance to an extent not found in other European colonies.

In many of their African colonies the British sought to collaborate with the chiefs in establishing their rule, but 'indirect rule' of this kind held no attractions for the Portuguese. They made few efforts to win over the paramount chiefs in order to administer the colonies from under the canopy of a traditional authority. Instead, they planned to rule the conquered areas directly themselves. Why did they adopt the expense of direct rule and avoid the indirect solution

7. Clarence-Smith (1975), pp.130, 171, 311.

* Joaquim Mouzinho de Albuquerque was one of the strongest protagonists of colonial autonomy and right-wing monarchism. Born in 1855, he served in the colonies from 1886 till 1898, his most famous action being the capture of Gungunhana at Chaimite in December 1895. He was High Commissioner of Mozambique 1896-8. After an appointment as tutor to the Crown Prince, he committed suicide in 1902.

which might have been expected to appeal to a country with few resources? The answer lies in the history of indirect rule in these colonies. Since the fifteenth century the Portuguese had sought influence in Africa less by conquest and settlement than by attempting to influence and control African chieftaincies. In both Angola and Mozambique they tried to establish a system of client chiefs who would serve the interests of Portuguese traders and missionaries, but too often they discovered that their support for a particular chief did not help to maintain his authority but led instead to a shift of allegiance to a rival chiefly lineage. The eventual collapse of their attempt to establish a form of indirect rule in the territories of the Manicongo in the sixteenth century and the Monomotapa in the seventeenth are simply the best-known of their failures.

Alliances with chiefs were always ambiguous, for it was never entirely clear whether they were accepting Portuguese sovereignty or whether it was the Portuguese traders, settlers and *sertanejos* who were acknowledging the overlordship of the chief. This ambiguity lay at the root of many of the 'rebellions' in the pacification era. Long experience of indirect rule had convinced the Portuguese that it provided a solution built on very shifting foundations. To this was added the realisation that it was the chiefs who often organised resistance, for instance among the Ovambo. Pacification thus became synonymous with the destruction of chiefly power and not with its maintenance. Finally, the immediate economic objectives of colonial rule — labour and tax — would not, it was believed, be best obtained from powerful and partly independent chiefs who might interpret their role as providing protection for their subjects and who would certainly expect to share in the product of African taxation. Therefore, although the collaboration or acquiescence of various groups was frequently bought by granting a temporary indirect rule, it was only in Guiné, where the government was not concerned with recruiting labour, that indirect rule was applied in a systematic way. The Fula chiefs of the interior enjoyed a semi-independence and were left unmolested by the Portuguese administration up to the time of independence.

The politics of pacification

Although the Portuguese opted for a military solution to the problems posed by pacification and African resistance, they had to give some thought to the embryo administration that would remain when the punitive column had received the 'vassalage' of the local population and then moved on. In areas over which they claimed sovereignty, nineteenth-century Portuguese governors had established officials whom they called *capitaes-mores*. These officials had judicial and fiscal powers, and had access to supplies of firearms from the government. In keeping with Portuguese practice, many of the *capitaes-mores* were men of mixed or pure African descent, drawn from among the leaders of local collaborating groups. Some, however, would be Portuguese officers, and as the pacification proceeded the *chefe* of a military post became, increasingly often, a white man. Whatever his own ethnic origin, he was unlikely to have any European troops or police at his command, and his authority rested entirely with the black *cipais* under his command. Once a military post was established it was the responsibility of the officer in charge to bring as much of the local population as possible to accede to the demands of Portuguese colonial government. The duties this government placed on its officials were legion. From his official report, it is clear that the governor of the Tete district of Mozambique in 1911 had to perform a full range of governmental functions, dealing with finance, taxation, prices, roads, trade licenses, claims, posts, telegraph, public health, prisons and meteorology. In addition, he was inspector of the *prazo* concessions, acted as a government labour recruiting agent, and had to try to maintain law and order in his district. To achieve this he had an adjutant and a secretariat of six, and a further six in the trade and justice departments. This staff included interpreters. It is small wonder that he found it necessary to write:

The region of Barue is too large to be administered directly by a single individual, . . . and however active the *capitão-mor* may be, it is not possible for him to assess and collect the head tax in a proper manner within the twelve months of the year.[8]

The first priority of any official was to collect tax. In Zambesia a head-tax (*mussoco*) had been traditional, but elsewhere the tax levied was a hut tax, called *palhota*. The levying of this tax had a threefold significance. First it was a symbol of submission. A region was only considered pacified when hut tax could be collected, and refusal to pay tax was a recognised way of declaring oneself to be in rebellion against the government, and was seen as such by the African population. Secondly, the tax had a vital fiscal purpose as it was designed to bail out the bankrupt colonial administration and, more than that, actually to provide a surplus which could be sent back to Europe. Thirdly, the tax had a socio-economic purpose or, as the Portuguese themselves would have said, a civilising purpose. It was designed to introduce Africans to the joys of living in a

8. Distrito de Tete, p.35.

capitalist society by creating an artificial need for them to earn cash.

Into a pacified area the tax collector was closely followed by the labour recruiter. In many areas this should be seen as symbolic rather than a matter of fact, for the growth of migrant labour frequently came earlier than pacification or the enforcement of Portuguese labour laws. This, as we shall see, is of crucial importance in understanding the development of Portuguese colonial policy. In the lives of the Ovambo of southern Angola and the Thonga, Chopi and Shangaan of southern Mozambique migrant labour established itself independently of Portuguese compulsion or encouragement. Wherever migrant labour was unknown, however, the Portuguese were determined to introduce it as one of the first acts of their colonial administration.

The effects of migrant labour will be discussed later, but here it is only necessary to ask why the Portuguese accorded it such high priority. First, labour was seen as the most easily accessible natural resource which could be tapped to make the colonial administration less dependent on metropolitan subsidies. Labour was sought by contractors for South African, Rhodesian and German mining concerns, but also by concessionaires who intended to invest in the Portuguese colonies themselves and for whom the availability of labour was the chief attraction of Angola and Mozambique. The second reason was the government's own needs. The building of roads, railways and ports, so important if Portugal was to fulfill her international obligations, required heavy inputs of labour. Thirdly, however, the campaigns of pacification themselves generated a demand for labour because carriers had to be recruited for the endless operations in the interior, and levies of black troops and *cipais* were raised in the conquered areas. Carrier service was, indeed, the largest single labour requirement, and clearly became an intolerable burden during the First World War. Conversely the development of roads and railways in the 1920s led to a rapid decline in the need for carriers and to a corresponding slackening of the demands for labour made on the average African family.

The military post charged with raising tax and recruiting labour was not the only means used by the Portuguese to establish colonial rule. Considerable parts of Angola and rather more than half of Mozambique were granted to concession companies who assumed extensive governmental functions. These ranged from the quasi-sovereign powers of the chartered companies to the limited police and fiscal duties of the *prazo* concessionaires in Zambesia. Many of these concessions were granted before pacification was complete, and the concessionaires were left with the problem of asserting their authority in the interior. Few of them had sufficient resources for this task, while their attempts to extract profit from unpacified and frequently unexplored territory allowed the ripest abuses of power to flourish.

Why was unrest endemic in Mozambique?

The foregoing analysis of the factors involved in the campaigns of pacification may explain in general terms why this phase of Portuguese colonial history was so prolonged, why many parts of Angola and Mozambique had to be pacified again and again as resistance continued to flare up. However, each colony had its own distinctive historic relations with Portugal, and the pattern of collaboration, resistance and ultimate pacification differed from region to region.

In only one major area did the Portuguese achieve swift and decisive military success, and that was in Gazaland in southern Mozambique. In the 1830s and 1840s Mozambique south of the Zambesi had been overrun by at least three different Ngoni armies. Only that commanded by Soshangane attempted to settle, however, and the great, sprawling Gaza state was established with claims to sovereignty over all the peoples between the Limpopo, the Zambesi and the Rhodesian high veldt. The kingdom had a central core of Shangaan clans organised into regiments and dependent on a cattle economy, but on the periphery the subject peoples and client states merely recognised Gaza overlordship and paid tribute. Among these were the Portuguese *muzungos* of Sena on the Zambesi. The first man, therefore, to impose the rudiments of political unity south of the Zambesi was not a Portuguese, nor a member of some long-established and venerable chiefly clan, but a foreign conqueror from Natal. The Gaza kingdom fitted the classical model of African sub-imperialism which in so many areas preceded partition by Europeans.[9]

By the 1870s, the Gaza kingdom had begun to contract. Many of the tributary chieftaincies were being drawn towards other centres of power and much of the low veldt between the Zambesi and the Pungue had effectively fallen under the sway of the Indian adventurer, Manuel António de Sousa. The Portuguese in Lourenço Marques and Inhambane were also increasingly effective in extending their protection to the neighbouring peoples, and these also detached themselves from Gaza rule. In 1884, when the old king Umzila died, not only had much of the periphery fallen away but the old Ngoni core of the state had begun to dissolve. Umzila's successor, Gungunhana, faced threats from three directions. There were

9. Liesegang.

rivals for the throne who had a better claim than his own; there were the growing internal disintegration and the mounting pressures from outside. These threats had to be met simultaneously and they preoccupied the king throughout his reign of eleven years.

In 1885 Gungunhana signed a treaty with the Portuguese which in his eyes guaranteed the independence and sovereignty of his kingdom, although it was typical of many such treaties signed by African kings in that it gave Portugal a privileged position *vis-à-vis* other foreigners. In 1889 the king moved his head kraal south to Manjacasse in the Limpopo valley. This move, dramatic in the scale of human organisation that was required, has always been attributed to a desire to regain control over the southern peoples who had gravitated towards the Portuguese port of Lourenço Marques, and the allurements of the labour touts from South Africa. The arrival of Rhodes' pioneer column on the high veldt placed the shrinking Gaza empire in a crucial strategic position between Rhodesia and the sea, and intense rivalry followed between agents of Rhodes and the Portuguese, which continued even after the formal demarcation of frontiers in 1891 had left most of Gazaland in Portuguese territory.

The Portuguese were uncertain how to deal with the apparently formidable military monarchy of the Gaza. They feared Rhodesian intervention if fighting broke out, and for four years permitted a situation of indirect rule to persist. North of the Sabi, for instance, the Gaza *ndunas* continued to collect tribute which was shared with the Mozambique Company. The relationship was to remain highly unstable, however, as chiefs could only be kept tributary to Gungunhana, and his own warriors could only be kept loyal, through periodic armed raids. The peoples raided naturally tended to appeal to the Portuguese authorities for protection, and tried to throw off Gaza overlordship. Following a local rising in 1894, the Portuguese decided on a major war to destroy Gaza power once and for all. The expeditionary force assembled by the high commissioner, Antonio Enes, was large by Portuguese standards, consisting of 2,000 troops. It won two decisive battles at Coolela and Chaimite in which the Gaza armies were slaughtered and Gungunhana was captured. A further campaign had to be fought in 1897 to eliminate the remnants of the Gaza military machine, but thereafter the region south of the Sabi was pacified.[10]

The speed and decisive nature of this pacification are so exceptional in the story of Portuguese colonial rule that some explanation is called for. First, although the Gaza had acquired some experience of Portuguese fighting and diplomatic methods by the 1890s, they

10. Wheeler (1968).

were not adept at the sort of tactics required for dealing with the Portuguese, as were the peoples of the lower Zambesi or the Muslim sheikhs of the coast. As the Zulu discovered in 1879 and the Matabele in 1893, massed formations and set-piece battles were a disastrous military mistake against mounted troops armed with maxim guns. Secondly, many of the peoples south of the Sabi had already been subdued a generation earlier by the Gaza who had subjected them to tribute and to periodic raids for manpower and cattle. When the Portuguese defeated the Gaza, they found the other peoples of the region, so to speak, already conquered for them and relatively inured to tax and tribute. Third, and most important however, were the social and economic changes which had already in the 1860s begun to affect the *Sul do Save* region. As the Gaza empire contracted, so it became increasingly difficult for the cattle-based economy to replenish itself from raids. The custom of migrating to seek work in South African mines or on plantations was already making inroads into the traditional economies of the Thonga and Chopi of the south, and many young Shangaan men began to make the journey as well. The authority of chiefs and the cohesion of the lineages began to weaken, since neither could exert economic control over the individual entrepreneurship and private cash incomes of those who went to the mines. Enes had believed that the monarchy would soon collapse through internal weakness, and although Portuguese military prestige demanded that the strength of Gaza military power in 1895 be emphasised, it is likely that the Portuguese maxim guns merely delivered the *coup de grâce* to a state already in an advanced state of disintegration.

The Zambesi valley and the coastal lowlands of northern Mozambique presented entirely different problems, for they were areas which had felt Portuguese influence since the sixteenth century. Resistance here had its origins in wars and rivalries dating back for centuries, and the region was not fully pacified until 1920. Some of the Makua and Yao chiefs between the coast and Lake Nyasa were of importance, and south of the Zambesi the anicent chieftaincy of Barue maintained some independent significance until 1880, but apart from these, economic and military power rested almost exclusively with the Muslim ruling lineages of the coast and the great *prazo* families whose domains stretched from the Licungo to Quelimane and then up-river to Zumbo and beyond. The sheikhs and the *prazo senhors* controlled a valuable trade in ivory and slaves which came from the interior; they also taxed their subject-peasantry and were able to import firearms and even artillery from their Portuguese mercantile collaborators. Their heavily fortified towns, called *aringas*, were extremely difficult to attack, and generally they were masters of the arts of guerrilla warfare.

The Portuguese had learnt the lessons of their disastrous Zambesi campaigns in the 1860s, and after 1875 they cautiously sought opportunities to build up alliances which would enable them to isolate the ruling clans and destroy them piecemeal. The model for this policy was the extremely successful attack on Angoche in 1861 when one of the *prazo* warlords had been used by the Portuguese to attack the island stronghold of the most important of the Muslim sheikhs. In the 1870s and 1880s the Portuguese increasingly came to depend on the co-operation of two great *muzungos*, Manuel António de Sousa and Ignacio de Jesus Xavier. De Sousa's black army was used in the conquest of Barue in 1880 and in the suppression of the Massingire rising on the Shire in 1884, while the two combined with a Portuguese expeditionary force to isolate and destroy the da Cruz in Massangano in 1887-8. The Portuguese also sought to use de Sousa for the conquest of Manica and the high veldt regions of Rhodesia. However, all that had been achieved towards the pacification of Zambesia since 1880 was undone when de Sousa was captured by Rhodes' men in Umtasa's kraal in September 1890. With the warlord in captivity, his personal empire fell apart. Power devolved on his *chicunda* captains and the chiefs of Barue used the opportunity to regain their independence and to hold onto it precariously for another decade. Unable to provide white troops, the Portuguese had to seek other allies and they turned to the Ngoni chiefs of northern Zambesia and to the black soldiers who had originally been assembled by Silva for the attack on Angoche in 1861 and who now formed a military élite ruling his *prazo* of Maganja da Costa. Some of de Sousa's captains sided with the government, others joined the opposition. During the height of de Sousa's power in the 1880s the Barue chiefs and spirit mediums allied with other threatened Shona states like Mtoko and with the da Cruz clan to bring into existence a broad-based coalition of interests. However, with the establishment of the British South Africa Company in Rhodesia and with de Sousa's death in 1892, the main incentive and the main opportunity for unity were gone. In particular the warring factions among the Barue chiefs were unable to reconcile their differences, with the result that in 1902 two swiftly fought campaigns crushed their lingering independence and at the same time eliminated the power of Macanga, a semi-autonomous state north of Tete which was ruled by a chiefly dynasty of Afro-Indian descent.[11]

However these military successes had been won against people

11. For detailed accounts of the pacification of Zambesia, see Newitt (1973). Isaacman (1976); Vail and White (1980).

who did not have centralised state systems, and they failed to bring peace. The inhabitants of the valley were traditionally organised in small chieftaincies and were accustomed to the domination of warlords who could establish their power in a locality with a handful of men, a few guns and a stockade. The old *prazo* families and their bands of *chicunda* soldiers had behaved not unlike bandits, and banditry remained endemic in the valley, attracting much popular support as the Portuguese tried to introduce taxation and labour recruitment. In 1917 banditry once more became rebellion, spreading from Barue both up- and down-river and causing the Portuguese maximum embarrassment due to the fact that their military strength, such as it was, was deployed in the north against the Germans. The Barue rising and its associated disturbances were suppressed by recruiting Ngoni warriors and turning them loose against the dissident populations. By 1920 the Zambesi valley was quiet and this time there were to be no further armed risings for fifty years.[12]

Unrest in Zambesia in the twentieth century can at least partly be attributed to the labour recruiting practices of the Portuguese, but there is never a simple correlation betweeen the existence of grievances and the violent expression of opposition — indeed the relationship between grievance and resistance often only exists in the mind of the historian. Resistance has much more to do with the capacity to resist than with the desire to do so. The military élites of Zambesia, the old *prazo* captains with their *chicunda* soldiers, and the Barue chiefs with their caches of arms and their stockades in the barren, broken escarpment country were not going to take easily to peaceful pursuits. They had lived in a predatory way for centuries and intended to continue doing so. Against them the Portuguese could not deploy a disciplined European force or a disciplined European administration. Indeed, in their desperation to find some viable way of pacifying Zambesia, they maintained the old *prazo* divisions and leased them to private companies. These in their turn sub-leased them to the old *prazo* élites and employed them to collect the head tax, thereby prolonging their existence. It took a whole generation from the death of de Sousa in 1892 until banditry and the predatory pursuits of these military élites had been finally eliminated — until, in other words, the leaders of the old *chicunda* war bands had literally died out.

Resistance to Portuguese rule was also endemic among the Muslims of the northern Mozambique coast and their Makua and Yao allies.[13] Here the crucial factor was the survival into the

12. Ranger; Isaacman (1976).
13. Lupi; Mello Machado; Newitt (1972); Hafkin.

twentieth century of an independent trading economy, very profitable for the ruling groups and for certain sections of the Portuguese mercantile community but anathema to the colonial authorities. The coastal estuaries were inhabited by people of Makua origin who were largely Islamised and who accepted the political authority of sheikhs who had family, cultural and economic ties with the ruling families of Zanzibar and the Comoro Islands. They controlled a seaborne commerce in ivory, slaves and some agricultural products which were brought by caravans from the interior. The chief caravan operators were the Yao from the Lake Nyasa region and, in the north, the Makonde. The whole region was marked by a lack of large political units and by an endlessly shifting pattern of alliances and rivalries between the sheikhs, the Makua chiefs, and caravan leaders and Portuguese traders and officials. The Portuguese had claimed control over the coast ever since the sixteenth century, but in practice they had accepted nominal recognition of their overlordship from the sheikhs to whom they granted titles and sold firearms. The sheikhs for their part depended on the Portuguese not only for their arms but also for support against intrusive Makua groups which periodically moved towards the coast in search of better land and a share in international trade.

The official abolition of the slave trade in the 1840s greatly increased the tension between the Portuguese authorities and the coastal rulers who were supported by the Indian and Portuguese trading community Opposition to abolition centred round the ruling family of Angoche which in the middle of the century threatened to create a large Islamic monarchy, independent of Portuguese influence. In 1861 the Portuguese persuaded one of the most powerful of the Zambesi *muzungos*, João Bonifacio Alves da Silva, to attack Angoche, which he did storming and burning the town. A Portuguese military post and customs house were set up, but this exerted little influence inland and the Angoche ruling family continued active in the slave trade and as a focus of opposition. In their defiance of the Portuguese they were joined by the Namarral Makua, a group which had entered the coastal region in 1865. Together these two made a successful living by raiding their weaker neighbours, and others whom they suspected of collaboration with the Portuguese, and by selling slaves to the Comoro Islands and Madagascar. The Portuguese mounted several more or less unsuccessful expeditions against these élites, the best-publicised being Mouzinho de Albuquerque's attack on the Namarral in 1896, but effective occupation was hindered by the fact that after 1893 the territory north of the Lurio river came under the control of the chartered Niassa Company. The Company, with its extremely precarious finances, was not anxious to take any action which would disturb the caravan traffic from which it derived customs income or which might force it to discontinue its lucrative trade in firearms. Indeed, many Portuguese interests opposed military pacification completely, pointing out that the region was relatively quiet and prosperous as long as the authorities made no moves to collect taxation.[14]

The region south of the Lurio was finally occupied between 1910 and 1914 when a number of punitive columns were launched against the dissident Yao chiefs and coastal sheikhs. These expeditions were more successful than their predecessors because the Portuguese were able to secure the collaboration of many of the local chiefs to hunt down and kill or capture the rebel leaders. No sooner, however, had Farelay of the Angoche ruling house, chief Marave and the Namarral chiefs been defeated than the First World War broke out. In 1917 Zambesia rose in rebellion and in 1918 Makua territory was invaded by the Germans, to whom many of the chiefs, who had only recently submitted to Portugal, transferred their allegiance. The whole region had to be re-occupied at the end of 1918 by British, South African and Portuguese forces, and the Portuguese forces took fierce reprisals against many of those who had collaborated with the Germans. Finally, in 1922, a column entered the territory in the far north of the Makonde who either submitted without any fighting or crossed the frontier into Tanganyika.

As in Zambesia, much of the endemic resistance in the north of Mozambique appeared to be the result of Portuguese attempts to impose taxation and labour recruitment. However, on closer observation it can be seen that this was a continuation of the pre-scramble conflicts. The most recent historian of this region has pointed out that the opposition was organised by a narrow class which continued to benefit from the clandestine slave trade and which feared for its economic position if Portuguese rule were established:

The rulers of the sheikhdoms, chiefdoms and sultanates were essentially parasitic in their relationship to the African land and people. Producing little themselves, they had no organic relationship with the regions in which they were situated. The revolts were reactionary, in the same sense that they represent the strivings of an elite to preserve a situation in which they alone profited.[15]

In its final stages, resistance among the Makua appears to have lacked widespread popular backing; the dissident chiefs were totally isolated before they were captured. Probably this can best be explained by the rapid growth of cash-crop farming which provided

14. Hafkin.
15. Hafkin, p. 400.

the population of the coastal lowlands with a new source of livelihood, while the Makua who lived inland along the borders with Nyasaland were expressing their opposition by wholesale emigration, avoiding in this way both of the hazardous alternatives open to them if they stayed: armed resistance or submission to Portuguese colonial demands.

Three factors, therefore, emerge in the history of Mozambique to explain the endemic nature of resistance: first, the fragmentation of political authority, which favoured guerrilla warfare and made it difficult for the Portuguese to strike at any one centre of opposition; second, the tactless demands for tax and labour from areas where no adequate military or administrative presence had been established; and third, the resistance of reactionary élites, the *chicunda* war leaders of Zambesia and the slave-trading sheikhs of the northern Mozambique lowlands, with everything to lose from colonial rule.

Why was resistance endemic in Angola?

The wars of pacification cannot be said to have been over in Angola until 1924, and, as in Mozambique, they were mostly extensions of rivalries and confrontations which had their origins centuries before the scramble for Africa began. Although the Portuguese met with both resistance and collaboration in every region of Angola, the most persistent opposition was concentrated in two areas, the Kongo and Dembos region north and north-east of Luanda and Ovamboland east of the Cunene in the extreme south of the country.

The Portuguese had traditionally exercised influence in the Kongo region through a sort of indirect rule. They made treaties with the BaKongo kings, the main object of which was to secure the Portuguese trade monopoly. A Catholic mission was frequently present at the court, and Portuguese and Catholic influence over the royal family was maintained as a matter of policy. This relationship proved unsatisfactory to all parties. The trade of the region escaped the crude attempts to establish a monopoly, and provincial chiefs developed their own commercial contacts with illicit European or African traders. This in turn weakened the economic power of the Kongo king, while his prestige as a ruler was undermined by repeated Portuguese interference in succession disputes and the internal affairs of the dynasty.

The abolition of the slave trade threatened severe disruption to the economic interests of the ruling élites, and weakened still further the basis for co-operation with the Portuguese. At the same time, recognising this, the Portuguese tried to establish a more formal type of rule, building a military station at Ambriz in 1855 and trying to introduce the collection of taxes. The kings protested that theirs was not a relationship which obliged them to pay tribute, but rather that it was an alliance between equals;[16] there was talk of treaties imposed on Kongo princes who were ignorant of the meaning of the text. It was the insecurity of Portugal's position in the north of Angola which led her to sign the abortive treaty with Britain in 1882 which would have given her claims international sanction. This sanction was eventually obtained for Cabinda and the south bank of the Congo river in the Berlin Act of 1885, but with it came a nominal international supervision, for northern Angola was deemed to fall within the conventional basin of the Congo and to be subject to the special international agreements over tariffs, trade, slavery and missions which were accepted in Berlin.

The international interest which was focused on northern Angola made the Portuguese very sensitive to what occurred in that region. In 1878 Baptist missions had been sent out, and under cover of the Berlin Act their stations spread throughout Portuguese Congo. These missions became a rival focus of authority undermining the influence of the nominally Catholic Kongo kings and the Portuguese representatives at their court. Chiefs who accepted Protestantism or allowed their subjects to attend the Protestant missions did so as an assertion of independence as much as from religious conviction.

After 1885 the Portuguese took steps to secure their borders with the Congo Free State, and their progress was eased by the requests for protection which they received from those who suffered from the raids of Free State officers.[17] It was also eased by the fact that during the boom in the rubber trade at the end of the nineteenth century and the beginning of the twentieth, the Portuguese ceased their efforts to collect hut tax, and concentrated instead on the customs revenues which could be levied at the ports. During these years trade boomed in the Kongo region, missions were founded, and the twin effects of cash earnings and the Protestant ethic acted as solvents to the traditional structure of BaKongo society. In 1906, under orders from Lisbon, hut tax once again began to be demanded, despite warnings from local officers that Portuguese authority counted for nothing in much of the interior. When Henrique de Paiva Couceiro became governor-general in June 1907, effective Portuguese control was still virtually confined to a string of posts along the Congo river and the Atlantic coast, with São Salvador the only inland station. In the Dembos hills immediately north-east of Luanda, the Portuguese writ was openly defied. 'The whole region', wrote João de Almeida

16. Wheeler and Pélissier, p.88.
17. Felgas, p.154.

in an official report, was in revolt, no

> European being permitted passage by their rivers or to penetrate their lands. Even natives were forbidden access if they wore any European article. The regions adjacent to the plantations had become veritable asylums for escaped contract labourers, deserters and criminals.[18]

Paiva Couceiro organised a pacification campaign which had five main objectives: the placing of military garrisons, road construction, political contacts, missionary work and agricultural instruction. In the event his pacification simply took the form of organised forays by what he described as a 'flying police column' into the interior of Dembos and the northern Kongo regions. As these columns, mostly of black troops, raised the flag and collected hut tax in one chief's territory, it was the signal for others to resist. By 1913 endemic armed resistance had become open revolt throughout the Kongo language region, and a common leader had emerged in the person of a minor, mission-educated chief called Alvaro Tulante Buta.[19] Communication between the interior and the coast was cut and the capital, São Salvador, was burnt. The Congo region was not quiet again until 1916 when Buta was tricked into surrendering to the Portuguese.

In its final phases discontent in the BaKongo region came to focus clearly on the demands of the new Portuguese colonialism, hut tax and labour recruitment. Many chiefs objected to being asked for hut tax when they had been accustomed to receiving payments themselves from Portuguese traders;[20] others protested at the uneven application of the laws, for the Portuguese tended to collect tax from the compliant and ignore the refusal of the recalcitrant areas. Opposition to labour recruitment specifically mentioned the dislike of serving outside the Kongo language area. However, behind the resistance lay long-standing tensions between provincial chiefs and the Kongo king whom they accused of being a Portuguese-controlled puppet, but whose potential economic power they feared. Moreover the Protestant missions undoubtedly did little to help the establishment of Portuguese authority. The greatest factor, however, was probably the economic uncertainty that followed the down-turn in the rubber trade after 1910, at a time when Portuguese demands for tax were rising. Finally the unrest was fanned into flames by the methods the Portuguese used to achieve pacification. To demand

18. Paiva Couceiro, p.49.
19. Carson Graham, chap. 5; Pélissier (1977), pp.232-48; Felgas, pp.166-74.
20. Felgas, p.157.

taxation before establishing an administration and then to try to pacify the territory by unleashing columns of predatory black troops on the recalcitrant areas was the clumsiest and least effective policy that could have been pursued.

Many of the same factors applied in the extreme south of the country. During the last quarter of the nineteenth century, Portuguese and Boer settlers established themselves on the Huila plateau inland from Moçamedes. Although some attempts at co-existence with the African population were made, the settlers soon expelled the Nyaneka from their lands, and by the end of the 1880s had made Huila into the 'white highlands' of southern Angola. Beyond the Huila plateau to the south and east lay the flood plains of the Cunene and the Okavango, and east of the Cunene was the homeland of the Ovambo.[21] The Ovambo economy was based essentially on cattle ownership, but during the nineteenth century long-distance trade became increasingly important to them and was the object of rivalry between the major Ovambo kingdoms. By the end of the century they were exporting many of their valuable cattle in order to obtain guns, liquor and other imports, and their cattle stocks were replenished by intensifying the raids on their neighbours.[22]

The Portuguese had originally claimed the whole Ovambo country as lying within their sphere of influence, but in 1886 had been forced to accept a frontier line drawn by the Germans, which left half of Ovamboland in German territory. The Germans never made any secret of their desire to acquire all southern Angola, and their traders and emissaries were active trying to win Ovambo support against the Portuguese. At the same time the Holy Ghost Fathers established missions east of the Cunene, which from the first tried to maintain an independent stance against Portugal. Fearful of entirely losing control of the south, the Portuguese were in no position to allow the Ovambo the autonomy which experience and common sense dictated. Moreover, in 1904 the Kwanyama section of the Ovambo inflicted a crushing and humiliating defeat on Portuguese forces at Cuamato.[23]

This is the background to the raids and counter-raids between Portuguese and Ovambo which lasted from 1904 to 1915, but it is not the full story of these bloody wars. On the Portuguese side the continuous state of war came to be a major factor in the economy of the south. Military contractors, Boer transport riders, storekeepers, railway personnel and farmers all came to depend on military

21. The most recent general study of the Ovambo is Lima (1977).
22. Clarence-Smith (1975), p.144.
23. Pélissier (1977), pp.447-52.

expenditure and it was this also which supported the provincial treasury. Indeed, when peace did come in the 1920s, its first effect was to accentuate the economic depression in the south. On the Ovambo side considerable economic and social changes underlay the resistance. These were destroying the traditional socio-economic structure more rapidly than any measures taken by the Portuguese. The prosperity of trade in the late nineteenth century had put money in the hands of the Ovambo and had given some of the kings a taste for expensive imports. Firearms had been imported on a large scale, and the kings took the opportunity to tighten their hold over their people, increasing their exactions of tribute and driving many to emigrate to seek work with the Portuguese and Germans. This trend was intensified when Portuguese control of the surrounding areas prevented the Ovambo from raiding their neighbours, and when in 1911 drought destroyed the herds and cattle pastures.[24]

There is some evidence that it was resistance to the Portuguese that stayed this disintegration and enabled the chiefs to maintain their position of leadership. The proximity of the Germans also enabled the Ovambo to avoid a Portuguese stranglehold. Individual Ovambo could easily migrate south, and imports could reach the country from the Germans as well as the Portuguese. It is possible that arms also reached them from German sources. The end of Ovambo resistance came when these props to their independence were removed. After the disaster at Cuamato, the Portuguese had concentrated their efforts on sealing their border with South West Africa, but it was only in 1912 that the arms trade was finally banned and in 1915 that the defeat of the Germans by J.C. Smuts removed their accomplice to the south. Further droughts in 1913 and 1914 finally destroyed Ovambo economic reserves and allowed the ultimate campaigns to become a struggle for the control of the few wells that supplied the countryside. Once these were seized by the Portuguese, the end was inevitable.

The pacification of Guiné

Guiné was also effectively pacified during the years of the First World War. The colony had been separated from Cape Verde in 1879 and since then it had been administered from the old trading port on the island of Bolama. Portuguese trading stations, some dating from as early as the seventeeth century, were to be found in the river estuaries to the north and south of Bolama, but the frontier agreement with France in 1886 had deprived Portugal of her position

24. Clarence-Smith (1975), p.388–92.

on the Casamance river and had indemnified her with some land to the south where she had no presence at all.[25]

Guiné had always been a trading colony, and by the end of the nineteenth century its commerce had recovered from the abolition of slave trading. Skins, wax, palm-nuts and rubber were being exported, but the real growth occurred in the groundnut trade and in the internal commerce in rice. Groundnut production and marketing brought many of the peoples of the Guiné rivers into the European economic orbit long before any formal administration had been set up.[26] Moreover, pacification was not to alter the situation greatly and the growing of groundnuts and rice for the market remained the principal agricultural activity of the Guiné population up to independence. The Portuguese contented themselves with controlling the marketing of these products as far as they could, and never tried to establish large-scale plantations. Nor did they have any mines or other enterprises which required labour, so that the recruitment of contract workers was never a major aspect of their policies. Hut tax, however, did feature in their plans for the colony, and the first attempts to collect it were made in 1901, giving rise, as elsewhere, to strong resistance from those peoples who had had long experience of trading with Portugal, but who regarded themselves very much as equals and saw no reason why they should recognise the overlordship of the small and weak Portuguese military posts.

In particular, the Portuguese faced opposition from the Papel people of the Bissau region. The Papels had been accustomed to dominate the trading post at Bissau, and subjected it to continuous military pressure, blockading the town in 1891, 1894 and again in 1908. Against them the Portuguese had little success, and suffered major military setbacks when they tried to mount formal punitive raids. The elimination of this persistent opposition again had to wait until the First World War. Only then was Portugal prepared to outlaw the gun traffic and to deprive the Guiné peoples of the means to resist. The destruction of Balanta and Papel military power was eventually achieved only by the recruitment of African warriors. Teixeira Pinto, the officer who planned the pacification in 1912, enlisted the aid of a Senegalese adventurer, called Abdul Injai, whose armed followers were employed very effectively to hunt down resisters in the forests while Portuguese gunboats patrolled the rivers. Abdul Injai himself proved difficult to control, as he assumed that the areas he had conquered were his to plunder. He was not

25. Teixeira da Mota, vol 2.
27. Anuário da Guiné; *Portuguese Guinea*; 'Report... on the Trade of Portuguese Guinea'.

finally removed until 1919.[27]

Inland, the Portuguese fought no pacification campaigns. Here they entered into negotiations with the Fula chiefs and established a form of indirect rule which left the Muslim population very much to its own devices. They were rewarded with relative peace and security in the interior throughout their brief rule in Guiné. In the south there were no centres of resistance, but apparently the collection of hut tax remained a problem even in the 1930s when police had to be used on a number of occasions in the Bissagos Islands.[28]

Conclusion

Although resistance persisted in parts of Angola well into the 1920s, it is difficult to escape the fact that it was the years of the First World War that saw the decisive confrontations and the ultimate Portuguese victories. Is it merely coincidence that resistance movements in Guiné, in Angola among the BaKongo and Ovambo, and in Mozambique among the Barue Tonga, Yao and Makua, all reached a climax between 1914 and 1918 and that it was during those years that they suffered their final defeats?

Probably the events of the First World War had little direct effect except in northern Mozambique, which became a battlefield between Allied and German forces. What was decisive, however, was the decision taken after 1912 to ban the trade in firearms. It is a measure of the influence which trading interests wielded in the Portuguese colonies that trade in arms continued almost to the end of the pacification period. It was some years before the ban, once imposed, became fully effective, but it eventually tipped the scales against further successful armed resistance.

These years also saw the collapse of the prosperity of important sectors of the African economy. After 1910 the export of wild rubber fell steeply, first in price and then in volume. With it fell the independent caravan trade and the political and economic dominance of the caravan leaders. At the same time, southern Angola was hit by recurring droughts which undermined and finally broke the cattle economy of the Ovambo and drove the population to seek work within the European sector of the economy. These disasters hastened the decline of the communal economies and of the social systems dependent on them.

One must be cautious in drawing conclusions concerning the fifty-year span of the era of pacification. The economic and social

27. Teixeira Pinto.
28. Lyall, chap. 19.

changes that created modern Africa were already in progress before 1875, and did not depend on the formal establishment of colonial rule. Nor is it necessarily true that the wars of pacification diverted Portuguese resources from much needed economic infrastructure. One estimate has it that between 1904 and 1910 the pacification of southern Angola alone had cost the equivalent of £1 million and had absorbed virtually all the colony's income.[29] Without the wars, however, it is quite possible that government expenditure would have been very much lower and that the general level of economic activity would have been depressed. The needs of the military led to the building of railways, the opening of roads and the development of river navigation. Military posts scattered throughout the country were consumers of local production and often formed the nucleus of future urban development. It is difficult to imagine investment on this scale taking place if the metropolitan government had not convinced itself of its military necessity.

Among both the white and black populations of the colonies, the effect of the wars was to enhance the importance and prestige of the military élites. Much of the resistance to the Portuguese was organised by the traditional warrior classes for whom warfare was a predatory activity bringing booty, slaves and captured cattle. The same situation prevailed among those groups that collaborated. For them also, warfare was a profitable activity. While the wars continued there was little danger of rivals emerging from among those who had grown rich in the market economy or who had been educated on the missions. With the coming of peace, however, these men rapidly came to the fore and supplanted the old chiefly ruling class. In this sense the period of resistance may have slowed down the pace at which African society was changing, and, by delaying the emergence of a new élite, put the Portuguese colonies a generation behind their French and British neighbours in the development of political consciousness.

29. Hammond, p.287.

4
THE RULE OF THE CONCESSION COMPANIES

The economic relations of Portugal and Africa at the end of the nineteenth century

In the last quarter of the nineteenth century Portugal was overwhelmingly a country of farms and small workshops. In 1890, 77 per cent of the working population was employed in agriculture and less than a quarter of those employed in manufacturing worked in factories with more than ten workers. This picture is reflected in Portugal's relations with the rest of the world. In 1865, 89.9 per cent of her exports were of agricultural produce and 40 per cent (a figure which remained fairly constant till 1879) of these consisted of wine — an industry in which there had been some capital invested. Great Britain took between 51 and 66 per cent of these exports, and it was British capital that controlled the Oporto vineyards.[1]

In the last years of the century there was a great increase in manufacturing. Indeed it is fair to say that Portugal's modern industrial sector was conceived in the twenty years after 1884, when many of the companies were founded which, like Companhia União Fabril (CUF), were later to play a major role in Africa.[2] In particular there was a great expansion of the cloth industry so that by 1911 20 per cent of the industrial labour force (and 38 per cent of those working in units of more than ten workers) was employed in textile manufacture. It seems that this growth was, in part at least, export led and that the colonial market was of critical importance. Between 1891 and 1899 cloth exports to the colonies rose from 100 to 2,337 *contos*.[3] The colonies played a correspondingly important part in sustaining the wine industry. In 1889 they took only 3.07 per cent of Portugal's wine exports, but as the European markets declined due to foreign competition, the colonial share of wine exports increased dramatically. In 1900, 15.06 per cent of wine exports went to the colonies, and by 1904 this had risen to 30 per cent. In 1900, wine and cloth between them made up 70 per cent of Portugal's exports to her colonies.[4]

The economic relationship of the colonies and the mother-country

1. Costa, p.18.
2. Costa, p.25.
3. Costa, p.26 1 *conto* = 1,000 escudos or 1,000 milreis.
4. Castro, p.216.

The Rule of the Concession Companies

has to be seen in a special focus. Colonial trade amounted overall to a small, even diminishing, proportion of her total trade (6.56 per cent of total trade in 1896, 8.8 per cent in 1910 and 6.7 per cent in 1920);[5] moreover, colonial budgets had to be regularly topped up by aid from the Lisbon treasury until the 1920s (for example, between 1888 and 1894 the Mozambique government was being subsidised by 25.5 *contos* a month).[6] This might give the impression that the colonies were not economically important to Portugal. However, her trade with Africa was heavily in surplus, and this surplus was important as trade with the rest of the world was in deficit, and the deficit tended to grow year by year. This trade was also of crucial significance for the two key industries of wine and textiles which were the mainstay of the economy's export sector.

At the end of the nineteenth century, then, Portuguese businessmen were principally interested in the commerce of the colonies, and this commerce was vital also for the government, which derived much of the income of its African colonies from customs revenues. Many of the policies pursued, therefore, recognised the importance of maintaining a thriving trade. Not all, however, were equally successful.

In 1892, a protective tariff was established which favoured trade between the colonies and Portugal, creating a classic mercantilist relationship. However, the tariff could not be applied universally. In Mozambique a separate commercial agreement with the Transvaal allowed free trade between the two countries;[7] the chartered companies in Mozambique were allowed to set their own tariffs; in Angola the northern Kongo district had a separate tariff régime determined by the international agreements on the Congo basin. The different systems caused a chaotic situation. In Zambesia, high Portuguese tariffs contrasted with the generally lower prices of imports in British Africa, and encouraged smuggling and emigration.[8] In Angola the tariffs damaged exports. Nearly 100 per cent of the colony's exports went to Portugal, and there was no way of disposing of any surpluses when Portugal could no longer take them. It even proved impossible to export to other colonies, and in 1906 the British Consul reported that the Portuguese Congo imported sugar from Portugal while Luanda surpluses were unsold, and that Luanda imported timber from South Africa while the same commodity was being exported to Portugal from the tropical forests in

5. Castro, p.214.
6. Mouzinho de Albuquerque, pp.50–1.
7. Katzenellenbogen (1981).
8. Wiese (1907).

the north. It is not even certain that the tariff effectively protected Portuguese manufactures. Foreign exporters adopted the practice of 'nationalising' their goods by having them shipped via Lisbon.[9] It was the general — though not of course disinterested — opinion of foreign observers that the tariff caused colonial commerce to stagnate without allowing the economies of either Portugal or the colonies to benefit by the protection.

The tariff remained the core of Portugal's economic policy in her colonies, but other measures designed to promote trade came into conflict with the political objectives of the government. In 1896, for example, the decision was made to stop collecting African hut tax in the belief that this would promote the caravan trade and that customs dues would make up for the lost revenues. This policy was pursued until 1906, when hut tax was once again collected as a means of cutting the colonial deficits and putting pressure on the Africans to volunteer as wage labourers. There was a similar conflict of interest over the decision to allow the foreign recruitment of labour. Recruitment for the South African mines was encouraged in Mozambique, this being the simplest way of boosting the revenues of the colony and Portugal's sterling balances. However, local interests claimed that Mozambique's own economy was thereby starved of labour.

In these instances the fiscal needs of the government overrode local economic interest — in the case of firearms, the decision went the other way. Supplies of firearms and liquor were believed to be essential for the maintenance of commerce with the quasi-autonomous African societies of the interior (as late as 1908 rubber brought by caravans from the interior formed 60 per cent of Angola's exports).[10] The firearms were used against Portuguese forces and prevented pacification from becoming a reality. However, because of the influence of the commercial interests, the government imposed no serious restrictions on the trade until 1912.

If the interests of government and business clashed, so also did those of different sectors of private enterprise. This was particularly seen in the struggle of the Angolan planters against the Lisbon capitalists who had invested in the São Tomé cocoa plantations and the wine trade. The highly profitable cocoa plantations demanded a ready supply of cheap labour, which was supplied from Angola. The Angolan planters, themselves eager to employ semi-servile labour, joined the international campaign against 'São Tomé slavery' in order to stop the loss of contract labourers abroad. They had some

9. Report on the Trade and Commerce of Angola, (1906).
10. Pélissier (1977), p.177.

success in controlling the traffic, and briefly — between 1910 and 1913 — had it banned.[11]

The struggle with the Lisbon wine interests was less successful. In 1889, a high tariff had been imposed on imported liquor as a result of international action decided on at the Brussels Conference. The result was boom conditions for producers of spirit within the colonies, and in particular for the sugar producers of Angola and Mozambique. By the early part of the twentieth century, spirit production had become the main economic enterprise of the white settlers in the colonies. The sale of spirits, however, had many enemies. Philanthropists pointed to the appalling effects of drunkenness, and administrators to the disruptive effects that the trade was having on the stability of African societies. Behind these, however, were the Lisbon wine interests anxious to corner for themselves the drink market in the colonies. In 1901 they had persuaded the diplomats who were drawing up the agreement with Britain over the supply of labourers to the Rand to press for a clause making it compulsory to serve the Mozambican workers with Portuguese wine. This had failed, but they continued to be active in the campaign which gathered momentum against the liquor industry. In 1906 a new excise was introduced and measures were taken to phase out local spirit production. In 1911 it was finally outlawed.[12] The economic policies of the colonial authorities, therefore, had to try to reconcile the often conflicting interests of settlers, Lisbon merchants and colonial administrators.

The considerable commercial interest which the Portuguese had in Africa was not matched by capital investment. Portugal herself was only just beginning to develop large-scale capitalised industry, while the banking sector was still divided into a large number of small operators who made their profits through speculation or through servicing the needs of the government. Much of the infrastructure development in Portugal itself had been the work of foreign capital. Capital investment in the colonies was, however, seen as crucial. Railways, ports and other public services had to be built in order to fulfil international obligations, and investment was seen too as a necessary aid to pacification and the development of the productive resources of the colonies. However, Portuguese capital was seldom willing to invest in colonial enterprises. Where Portuguese capital was attracted, it was usually in some kind of official relationship with the government. The Trans-African Railway Company, for example, began in 1886 (although its line turned out to be the most

11. Duffy (1967), p.208.
12. Hammond, pp.304-10.

expensive built in Africa, and both investment and profits depended on government subsidy); the steamship line, Empresa Nacional de Navigaçao, required favourable government contracts, while the Banco Nacional Ultramarino obtained the exclusive right to issue colonial currency and lived from the manipulation of exchange rates. The colonial and metropolitan treasuries were usually the losers from these operations, and this sort of investment had little to do with developing the resources of Africa and much with achieving access to political spoils.

The lack of Portuguese capital faced the government with the prospect either of opening the colonies to foreign capital or of playing a major role itself in investment. At the end of the nineteenth century the second of these options was scarcely possible. In the twenty years from 1885 to 1905, the years when Portugal was under maximum international pressure and when Africa was partitioned, the Portuguese government went through a severe financial crisis which required drastic cutting of government expenditure and a restructuring of her foreign debt. Extensive state investment in the colonies was ruled out, with the result that foreign capital was introduced, not only to carry out infrastructure and agricultural investment but to take over the basic functions of government.

By 1904, foreign control of the colonial economies was far advanced. In that year, capital investment by private companies was estimated at 44,826 *contos* (approximately six times the annual revenue of the colonies). Of this 46 per cent was in Angola, 29.7 per cent in Mozambique and 23.5 per cent in the cocoa plantations of São Tomé. The investment in São Tomé was largely Portuguese, but the overwhelming majority of the rest was foreign. More than half of this capital was represented by only six companies: the Niassa, Mozambique and Zambesia Companies, the Moçamedes Company, the Benguela railway and the Mozambique Sugar Company which later became Sena Sugar Estates.[13] This dominance of foreign capital was maintained throughout the period of the Republic. Yet the peculiar conditions in which the capital was employed meant that much of it was never devoted to productive investment at all. Indeed, the greatest criticism that can be made of the foreign concession companies is not that they introduced a capitalist régime but that they actually hindered the introduction of capitalist modes of production.

A modern feudalism

It is important at this stage to distinguish two sorts of foreign

13. Castro, pp.287-9.

concession. First there was the concession granted for a specific commercial investment. Frequently such concessions were for the building of public works, but some were for the establishment of industrial or agricultural enterprises. Not all concessions were obtained by *bona fide* investors. Many would be sought by individuals or syndicates who intended to sit on their concessions until they could be unloaded at inflated values: sometimes too they sought to profit, not by the ostensible object of the concession, but by the fringe benefits that were written into the contracts — for instance, from the land grants or commercial rights. These contracts often gave the concessionaires quasi-governmental functions such as control over labour supplies in the locality, the responsibility to settle white colonists (which was a condition eventually imposed on the Benguela Railway Company), or the responsibility for communications and public health measures. The more successful of these concessionaires, like Sena Sugar or Diamang, formed virtually self-governing enclaves providing a full range of government services as well as undertaking agricultural and industrial enterprises. However, these concessions are essentially different in character from the second category, which might be described as 'general' concessions.

These 'general' concessions were usually defined in terms of a certain area of land where the concessionaire would enjoy wide but generalised economic privileges, in return for undertaking some or all of the functions of government. Such concessionaires might range from the great chartered companies down to the small *prazo* leaseholders of Zambesia, but they were fundamentally different from the first category in that they did not receive their grant for a specific economic purpose or to undertake limited and defined investments. They were generalised concessions which the concessionaire was to exploit as he could.

The decision to grant these generalised concessions was made on purely political grounds and was not the result of pressure from investors or commercial interests. In the 1880s Portugal was claiming all of central Africa, but was at the same time fearful of losing all of it. The concessions were, first and foremost, a device for holding on to as much of Africa as possible and for providing, at any rate the façade of effective occupation. That these were the objectives can be demonstrated by the fact that they were granted between 1888 and 1894 in the very years when central Africa was being partitioned and the conflict with Britain was at its height.

If Portugal's main object in making these concessions was to hold on to her territory, then they can be said to have served their purpose. But seen as the principal agents of development, of pacification, of administration and of investment in infrastructure and production, they were failures. The policy they pursued was not really suited to the evolution of capitalism at all but was a kind of corporate feudalism.

What is meant by the term 'corporate feudalism'? Feudalism here is taken to mean a system where governmental functions are performed by individuals or corporate bodies in return, not for direct control of the means of production, but for control of the surplus production of the inhabitants. Feudalistic forms abound in the early history of the Iberian empires. *Encomiendas* in Spanish America, Brazilian captaincies, Indian *aldeas* and the *prazos da coroa* in Mozambique all involved to a greater or lesser degree the devolution of government functions in return for the enjoyment of local economic privileges.

In western Europe, overseas expansion early produced a highly successful mutation of this species of colonial feudalism, the chartered company. The great companies like the Hudson Bay Company and the Dutch East India Company held sovereign rights over vast tracts of land and millions of people. They had administrative and defence duties, and enjoyed the fiscal advantages of running an administration as well as their lucrative trade monopolies. The most successful of these companies, of course, did not depend to any appreciable extent on fiscal income, but made their profits by investing capital and by introducing a wholly new dominance over world commodity markets. Indeed, the English East India Company did not acquire any territory, nor did it act as a sovereign power, for nearly a century after its foundation. However, the chartered companies that were hastily created in the nineteenth century to fill an administrative vacuum in Africa were never viable purely as commercial concerns. From the start their very existence depended on the profits they could derive from their governmental functions. Like feudal seigneurs they provided justice and administration of a sort, but although they gave investment opportunities to subconcessionaires, their own viability depended on taxing the surplus production of the local population. In this sense their rule must be seen as a modern feudalism.

Feudal régimes in the colonies quickly proved to be highly unsatisfactory for the governments which created them. Most of the captaincies created by Portugal in the fifteenth and sixteenth century were reformed or ended completely within a generation, while the Castilian crown had to fight a war to limit the pretensions of its loyal *encomenderos* in Peru. The feudal rule of the chartered companies in Africa also proved an embarrassment to the metropolitan powers. Admittedly, they answered for the time being the critical problem of what to do with the millions of square miles of territory so heedlessly acquired in the course of a morning's work, but this convenience value seldom lasted long. Soon maladministration, bankruptcy and anarchy raised in urgent terms the question of their future. Within a decade, the affairs of the Niger Company and the Imperial British East Africa Company had to be wound up. The British South Africa Company nearly went the same way and survived only with its pretensions severely clipped. The German colonial companies proved even more *fainéant*, and disappeared by 1890, having proved incapable of ruling. In the Portuguese empire the rule of the concession companies, although arguably no more efficient, proved longer-lived, most of them surviving until the time of Salazar. The last disappeared only in 1941.

The Mozambique Company[14]

Of those who took up the great general concessions, the Mozambique Company was the longest lived and the most successful. The Company evolved from the speculative concessions obtained in Zambesia by the penniless but well-connected Joaquim Paiva de Andrada — in his ambitions, if not in his financial resources, the Portuguese Cecil Rhodes. The Company was founded in 1888 and received its charter in 1891. Its territory included all Mozambique between the Zambesi and the 22nd parallel with the exception of the land to the west of the Luenha and Mazoe rivers. Its most urgent task was to uphold Portuguese claims in the sensitive region that lay between the high veldt and the sea. It had to build a railway to the highlands, and pacify and administer a region that was still totally outside Portuguese control. The Company had few assets with which to achieve these objectives. It attracted a certain limited amount of French and British capital, but with the loss of most of Manica to the British in 1891, it was left with few resources to exploit except the labour and the fruits of the labour of its African population.

It experienced great difficulty in pacifying its territory, and throughout the 1890s devoted little effort to trying to do so, concentrating instead on developing the port of Beira and the rail communications with Rhodesia. The railway was eventually opened in 1898. Throughout this period, the Company's territory along the Zambesi was in the hands of black *chicunda* war chiefs, while the chieftaincy of Barue was totally independent, the prey of rival chiefly factions and, increasingly, of white adventurers. The pacification of this

14. For the history of the Mozambique Company see Vail (1976); Neil Tomlinson (1979); Nunes.

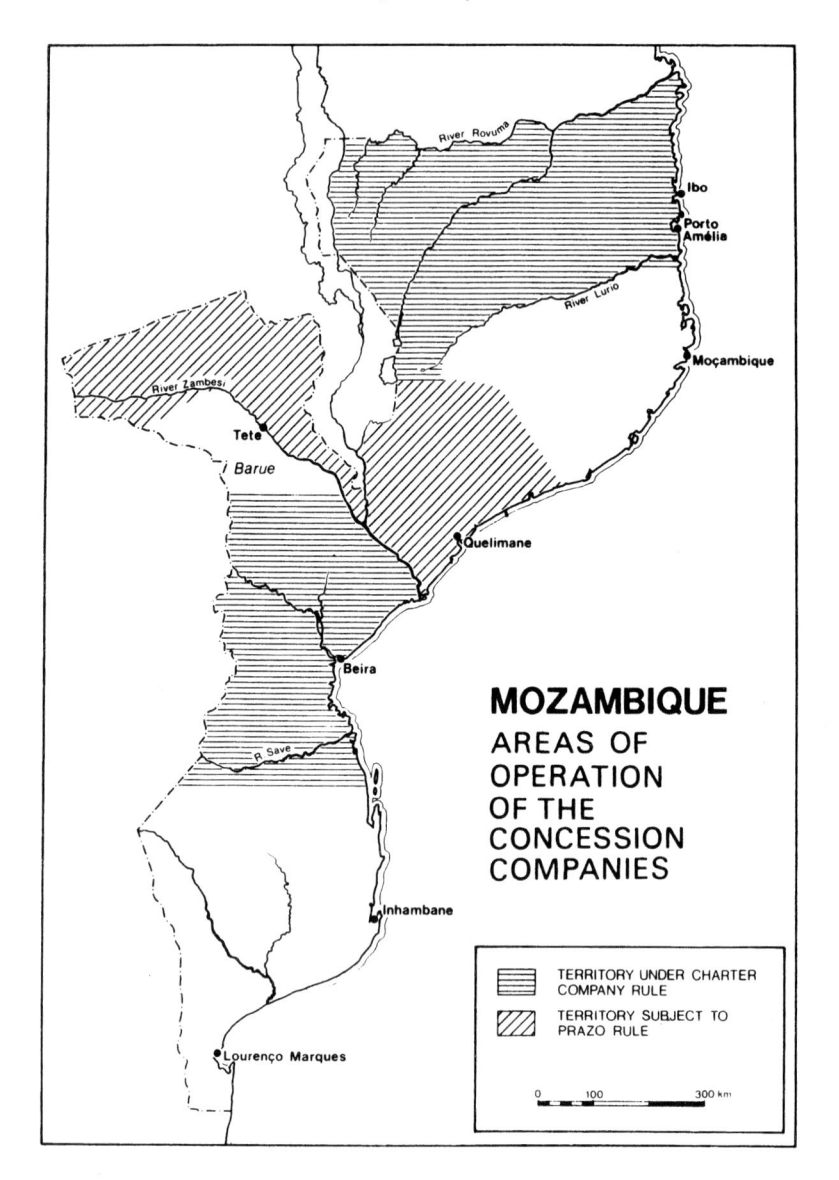

MOZAMBIQUE

AREAS OF
OPERATION
OF THE
CONCESSION
COMPANIES

TERRITORY UNDER CHARTER COMPANY RULE

TERRITORY SUBJECT TO PRAZO RULE

northern part of its territory was eventually carried out by the most accomplished of Portugal's bush commanders, João de Azevedo Coutinho, but as a consequence of the aid that the Company had had to seek from Lisbon, Barue remained under direct government administration.

At first, the Company experimented with taking a direct part in economic development. It founded plantations and a few industrial enterprises, using its administrative authority to supply itself with cheap labour, but direct economic activity ceased by the middle of the second decade. The Company then sought to make profits by exploiting its 'sovereign' rights. Customs and transit dues, taxes, fees, licences and, increasingly, African taxation not only paid for the administration, but enabled the Company to show a moderate profit. To increase tax and customs yields, the Company sought to encourage economic enterprise in others. It sub-leased its land to plantation companies, and at least two of these became creditable successes — Sena Sugar Estates and the Companhia Colonial de Buzi. Both came into existence by swallowing other smaller and less successful concerns, and profited by the relatively plentiful supply of labour to establish their cheap sugar in the world markets. There was also a colony of white farmers who grew maize in the Manica highlands.

Production for export was a major objective of economic policy, and it is interesting to measure the Company's success by this criterion. In 1904, sugar constituted 43 per cent of the Company's exports, a significant proportion of the rest being made up of wax, oil seed and rubber, which were largely the result of African agriculture and collection. In 1914, 45 per cent of exports were sugar and 8 per cent was maize, showing the emergence of another sector of the colonial economy.[15] Total exports in that year were five times the value of those in 1904. In 1924, 65 per cent of exports were sugar, and the only other significant exports were maize (19 per cent) and cotton (9 per cent), but owing to the collapse of the *escudo*, the value of these exports was only a fraction of their value in 1904.[16] In 1934, 56 per cent of exports were sugar.[17] Cotton, fruit and timber each amounted to 3.6 per cent and the only other significant export was provided by gold (17 per cent). Until 1924 the value of the Company's exports had been roughly equivalent to those of the rest of Mozambique and of Angola, and in 1922 their value had exceeded

15. *A Manual of Portuguese East Africa.* p.298.
16. *Report of the Commercial. . . Condition of Portuguese East Africa* (1927), p.40
17. *Economic Conditions in Portuguese East Africa* (1935), p.66.

both. After 1924 they declined relatively, and already by 1928 were less than a third of the value of the exports of the rest of the colony. It is difficult to escape the conclusion that sugar was the only true success in fifty years of Company rule.

The success of the Company, such as it was, rested on the ready supply of cheap labour, and as the Company itself withdrew from direct economic activity, its main contribution to development was its ability to supply employers with labour. Labour was both recruited under the terms of Portuguese labour laws and obtained in the open market, although the two are not really distinct methods since the open labour market was stimulated by the fear of compulsory recruitment. The labour force rose from 80,000 labourers a year (each doing a three-month contract) between 1911 and 1917 to 138,000 (each doing a six-month contract) in 1928. In the 1930s the depression led to a decline in the labour demand. The Company claimed that it was utilising nearly 100 per cent of its domestic labour reserves, and a large proportion of its labourers were imported from outside its territory. There is reason to believe that this was not entirely the case. As well as wanting African labour, the Company wanted African taxes, and for this purpose it was anxious to attract immigrants. This it apparently succeeded in doing, and hut tax receipts formed a steadily increasing proportion of its income. In 1904, African tax formed 23 per cent of Company income (in 1932 it was 34 per cent).[19] Immigration was probably encouraged by lessening the labour demand in comparison with neighbouring territories, and by turning a blind eye to evasion. The extensive labour imports from outside the Company territory were obtained by convincing the government that its own labour resources were being used to the full. The Company also refused to allow South African labour contractors to recruit in its territories, and set an example to the rest of the colony in retaining its labour resources at home. The application of cheap labour allowed the export sector to grow while world prices were favourable, but already by the 1920s it was becoming apparent that the economy was severely undercapitalised and that virtually no industrial sector had emerged at all. This was a problem which was to be faced elsewhere in the empire.

During the first decade of the twentieth century there was a duel for control of the Company, which was eventually won by British financial interests; these continued to rule the territory until 1941. Although the Company authorities collaborated closely with the

18. Neil Tomlinson (1979).
19. *Economic Conditions in Portuguese East Africa* (1935), p.51; *Anuário de Moçambique* (1917), p.626.

Portuguese and did not give way to pressure for labour-recruiting facilities, British influence was nevertheless very strong. The currency in circulation was sterling, British goods dominated the market, and English-language newspapers appeared on the streets of Beira. It appears also that the close connection with Britain led to a considerable coup as far as the Company was concerned, when the British government was persuaded to build the Nyasaland railway through the Company territory to Beira and to construct the Zambesi bridge without which the railway was next to useless. The development of this transport infrastructure was indeed the main claim of the Company to have developed its territory. For the most part it had invested little, and had lived on the product of African labour and African agricultural production, thus largely justifying the description of it as a form of corporate feudalism. Its influence on Mozambique as a whole was divisive. While it continued to exist, Mozambique could not evolve as a single state, for the Company had its own labour organisations and administration, built its communications to link with British Africa, had its own separate tariff structure and tax system, and even had a different currency.

The Niassa Company[20]

The Niassa Company came into existence in 1894 and its purpose was to justify Portugal's claim that she occupied the northern part of her east African colony. Most of the region north of the Lurio river was unexplored by whites at the time of the partition of Africa and there was no question of its having been pacified. One Portuguese town existed on the coast, the picturesque slaving port of Ibo, already almost entirely in the hands of Indian traders who were beginning to tap the agriculture of the interior for cashew and groundnuts. This area of the coast had no economically important interior and hence no transit traffic; it had no minerals and was not greatly desired by other European powers. Neither the prospect of financial dividends nor the pressures of great power rivalry caused investment funds to be channelled in its direction.

From the start, the Niassa Company was little short of a fiasco. It was undercapitalised, and its shareholders soon quarrelled among themselves and set up rival boards.[21] Litigation ensued in which the Portuguese government became involved, and it was not till ten years had elapsed that these problems were ironed out and the

---

20. For the history of the Niassa Company, see Vail (1976) and Neil Tomlinson (1977).
21. Vail (1976) and Mouzinho de Albuquerque, p.47.

Company could assume its governmental role. British influences had triumphed in the boardroom struggle, and once this issue had been settled, a controlling interest was purchased by the South African mining company, Lewis and Marks. Their interest in the territory was its labour, and for a few years they organised recruitment on a large scale. However, in 1913 the South African government banned the use of labour in the mines which had come from tropical regions, and the Company was bought out by German interests. On the outbreak of war in 1914, it was German capital which controlled the Company.

In all this time scarcely anything had been attempted in the way of fulfilling the Company's administrative and economic obligations. 'The employees of the Company collect customs dues from which they pay their own salaries, and that is all the administration consists of,' wrote Mouzinho de Albuquerque in 1898. A few military and administrative posts were set up in the interior to levy taxation and to collect labour, but in many areas the Company's writ did not run at all. On the coast a few plantations were established by Company employees who, from the governor downwards, spent more of their time running their private businesses than in administering the Company's territory. The economy of the region continued to depend on the communal agriculture of the Makua and Makonde inhabitants and on the export of rubber and agricultural surpluses brought to the coast by African caravans or Indian merchants. The exports were shipped from Ibo or Porto Amelia, which the Company had founded in 1904, and a few *escudos* of customs revenue found their way into Company hands. A year before the end of the Company's rule in 1928, its foreign trade amounted to barely 1.5 per cent of the trade of the Portuguese empire.[22]

During the war British interests took over the Company and the campaign against the Germans in 1918 led for the first time to the effective occupation of much of the interior, the Company's officers reaching the Makonde plateau in 1922. Even the seasoned colonials who accompanied the expeditionary force found the Company's rule unattractive. Chiefs thought to have collaborated with the Germans were eliminated, and force was used to collect the hut tax which was the Company's only significant form of income. Underpaid officials were guilty of violence and corruption, refugees flooded into Tanganyika, and the scandalous state of the Company's territory began to cause embarrassment to the British government.[23] Owen Philipps, Lord Kylsant, who owned a controlling

22. Salgado, p.201.
23. PRO FO 371 5491 (1920), G. Lardner Burke to CO.

share in the Company, claimed that it was impossible to raise the money to carry out development, because the charter was due to expire in 1929. Equally embarrassed by the state of the territory, the Portuguese government refused to renew the charter, and in 1929 the Company came to an ignominious end.

The misrule of the Niassa Company was not considered acceptable by contemporary opinion; it did not meet the minimum standards which even the least sentimental colonial demanded. Yet no effective action was taken against it. Its charter was not ended prematurely, nor did it suffer the same fate as King Leopold's Congo. Why was this? An easy answer would be that, except for a brief period after 1913, the Company was British-controlled and, as the mainspring of international indignation about colonial scandals tended to be British, the Niassa Company's activities were ignored for safer targets like Congolese Red Rubber or São Tomé slavery. However, before the war there was deep ignorance concerning Niassa. It was the work of the Admiralty Intelligence division[24] and experience of British officers fighting in Africa which effectively opened up this part of Mozambique and led to the questions in Parliament and letters to the Foreign Office. By that time it was appreciated that the charter would run out in 1929, and it was not surprising that no effective head of steam could be built up to anticipate that happy event.

The rule of the Niassa Company was a further clear case of corporate feudalism. The Company invested little and embarked on few productive economic enterprises. Its profits, such as they were, and the expenses of its operations depended wholly on money and labour rents paid by African peasants from their own economic surpluses.

The Zambesi prazos[25]

The Zambesi *prazos* were also generalised concessions, and clearly belong with the chartered companies, but they were strange institutions of which the roots lay deep in the history of the region. They consisted of approximately 140 land concessions lying along both banks of the Zambesi and occupying most of the land between the two charter companies, with the exception of some directly administered state territory inland of Mozambique Island and south of Tete. The *prazos* had for centuries been the domains of the Zambesi *muzungos* and their slave armies, and more than once in the nine-

24. *A Manual of Portuguese Nyasaland.*
25. The outstanding discussion of the *prazos* in the twentieth century is Vail and White.

teenth century attempts had been made to abolish them. However, the power of the *muzungos* had remained, and they had defied the feeble efforts to establish a regular form of government. A commission of inquiry, convened in 1889, had recommended that the *prazos* should be retained to form the basis for a new administration, and in 1892 the leases had been put up for auction. The leases were originally to have run for fifteen years, but this was eventually extended to twenty-five. The renters became in effect chartered companies in miniature. They collected the head tax, administered their *prazo*, provided the police force, regulated commerce and had formal obligations to set up schools and 'civilise' the population. Originally there were to have been two categories of *prazo*, those in pacified and unpacified areas, and different obligations were to have been attached to each. There is no doubt at all that the intention was to promote agriculture in Zambesia. The renters were specifically debarred from living merely off the profits of African tax, and had to take a percentage in the form of labour, which meant that plantations had to be established. This has to be seen in the light of Portugal's lack of capital for investment. António Enes, the designer of the system, was attempting to make this part of Africa generate its own capital, in the form of money (obtained by taxation) and labour. For those investigating the problems of underdevelopment the idea is of considerable interest, the reality however turned out to be very different from the hopes invested in it.

When the auctions for the leases took place, the *prazos* nearest to the coast, where transport was less of a problem, where the population was thickest and where the rainfall and soil fertility were highest, were taken up by five land companies who rented an average of four concessions each, and who appear to have derived what capital they possessed from British, German, French, Belgian and Swiss sources. No bids were put in for 110 of the 140 *prazos*, most of which lay in the thinly populated and unpacified territory further up the Zambesi. Eventually a company was formed to take over the majority of these *en bloc*.

The Zambesia Company, which assumed this responsibility, therefore became in effect Mozambique's third charter company. Its territory compared in size with that of the Mozambique Company, and although its powers were not those of a sovereign *companhia majestica*, it nevertheless had extensive police and administrative functions, as well as control over the labour and taxation of the inhabitants. For the first ten years of its existence, the Zambesia Company ruled its concession by subcontracting the collection of tax to whoever felt able to undertake the task. A motley collection of adventurers, former slave dealers and ivory hunters took up the challenge. None of them had much idea of investing the money or the labour in productive enterprises, and were merely anxious to line their pockets by selling labour to touts from British Central Africa and by keeping for themselves a large portion of the tax collected. A substantial part of the region was left in the hands of the chief of Macanga, a warlord of Afro-Indian extraction called Pereira, one of the most notorious opponents of Portuguese government rule during the era of the Zambesi wars.

After the campaigns of 1902, which crushed the independence of Barue and Macanga, rather more settled conditions prevailed. Making use of the fiscal labour at their disposal, the Companies began numerous plantations, producing sisal, sugar and copra and experimenting with tea, coffee and cattle farming. Most of this production took place on the lower Zambesi and many of the *prazos* were used simply as labour reserves. This was especially true of the territory which remained in government hands. During the second decade of the century, production of tropical export crops increased on the Zambesi estates, the most impressive growth being on the plantations of the Boror Company. By 1930 it had planted over 2 million coconut trees, produced up to 6,000 tons of copra and 1,500 tons of sisal fibre, almost the whole of this growth having taken place since 1910. As a result of this production, the port of Quelimane handled 43 per cent of Mozambique's exports (by value) in 1927.[26]

During the years of the Republic, there was a vigorous debate about the virtues of the *prazo* system. Its advocates were able to show that it had led to the only successful European economic enterprises in Mozambique, and they claimed that this was due to the fact that they were employing the labour of the country locally. They criticised the official government policy of allowing the labour of the southern districts, and of other government-controlled territory, to be creamed off by foreign labour contractors. Critics of the system drew attention to the scandalous administration of many of the *prazos* — scandals which have their place in that repository of tender consciences, the Foreign Office consular files, and which led to at least two official Portuguese inquiries, in 1909 and 1919 respectively.[27] According to the critics, Zambesia was being depopulated as people fled the region to avoid labour and tax obligations, and the government was getting a poor return relative to the large profits

26. Ribeiro, pp.62, 72.
27. *Provinicia de Moçambique: Relatórios annexo ao Boletim Official* (1909); Vail and White, pp.191-2.

collected by the Companies.[28] Finally, it was clear that a lot of the economic development was rather spurious if it was to be judged as a burgeoning form of capitalist enterprise. The copra of the Boror Company, for example, was largely produced by African peasants who rented the trees from the Company and who lived as squatters on their land.

The *prazo* administration continued until 1930, and was ended as part of the reforms of the Salazar administration. The *prazos* had enabled the colonial authorities to evade the responsibility of establishing an administration or of evolving policies for the future of this region. They had enabled undercapitalised companies to establish a sizeable plantation sector in the Mozambique colony, but they had also evoked the most emphatic and widespread reaction among the African population — mass emigration and the so-called 'Barue rising' of 1917.

Why had Enes' experiment not worked out better? Why had so little of the African tax and labour been ploughed back into the development of the region's agriculture? Partly the answer lies in the multiple holdings of *prazos* which allowed the Companies to concentrate the labour resources of several concessions in one narrow area of plantation development. Partly too it reflects the failure of the colonial administration to provide any adequate supervision of the concessions. Since the concessionaires also provided the administration in the localities, it was easy for them to avoid the application of the law. Their fiscal powers allowed them to establish quasi-feudal regimes and to avoid capitalist development. Many of them behaved just like feudal seigneurs, allowing the African peasantry to occupy their land on a basis of share-cropping and labour service, taking surplus production in the form of the head tax, securing 'contract' labour at cheap rates, manipulating local markets and controlling the sale of commodities. In all this there was little investment, little was created in the way of infrastructure, little mechanisation took place and little in the way of new skills was built up among the population.

The Moçamedes Company

Plans were laid to grant a number of general concessions in Angola as well as Mozambique, but in the event only the Moçamedes Company received a charter (in 1894). Although it was not established on the basis of any clear economic prospectus, the Moçamedes

28. See Newitt (1973), pp.367–76, and sources quoted.
29. Lyne, p.62.

Company really bears little resemblance to the Mozambique chartered companies. In particular, it did not control African taxation, police or customs dues, nor did its concession include the coastal ports.[30] Deprived of these fiscal rights and controls over the population, it was not able to evolve the corporate feudalism of the Mozambique companies and so draw its profits from surplus African labour and production. Instead, it was forced to invest and to exploit its geographical position in the atmosphere of rather fevered competition between British and Germans for influence in southern Angola. The original capital had been French-owned, but the Company was taken over by Rhodes, who appears to have wanted to used it either to build a railway from central Africa to the sea or simply to defeat the railway projects of his rivals. He only partly succeeded in this. As we have seen, in the end the Germans were prevented from building their railway connecting South West Africa to an Angola port, but Robert Williams' railway linking Katanga to Benguela, which Rhodes also opposed, did go ahead.

Having failed as a railway promotion company, the Moçamedes Company failed also as a mining enterprise, abandoning its attempts to mine gold in Cassinga. Eventually, once again in the hands of French owners, it made a modest success of establishing cotton plantations and, later, cattle ranches. Its privileged charter was ended, after having received one four-year extension, in 1923.

The development of specialised capital enterprise

Although Portuguese trade with Africa was growing in the last years of the nineteenth century, and although there was a class of planters and merchants already established in Angola who disposed of some capital, very little metropolitan Portuguese money was invested in the mainland colonies until the 1920s. Instead, the colonial authorities were approached by entrepreneurs of all kinds seeking specific concessions — for railway building, mineral extraction, land and property. In their desire to attract capital and some form of economic development, they granted many of these requests, though seldom with conspicuous success. The motives of the concessionaires were mixed. Some of them looked upon their concessions simply as an appreciating asset to be held until it could be off-loaded on a rising market; others looked to benefit from some windfall discovery or to profit from the land or commercial rights which accompanied their concessions. Where the intentions were honest, the concessionaires was usually attracted by the apparent easy availability of cheap

30. Clarence-Smith (1979), pp.17-18.

labour in the Portuguese colonies and by the monopolistic conditions which could be written into their contract. Because of these monopolistic rights, and their control over land, many of these concessionaires came to be virtually indistinguishable from those who held more generalised concessions.

Two early examples of such concessions were provided by the railways. Portuguese capital had not been forthcoming to build Portugal's share of the Lourenço Marques-Transvaal railway, and in 1883 the concession was granted to a not very reputable American called McMurdo. This man was able to raise finance in London to build the line, but was intent on using his concession to extort other gains for himself. He obtained an extensive land grant from the Mozambique government, and then held out for the right to build the Transvaal section of the line: In the end, Portugal repossessed the concession, though only after extensive litigation, and then found that she had to rebuild the track completely.[31]

The concession granted to Robert Williams in 1902 was again to prove unsatisfactory. Williams, once granted his concession, was unable to finance the railway since it faced too much opposition from Congolese, Rhodesian and South African sources. By 1908, he had constructed 205 kilometres, which effectively linked the plateau with the coast but came nowhere near providing the link between the copper mines and the coast through Portuguese territory, which was the railway's purpose. Instead, the mines were linked to the Rhodesian railway network in 1910. Although Williams' railway made little further progress until the 1920s, his concession included land and mineral rights within a 120-km-wide band on each side of the track, as well as taxation and commercial privileges. Many Portuguese saw this as creating what was virtually a British colony in the heart of Angola.[32]

In the end, both these railways were actually built, but other contracts were less satisfactory. American and Belgian capital, for instance, set up companies which obtained extensive prospecting rights for petroleum, copper and other minerals in Angola.[33] They achieved little. Paiva Couceiro likened their activities to 'the assault on a defenceless country by various groups of *francs-tireurs*, each acting independently'.

Of these foreign concessionaires, however, two proved outstandingly successful, fulfilling alike the hopes of the Portuguese administration and the expectations of their shareholders. Both invested

31. Hammond, pp.224-44.
32. Katzenellenbogen (1973), p.40, and Paiva Couceiro, p.89.
33. PRO FO 371 8374 (1922) Hutcheon to FO, 28.9.1922, for list.

Sena Sugar estates

The Sena Sugar Company grew up on the estates of the failed Opium Company, and was at one time known as the Mozambique Sugar Company. Successive mergers and reorganisations brought it under the control of James Hornung, an able and aggressive Sussex squire who had married a Portuguese wife. The Sena estates comprised *prazos* on the north bank of the Zambesi and on the south bank within the jurisdiction of the Mozambique Company, and it was there that the Company had its headquarters. Sugar being a labour-intensive crop, the Company made full use of its administrative control over African labour, and continually sought ways of acquiring more *prazos* and of creaming off labour supplies from other areas.[34] Where it differed from the other concessionaires was in the fact that Hornung used his opportunities to build a thriving modern sugar industry, adequately capitalised and properly equipped with technical infrastructure. On its estates the company achieved the kind of development which one imagines the colonial authorities had hoped for from all the concessions they granted. Pedro Muralha described the estates of the Company in 1924 before the decline on the price of sugar had set in. Commenting on the Company's new centre of production at Luabo, Muralha said simply: 'It did not limit itself to constructing a factory, it is constructing a city.' He described with enthusiasm the electric generators, the railway, the hospital, the refrigeration plant, the bakery, the telephone service and the workshops, all built by the Company. The Company was employing 8,530 labourers and farming 18,857 hectares of land. It had built 267 km. of railway on which twenty-five locomotives and 1,446 wagons were operating, and its fields were irrigated by forty-five irrigation pumps.[35]

Yet a word of caution is necessary, for the feudal elements were markedly present in this model capitalist enterprise. The company made extensive use of 'contract' labour; in other words it did not feel able to survive in a free labour economy, and in the early days it never tried to do so. Indeed, in 1924 it was involved in a contract with the government for the supply of 3,000 labourers at the very time

---

34. A history of Sena Sugar forms the core of Vail and White.
35. Muralha, pp.69–85.

when Portugal was trying to tell the world that the administrative involvement in labour recruitment was coming to an end. Perhaps its enterprises can be compared with those of an eighteenth-century Prussian junker amid his estate serfs rather than with a modern capitalist enterprise.

Diamang[36]

The Companhia de Diamantes de Angola ('Diamang') was, in one respect, just another mineral-prospecting company whose concession covered two-thirds of Angola and which was financed initially by Belgian capital. The Company, however, did find workable deposits of diamonds in the remote and unpacified Lunda district in eastern Angola, and began operations just as a Portuguese administration was being established for the first time. It was not surprising that the Company and government should be the dominant partner, since the former disposed of resources not available to the administration, while the nature of its activities required the strictest monopolistic controls. Although it had no charter and was not officially endowed with administrative functions, the Company became, in effect, the government throughout that whole Lunda province, and retained its dominant position until Angola became independent.

The large profits earned by the Company were invested in the creation of a communications network in the area and in building up the supporting industries and services needed for the extraction of diamonds. The Angolan government had always seen concession companies as institutions that could aid it in raising loans and financing government projects, and Diamang became the chief banker for the Angola government throughout the 1920s and 1930s. In return, it required assistance in the recruitment of labour. Hitherto the government itself had been the biggest employer of labour, and had officially frowned on the practice of employing administrative pressure to supply private concerns. Diamang was different; Angola's financial health was seen to be deeply involved in its success, and the flow of contract labour to maintain the Company's workforce of 10,000 was assured.[37]

The sale of diamonds and ultimately the rate of their extraction came to be controlled by the Diamond Corporation established by Ernest Oppenheimer.[38] Foreign capital had led to foreign monopoly

36. For an official history of the Company see *Companhia de Diamantes de Angola*.
37. *Companhia de Diamantes . . .*; *Portuguese West Africa* (1949), p.10; Galvão and Selvagem, vol.iii, p.354.
38. Gregory, pp.129–30, 234–5, 308–9; Lanning and Mueller, pp.58–60.

control. However, the need to extract the diamonds in a remote part of the country forced the Company to invest heavily in Angola itself and to develop the infrastructure and services that the industry needed.

Conclusion

Long before the 1920s, the Portuguese had come to realise that the policy of granting concessions had not been as successful as had been hoped. Ex-governors, planters and journalists interested in the colonies were among the foremost critics of the system which they saw as having delivered Portuguese territory into the hands of foreign capital, which had no 'national' sentiments and was concerned simply to extract wealth, leaving little productive enterprise behind it. Although the success of Sena Sugar and Diamang was undeniable, this has to be seen alongside the failures of other mineral-prospecting, sugar and land companies. The British consul in Mozambique, R.C.F. Maugham, was clear about what had gone wrong. He wrote of Zambesia:

Its development will not be achieved by large concessionary companies. They are too unwieldy, or rather the needs of the concessions entrusted to their governance are too numerous, intricate and multifarious to be supplied by even the most painstaking and conscientious of directing boards. Instead of two or three developing companies, we need two or three hundred . . . Throw open the country to industry and agriculture. Make its acquisition for legitimate objects easy to whomsoever will come and devote his time and his capital to increasing its value.[39]

The size of the concessions had led to a dissipation of expenditure and effort, with little achieved at the end of the day. However, the concessions had been made large in the first place because of Portugal's need to establish the concession companies as a territorial administration. Control over African tax and labour had been granted as a lure to investors and as a necessary part of their administrative role. The result had been that the concessionaires had been able to make profits from the tax and the sale of contract labourers. What productive development they had undertaken had been through the employment of cheap labour and not through capital investment.

The system had led to the perpetuation of quasi-feudal relations, semi-servile labour, low levels of productivity and a general retardation of the development of the colonies along capitalist lines.

39. Maugham, p.109.

5
THE AFRICAN POPULATION UNDER PORTUGUESE RULE, I

The autonomous development of African economies

The first chapter examined the response of the African peoples who lived in the Portuguese sphere of influence to four centuries of international trade. It was suggested that this trade did not distort the evolution of their economies as much as has been suggested, partly because only a few societies — and often only a narrow élite within even those — indulged in this trade, but also because African farming methods, due to their high productivity, left much surplus labour available for the different activities associated with trade. The importance of the African role in this trade was also stressed. Although European and Indian capital controlled supply and demand at one end, it was African chiefs who controlled it at the other, and the trade within Africa itself was organised very much in their interests.

The greatest disruption to this pattern of trade, and to the stability of the societies which depended on it, was caused by the abolition of the slave trade. This not only undermined the economic base of the caravan trade but led to shifts of political and economic power within African societies. Some adapted, but others tried to retain slave-trading, and their desire to maintain their old predatory economies was often the basis of their resistance to the imposition of colonial rule.

In general, as the abolitionists foretold, the abolition of the slave trade was accompanied by an expansion and diversification of legitimate trade between Africa and the outside world. This was partly due to changing demand in the western economies, which now sought supplies of groundnuts, palm oil, copra, etc., for industrial purposes, and to the expanding market for ivory both in Europe and the East; it was also due to the breakdown of the restrictive monopolies which both Africans and Europeans had tried to operate in the days of the slave trade, so that tariffs were lowered and the impediments to commerce generally removed.

The world market for African raw materials in the nineteenth century was concentrated either on forest products or on crops which could be produced as a by-product of subsistence agriculture. By the end of the nineteenth century, this trend had led in Portuguese Africa to a general strengthening of peasant economies, to a wider distribution of commerce and to the rapid growth of a cash sector. In the twentieth century, however, the dwindling world market for forest products, particularly wild rubber, was matched by a growing demand for some cultivated crops, so that the independent peasant producer continued to prosper. It was on him that the colonial régime came to focus its attention in the attempt to extract from him his surplus.

The collapse of world commodity prices during the great depression of the 1930s considerably weakened the independent African peasant economy, and led to a growth of wage-earning. This trend, however, was uneven, affecting some societies more than others, and was often also the result of adverse climatic conditions. At the same time, the Portuguese government introduced compulsory crop growing which further endangered the independence of the peasant sector but which helped to preserve the basic structure of village societies.

The evolution of a wage-earning, cash-oriented society had only imperfectly taken place in Portuguese Africa at the time of independence. Except in a few areas, Africans had not been driven from the land, and there had actually been extensive internal colonisation during the colonial period; colonial policies had aimed at providing labour for capital enterprises without creating a permanent proletariat. Migrant and contract labour had made extensive inroads into the African labour surplus, and compulsory crop growing still more, but in many parts of the colonies an autonomous African agricultural sector managed to survive.

It is this autonomy that must be stressed throughout. The Africans of Angola, Mozambique and Guiné were not simply objects to be manipulated by Portuguese colonial policies. They were affected by world markets and by the dynamic of their own internal development, more than they were by Portuguese colonial legislation. Much of this legislation, indeed, was a response to changes within African society and was not the cause of those changes. Equally, much of this legislation concerned the disposal of surpluses of wealth and labour, leaving the core of African economies and societies untouched; much of it also was very patchy, so that large areas of the colonies and whole sections of their peoples were relatively little touched by colonial rule.

The re-orientation of African trade and production

The abolition of the European slave trade might have fatally crippled the activities of the trade caravans, which connected the societies of the central African interior with the coast. This, however, did not happen, partly because the slave trade continued at a rather lower level, and partly because of the discovery of new commodities for the caravans to carry. The changes in long-distance trade cannot yet be charted with any accuracy, but it seems that in Angola there was a rapid increase in the exports of ivory after the 1840s, and this had the effect of opening the interior to hunters and traders as the elephants were pursued deeper into the backlands. In certain areas there appears to have been an expansion of the trade in cattle. This is particularly obvious in the south of Angola, where cattle exports from Moçamedes rose sharply in the 1880s,[1] and rather earlier in Mozambique where Lourenço Marques had already begun to develop into a major cattle port by 1820.[2] The exports of cattle and ivory not only paid for imports and provided cash incomes; they also had side-effects. The societies which produced the cattle, the Ovambo in southern Angola and the Ngoni of Natal, had to replenish their depleted herds, and this increased the intensity of their raids on their neighbours and their demand for firearms. Bands of armed raiders often doubled as hunters, and in this way trade increased the aggressive and expansionist nature of these societies. The extent of Ngoni raiding is well known; but the Ovambo also were formidable raiders, and as late as 1910 could harry the backlands of Benguela with raids originating hundreds of miles to the south.[3]

In the 1880s, cattle and ivory were both put into the shade by the spectacular growth of the trade in wild rubber. This product could be tapped in the forests of both Angola and Mozambique. It was produced carelessly and was a low-grade product, but for a short time it was much in demand and fetched very high prices. The rubber caravans frequently brought with them wax, which was also gathered wild in the forests of the interior. The impact of the rubber trade has been most closely investigated as it affected the Ovimbundu of central Angola. The Portuguese had traded with the Ovimbundu states for two centuries, but these do not appear to have played a major role in the slave trade. Their rise as caravan operators coincides with the decline of slaving when the old caravan leaders had fallen on hard times. By aggressive entrepreneurial activity, the Ovimbundu chiefs seized the initiative in the trade of the interior, drove most of the Portuguese from business, and came to dominate the caravans to the coast.[4]

1. Clarence-Smith (1975), p.144.
2. Hedges.
3. Paiva Couceiro, p.65.
4. Pössinger (1973).

The prosperity of the Ovimbundu long-distance trade appears to have lasted till the collapse of the market for wild rubber between 1910 and 1912, although it is unlikely that the caravans to the coast would anyway have survived the competition that the railways were beginning to provide. The prosperity of the caravans during the thirty years from 1880 to 1910 appears to have led to the concentration of wealth and political power in the hands of their organisers, who were frequently chiefs. This could be seen particularly in the growth of large towns as the families of those away with the caravans clustered for protection round the head village of the chief. This concentration in its turn helped to confirm the chief's authority and the power he was able to exert over land use and the disposal of economic resources.

In Mozambique, the caravans which had operated on the upper reaches of the Zambesi were crippled by the terms of the partition in 1891, which isolated the *chicunda* from their old hunting and trading grounds in the Rhodesias. In the northern part of the colony, however, caravans continued to come to the coast led by Yao or Makonde, again until the end of the rubber boom. However, as this coincided with the major campaigns of pacification in the interior and with the outbreak of the First World War, it is rather difficult to disentangle the inter-relationship of these events. If, in general, the continuation of the caravan trade tended to reinforce the old hierarchies and, incidentally, enable them to resist colonial rule, there were forces in northern Mozambique working in the opposite direction. In the last quarter of the nineteenth century, there was a great expansion of agricultural exports, in particular groundnuts, sesame and rubber. Groundnuts and sesame were produced by African peasants and marketed by Indian traders, who set up stores in the interior for the purpose.[5] This led to a rapid growth of a cash economy and to the emergence of a kind of economic individualism opposed to the traditional collectivisation of economic production. It is not impossible that this process accounts for the increasing isolation of those chiefs in northern Mozambique who wished to continue resistance to the Portuguese, and for the dwindling of support for them. An almost exactly similar process occurred in Guiné, where there was a large increase in the export of African grown crops at the end of the nineteenth century and in the first decade of the twentieth.

These changes had little or nothing to do with Portuguese policy. The Portuguese continued to collect customs dues at the ports, and professed to follow policies designed to promote trade. However, these policies were somewhat ambiguous in their intentions and

---

5. Vail and White, chap. 2.

limited in their effects. Equally difficult to assess is the part played by the colonial régime in the other great trend of the period, the growth of wage labour.

The Portuguese trading community had, of course, always employed a certain amount of labour. Carriers and soldiers had often been recruited from vassal chiefs, and this service was looked upon as part of the tribute they owed to Portugal. Other labour was done by slaves. Slavery was abolished in 1875, but servile labour continued to be available through a number of channels. Military service remained obligatory in Angola and the *guerra preta* thus recruited might be employed as a workforce. Ex-slaves were retained under 'contract', and their contracts were renewed again and again; then there was the system of redemption by which settlers and even missionaries 'redeemed' Africans from slavery and provided them with work. This system was a barely disguised continuation of the trade in slaves. Finally there was direct coercion by the administration, which compelled Africans to enter government service under the terms of the labour laws. Servile labour of all these varieties continued well into the twentieth century, and was particularly demanded by the white planters and concessionaires. However, to concentrate on this is to ignore the much more powerful trends which were beginning to create a free wage-earning labour force.

The first indications that wage-earning was entering into the lives of the population occurred in the 1850s, when agents of the Natal sugar planters began to recruit labourers in southern Mozambique. This source of supply proved successful, and South African railway contractors and mining magnates soon had their agents in the field as well. By the 1870s, many thousands of workers were leaving southern Mozambique annually to earn wages in South Africa.[6]

The cause of this migration has been much debated. The region from which the labourers came can be defined as the lowlands of Mozambique from Delagoa Bay to Inhambane. This area was barren, and its agriculture was precarious. It was easy for the population to outgrow the bearing capacity of the land, and by the end of the nineteenth century, game of all kinds was becoming scarce. It had long been accepted that younger sons of Thonga and Chopi families would migrate to establish new villages for themselves. Migration to seek wages could, therefore, relieve poverty and population pressure and at the same time allow the young men to establish their independence, earn *lobola* and free themselves from communal ties. It may be, however, that more specific pressures were at work. Compulsion may have appeared in the form of

6. Rita Ferreira, pp.11–13.

additional demands of tribute from chiefs who were anxious to obtain the bounties of the labour recruiters.[7]

Whatever the reason for the beginning of migrant labour, it was to become a pervasive form of economic activity. It acted as a supplement to the older forms of village agricultural economy. The migrant worker was expected to return to his village; the consumer goods he brought back increased its wealth, and his wages were often a vital addition to an inadequate living earned by the rest of his family from the soil. During the disastrous droughts and epidemics of the second decade of the twentieth century, the wages of migrant workers contributed substantially to the survival of many rural communities. At the same time, their independent economic position must have weakened communal ties and promoted economic individualism. The migrant worker was neither a peasant wholly involved in a pre-capitalist, communal economy nor a proletarian. His urban wages did not produce an urban society or an urban political consciousness.

By the time of the First World War, the migrant labour system had also begun to develop in southern Angola, another region still outside Portuguese control. Early in the twentieth century, the opening of the copper and diamond mines in South West Africa and the beginning of the work on the Moçamedes railway dramatically increased the demand for labour. The demand was met by the Ovambo, and by 1914 at least 10,000 of them were working for wages in the colonial economies.[8] Obviously, one factor in the growth of this wage labour was simply the opportunity to acquire the money to pay for imports. Among these, guns were of great significance, and the Portuguese continued to sell firearms to the Ovambo in order to stimulate trade and the further supply of labour. Important also was the decline in the cattle economy. Exports of cattle fell off after the rinderpest epidemic of 1897, and the cattle lands of the south were devastated by drought in 1911 and 1914–15. The expansion of colonial government made it difficult for cattle stocks to be recouped by raiding, as would have happened in earlier times. A third factor was the demands of the Ovambo chiefs for tribute, which became so excessive that many ordinary tribesmen were forced to flee. The most recent historian of the region has concluded that 'there are signs that many Ovambo were indifferent to the idea of European conquest as long as it freed them from the exactions of their rulers'.[9]

7. Young; Wield.
8. Clarence-Smith (1975), pp.388–9.
9. Clarence-Smith (1975), p.336.

Long before the establishment of effective colonial rule, therefore, the African population of parts of Mozambique and Angola were beginning to supplement their communally-based agriculture by collecting forest products, growing for the market and entering the colonial economy as wage-earners. These activities seldom interfered with the growing of basic subsistence crops, since they utilised surplus (frequently male) labour, while wage-earning likewise was carried out by men whose traditional activities of hunting and fighting were being increasingly restricted by the advance of the colonial government. These additional sources of income proved invaluable during the disastrous decades of 1895–1915, when epidemic, drought and famine brought many rural communities to the verge of destruction.

Portuguese 'native' policy

Portuguese 'native' policy was formulated during years when Portugal was scarcely master of the situation in her colonies, and was not free to conduct the sort of experiments in social engineering that theorists might have wanted. In the last quarter of the nineteenth century she was faced with the problem of pacification; with the urgent need after 1891 to cut colonial deficits; with the pressure of concessionaires and the metropolitan commercial classes for economic privileges; and with the autonomous social and economic changes which were affecting the African populations of her colonies. Yet although she was confronted with these pressing realities, her legislators never lost sight of idealistic objectives, and these coloured the colonial rhetoric and the language of decrees. There were, therefore, three distinct Portuguese 'native' policies, or rather a trinity in which one 'native' policy took on three different manifestations. First, there was the ideal, long-term objective of this policy, secondly, there were the actual provisions of the colonial legislation designed to form a framework for day to day administration; and thirdly, there was the policy that was actually carried out by the local *chefes do posto* (district officers) and the *regedores* (administrative chiefs).

The long-term objective of Portugal's policy remained fairly consistent throughout the last century of her rule. There was never any statement of, or commitment to, the paramountcy of African interests, as there was in British Africa. Instead the aim was to integrate the Africans with Portuguese society, making them Catholic, Portuguese in culture, and part of a wage-earning, market-oriented economy. This process was described as 'civilising'. An African could apply to the local administration for a certificate which would classify him as a *civilisado*, after which he theoretically enjoyed all the rights and obligations of a white Portuguese. By the end of colonial rule, relatively few Africans had achieved this formal state of being 'civilised', principally because they saw no advantage to themselves in abandoning the status of *indígena* (native).

It was with the man who was legally classified as an *indígena* that colonial policy can properly be said to have been concerned. The *indígena* was viewed in a variety of roles — as taxpayer, as labourer, as producer within a traditional economy, and as a potential *civilisado* — and the multifarious legislation which organised his affairs recognised the interrelationships of these roles. A comprehensive labour law was produced in 1899 and a land law in 1901, but the codification of all the decrees affecting the *indígena* was not carried out until the early days of the New State, and was embodied in the *Estatuto Político Civil e Criminal dos Indígenas* in 1929. The legislation was revised in 1954, when the term *assimilado* came to replace *civilisado*, but it was only fundamentally changed in the major reforms of 1961.

In 'native' affairs, therefore, as in so many other lines of Portuguese policy, there was a strong trend of continuity, in spite of the changes of régime and the appearance of fundamental difference in their ideologies. There *indígena* was considered to be part of a community ruled directly by a chief, and subject in the first instance to African customary law. He enjoyed access to communal land, paid the native tax, and was liable to perform a variety of services which might include acting as a carrier, serving with the police, labouring on public works, and acknowledging a general obligation to contract himself as a worker. Theoretically,[10] this policy aimed to educate the African and to lead him on towards his ultimate social destiny as a *civilisado*, but in practice it was designed to do three things — to maintain the structure of African traditional society, to provide income for the colonial exchequer, and to produce a ready supply of labour for government and private projects. In its general outlines this 'native' policy of the Portuguese was not dissimilar to that of other colonial powers, and Réné Pélissier has even said of the 1928 labour code:'*Il est rélativement avancé pour l'époque.*'[11] Yet Portuguese colonial rule had always been held to be in some way exceptionally corrupt, cruel and reactionary. These criticisms in part reflect the jealousy and frustration of those who vainly sought to wrest the colonies from Portugal's control; in part they reflect a traditional hostility on the part of liberal, Protestant Britons and

10. For an official account of Portuguese native policy, see Silva Cunha.
11. Pélissier (1978), p.137.

Americans towards what they believed to be an inherently corrupt Catholic tradition; but undoubtedly also they reflect the fact that the actual practice in the colonies departed a long way from the legal position set out in the legislation on 'native' affairs. As John Harris put it in 1914, 'Portugal may send a ship-load of regulations out of the Tagus every week and the planters will welcome them — as waste paper.' It is therefore on the realities, as far as they can be discerned, and not on the letter of the law, that any judgement must be based.

Land policy

As more and more of the colonies came under effective control in the early twentieth century, a decision had to be reached about land rights. In a decree of 1901,[12] the government recognised the right of Africans to the land which they habitually cultivated or occupied, and this right was restated at intervals throughout the twentieth century and enshrined in the constitution of the New State. An African could acquire individual rights in his land after twenty years' occupation. In 1918, a law permitted the designation of reserves in which land would be inalienable to private owners, and in 1927 some of the realities of African agriculture were recognised when land four times the extent of that in current use was considered to be in occupation. Unoccupied land could either be granted by the state to would-be developers of any race, or could be occupied by African farmers. The law nominally favoured the emergence of African smallholders, for those who took up concessions of vacant land and cultivated them could obtain remission of tax for a time and were exempt from labour and carrier service.

In only a few areas was there significant competition for land between Africans and white settlers. In Angola the establishment of coffee plantations in the Cazengo highlands after 1840 led to much of the local population being driven from the land — although a number of the coffee-planters were in fact African themselves. Likewise, the settlement of Boers and Madeiran peasants in the south after 1881 led to the Huila plateau becoming a sort of 'white highlands', with most African cultivators expelled or reduced to the status of squatters and labourers. From time to time in the twentieth century, further competition for land occurred. The coffee boom after the Second World War led once again to a fierce scramble for land in northern Angola, and although the law officially protected African occupants, there is little doubt that many were forcibly

12. Coissoro, p.417.

expelled from their holdings. Similarly, there were some removals from the land which was designated for *colonatos* in the 1950s.[13]

However, these regions where there was competition for land amounted to only a tiny fraction of the territory of the colonies. Far more striking was the rapid colonisation of vacant land by African farmers that took place during the twentieth century, resulting in far greater tracts of land being in African occupation than in the nineteenth century.[14] It is possible that this internal colonisation represents the restoration of some 'natural' population density, after a century or more of disruptive warfare and general insecurity for the agriculturalist. The nineteenth century had witnessed the wars of the Cokwe in Angola and the invasions of Mozambique by the Ngoni; pacification wars had devastated much of the Zambesi region, as well as the north and south of Angola; influenza in 1919, rinderpest and drought between 1895 and 1915, wrought havoc to human and animal populations alike. Such evidence as there is suggests an overall population decline and a tendency for people to concentrate around defensive centres, with the resultant abandonment of bush villages and gardens. This is most striking in Zambesia where the African population gathered under the protection of the fortified *aringas* of the Zambesi *muzungos* throughout the period of the Zambesi wars (*c*.1840-1902).

The settled conditions that followed pacification, and which became almost universal after 1920, led to a rapid growth of population. The return to cultivation was aided by the communications developed by the colonial authorities, which made it increasingly possible for the remoter inland areas to be profitably farmed. This process has been best documented in the case of the Ovimbundu. After the collapse of the caravan trade in the second decade of the twentieth century, the Ovimbundu took to the production of cash crops for the market, particularly maize and coffee. In their search for virgin land that would yield good crops, they left the larger settlements and moved south and east into thinly populated or unoccupied land, establishing small peasant farms based on a family nucleus. By the 1930s, the Ovimbundu had colonised vast tracts that were unsettled at the time of pacification, and had greatly extended the area of Angola which was theirs.[15] In 1960, the Ovimbundu made up 40 per cent of the Angolan population.[16]

A similar process took place in Guiné and Mozambique. In Guiné

13. Pélissier (1978), pp.153-6.
14. Pössinger (1973).
15. Pössinger (1973).
16. Pélissier (1978), p.78.

there was a great expansion of the Mandinga and Balanta agriculturalists in the years after pacification. In particular, the Balanta spread rapidly into the coastal regions, where they grew rice for the market and increased their domination over the fragmented and dwindling populations of Nalus, Falupes and Biafadas. In Mozambique the pacification of the lower Zambesi in the 1870s coincided with a reduction in the export tariff, and led to a great expansion of agriculture among the Lolo and Chuabo and Manganja peoples,[17] while in the north the end of the caravan trade saw the Makonde turn to cash crop production.[18] A similar trend appears to underlie the invasion of the Mozambique coastal plantations by squatters who worked for the companies in return for land to cultivate. Even in the Huila highlands of Angola, the 1920s saw a return of many of the Nyaneka to re-occupy some of the land wrested from them by the whites in the previous century.[19]

At the time of independence, the Africans were in general firmly in control of the land. Figures for 1960 indicate that in Angola, although there were three districts where whites held more than 10 per cent of the land, in the colony as a whole 97.3 per cent of it was either still vacant or was in African hands.[20]

Chiefs

As we have seen, except to a limited extent among the BaKongo and the Fula, the Portuguese had no intention of establishing any form of indirect rule in their colonies. Instead, pacification saw everywhere the disappearance of the African kings, many of them deposed or driven into exile. This was not, however, solely the result of military defeat and Portuguese conquest. In many areas, the power of the chiefs had been undermined by economic changes which deprived them of control over the economic resources of their people. Migrant labourers, for instance, quickly ceased to be amenable to chiefly control, while the Ovimbundu farmers also moved away from the influence of the chief's village and his control over communal land.

However, if the Portuguese had no time for the kings or the more important chiefs, they did assign a role to the village headman, whom they called a *regedor*. The *regedor* was seen simply as the government's agent in the villages. He was expected to aid the

17. Vail and White, pp.63–7.
18. Jorge Dias
19. Clarence-Smith (1979).
20. Pélissier (1978), p.155

government in the collection of taxes and in the recruitment of carriers and labourers. Later he had to co-operate with the compulsory cotton-growing campaigns. He enjoyed no privileges except exemption from taxation and labour, and even this was conditional on his carrying out the government's demands. He possessed no independent power or authority over his people. Few *regedores* were chosen from traditional chiefly families as none of these could be persuaded to take on such a hated task, and frequently former government soldiers were given the job. Traditional chiefs sometimes continued to be recognised by their people as leaders and arbiters alongside the government's *regedor*. The low status of the *regedor* meant that the white administrator had a much more direct control over the African population than his equivalent in most other European colonies.

This systematic destruction of chiefly influence is a notable and distinctive feature of Portuguese colonial rule. Alexander Barns, writing in 1928, after a tour of Angola, commented:

The policy of the Portuguese military administrative rule in Angola of recent years — indeed for many decades — has been to break up the power of the old chieftains, to break down the old tribal customs and to preserve nothing of the traditional native rights, thus leaving the native population a heterogeneous and leaderless mass of people, a fact which one cannot but deplore. The Portuguese may appear to gain by this resource at the moment in the ease which it gives in administering the country, but not in the long run, for like a riderless horse, the race, having no guiding hand, no home and traditional life, and not caring, becomes hopeless and sterile.[21]

Henrique Galvão, writing of the 1930s, when he had been a senior official in Angola, said simply:

It was one of the greatest errors of the Angolan administration in recent years in the field of native policy to have favoured the crushing of the chiefdoms and to have hastened the loss of prestige of the native chiefs — thereby depriving itself of the collaboration of the agents best able to assist a policy of natural assimilation.[22]

It is difficult not to agree with these two judgements. The Portuguese no doubt hoped to bind an influential part of the African population to co-operate with the régime through the process of assimilation. However, few Africans ever became assimilated, and the régime neglected to cultivate the support of any other class or group. It thereby lost not only political support but also a vital channel of communication through which it might have listened to

21. Barns (1928) p.159.
22. Galvão and Selvagem, vol iii, p.213.

the views of the black population and explained the objectives of the government. It was in part-recognition of this that the authorities made half-hearted attempts to give status and prestige to the catechists of the Catholic missions, but otherwise no convincing efforts were made to win over any influential sector of rural society.

The virtual elimination of the chiefs opened the way for alternative forms of leadership to emerge among the African population but, for reasons which are not entirely clear, this process was delayed and happened later in the Portuguese colonies than in those of other European powers.

Labour

African labour was seen as the greatest resource which the colonies possessed and the one whose value could most easily be realised. Labour resources are frequently among the principal assets of underdeveloped countries and they can be utilised both as a substitute for capital investment and as a means of accumulating capital. Because the Portuguese government lacked funds, and Portuguese capital was slow to invest in the colonies, measures were taken to develop this resource as soon as possible. At the end of the nineteenth century, African labour could be employed in a variety of ways. First and foremost was its potential for the production of export crops which would generate customs revenue and foreign exchange earnings. Much early legislation was directed to encouraging such production. For example, Africans in Zambesia were to pay part of their taxes in kind according to the regulations of 1892; the growing of crops for export could entitle Africans to exemption from the contract labour laws of 1899; and, briefly between 1896 and 1906, the collection of hut tax in Angola was suspended in order to encourage trade. Periodically during the early twentieth century, other measures were taken, a favourite one being the distribution of cotton seed to promote local peasant agriculture.

However, such limited encouragement to African producers brought only modest results, and was not welcomed by local employers of labour nor by those colonial administrators who wanted to put the finances of the colonies on a sound footing as quickly as possible. The colonial authorities principally wished to balance their budgets by raising money through African taxation, while the planters and concessionaires wished to employ African labour in their various enterprises. To a limited extent the desires of these two parties could be reconciled. Africans could be made to enter the labour market by means of taxation, while their employment for wages enabled them to pay government taxes.

However, this unity of outlook was rare. The government itself was an employer of labour on its public works projects, and in Mozambique sought financial advantages through permitting the export of labour to South Africa. The colonial élites were, therefore, in competition for labour, and this competition was to influence not only the labour legislation but the whole development of the economy and of the African role within it. The labour laws were supposed to apply throughout Portuguese Africa, but totally different labour employment practices grew up, often side by side — practices which corresponded to the different types of economic activity in particular areas, and not to any legal norm. Angola did not develop as a single economy; still less did Mozambique, divided as it was into totally separate administrations by the chartered companies. Any discussion of the labour experience of Africans has to recognise this diversity.

Although the labour laws were subject to frequent amendment, the core of the legislation remained unchanged from 1899 until 1961, with an important recodification in 1928.[23] This legislation stated that all Africans had a 'moral and legal obligation' to work. They could either exercise a recognised trade or profession, or they could 'cultivate on their own account land of a specified extent'; failing that, they had to contract themselves to an employer. The term used for a contracted labourer was *serviçal*, and in theory a *serviçal* could contract himself to whomever he pleased — a partly free labour market. If he failed to contract himself, he could be forcibly contracted by the administration. In addition to this, each African, male and female, was liable to work for the government either on public works, or in the police or as a carrier. Finally there was correctional labour. This was forced labour, paid at a lower rate, which Africans had to do if convicted of an offence. The offence might be non-payment of taxes, evasion of contract labour, or simply 'vagrancy'. According to the 1899 code, both men and women were liable to work, only those under fourteen and the old being exempt. In 1911 limitations on the liability of women were introduced, and these were further systematised in 1928. However, what is important about this legislaton is not what it said but how it was actually put into practice.

First, government labour. Compulsory labour for the state was demanded by most colonial régimes,[24] and was supposed to derive from the duty an African traditionally owed to his chief and

23. Silva Cunha.
24. E.g. Thomas; and see Orde Browne.

community. In the Portuguese colonies it was at first unpaid and extremely irksome; after 1928 it was always paid, and was restricted to such things as road works in the worker's own region. During the wars of pacification and the First World War, it was extensively used. Africans were recruited into local militias and police, or rounded up in large numbers to act as carriers. Both sorts of labour were intensely disliked, and loss of life on carrier service was high. A Zambesi planter declared that of the 25,000 carriers recruited for the campaigns against the Germans, only 5,000 ever returned to their villages.[25] Carrier service was also a highly unproductive form of labour, and after the war it was rapidly replaced by train and by motor transport. Labour on public works was the other major form of government service. In practice, it was largely confined to a local responsibility for maintaining the roads, and was frequently performed by women. How burdensome it was varied greatly from one area to another, and depended very much on the local *chefe* who ran the system.

When not on government service, an African had to be able to show that he was either exempt from work or was contracted to an employer. To show this, he was given a *caderneta* or pass-book, which recorded his labour and tax obligations. He could not move from his district without the permission of the *chefe* and without his *caderneta* being in order.[26] In theory, he was free to contract himself with any employer, but this freedom was closely circumscribed. For instance, on the Mozambique *prazos* up to 1930 he had to contract with the *prazo* concessionaire. In most parts of the colonies, the contract was effectively controlled by the local administrator, who arranged the labour supply for local employers. The British Consul in Luanda explained in 1922 how the system worked:

The authorities took an active part in securing labour for agricultural and other enterprises. Employers wanting hands would notify their requirements to the local administrator, who would procure the necessary labourers through tribal chiefs. The chiefs received 30 centavos for every labourer supplied, and the administrators also had a pecuniary interest in the transaction.[27]

Not only did the local administrators take bribes and payments, but they could also be persuaded to renew contracts and to turn a blind eye to failure by employers to fulfil the terms of employment.

Enormous variations existed in the way this system operated. In

25. Gavicho de Lacerda, p.14.
26. Pélissier (1978), p.134.
27. PRO FO 371 7211 (1922), Hutcheon to FO, 12.8.1922.

areas where slavery had existed before 1875, for instance in the old settled regions of Cazengo and Huila in Angola, contract labour was virtually a continuation of slavery. Planters sought to have the contracts of their workers continually renewed, and frequently recruited fresh labour by 'redeeming' Africans brought as slaves from the interior. The same applied to São Tomé, where, up to 1910, contract labourers were indistinguishable from slaves. At the other end of the spectrum was the development of a free labour market in the main sea-port towns like Lourenço Marques and Luanda, both of which saw the growth of a skilled labour force and a genuine African proletariat.

In between lay perhaps the bulk of the African population for whom, according to circumstances, periodic contract labour came to provide a supplement to their subsistence farming. There was a general tendency during the period up to 1945 for Africans to spend increasing amounts of their time working within the colonial economy, and for the importance of cash earnings to increase. A major reason for this was government coercion — and disguised coercion, for undoubtedly many of those who voluntarily came forward as labourers did so for fear of being contracted against their will. However, other factors were leading in the same direction. Growth of population put pressure on some farming areas, as did the impoverishment of the soil and the spread of plant diseases which followed a decade or so after the expansion of peasant agriculture; the decline in commodity prices during the great depression of the 1930s also forced Africans to seek paid employment. The gradual spread of mission education and technical skills acquired on contract labour also tended to loosen traditional communal ties, as did the greater independence and prestige of those who could command cash incomes, while the opening of roads and railways in the interior made it easier for more Africans to travel to the major centres of employment.

However, even if it is wrong to see coercion as the only force influencing African workers to enter the colonial economy, it clearly remained a very important one. Before the Second World War, the colonial economies could not, on the whole, begin to employ all the labour potentially available, so why was coercion necessary, and why were labour shortages so continuous a problem? The answer lies in three of the basic characteristics of the labour market in the Portuguese colonies. The first of these was the extreme unevenness of the demand for labour. In some parts of Angola and Mozambique there would be intense demand, whereas elsewhere demand scarcely existed at all. For example, there was frequently a high demand on the plantations of the lower Zambesi while there was practically no economic activity requiring labour in the Mozambique district to the north. Gradually as the colonial economies grew more unified, labour became more mobile and could be brought from greater distances to supply these pockets of high demand. However, there was another factor which continued to make demand erratic. This was the fluctuations in world prices for tropical products. These fluctuations could lead to very sharp booms and slumps. When the booms occurred, for instance in the demand for sugar in the period immediately after the First World War, large quantities of labour were required at short notice and coercion was resorted to.

The second major characteristic of Portuguese colonial labour was the difficulty of employing workers on long contracts. Although contracts tended to get longer, there was always a high turn-over of labour, which resulted in considerable difficulties in keeping numbers at a constant level — for example 120,000 workers are required to maintain a workforce of 10,000 on monthly contracts.

The third reason why coercion was required was that working conditions in the Portuguese colonies were notoriously bad and many employers stood little chance of attracting labour in the open market.

While it was always the general policy of the Portuguese colonial governments to encourage Africans to offer their labour, coercion was not looked upon as desirable and periodically attempts were made to do away with it altogether, at least for private employers. The man who identified himself most emphatically with the establishment of a free labour system was José Norton de Matos, governor-general of Angola in 1912–15 and high commissioner in 1921–23. In particular he campaigned against two widespread practices, forcible re-contracting and the use of administrators to recruit labour for private concerns. In 1913, while he was serving his first term in Angola, the law permitting freedom of contract was enforced, the use of compulsory military service to provide labour was abolished, and African producers were exempted from contract labour. Corporal punishment was also banned, and he established a Department of Native Affairs for the first time in Angola. Norton claimed that freeing labour actually led to an increase in the supply for all but the worst employers, and that even in the Moçamedes region, where many of the worst were to be found, all but 10 per cent of the labourers voluntarily re-contracted themselves.[28] One might well speculate, however, whether it was the blessings of free labour or the effects of the drought which maintained the labour supply in this area.

28. Norton de Matos; Clarence-Smith (1975), p.365.

These changes were against the interests of both administrators and settlers, and did not survive Norton's removal from office. When he returned as high commissioner in 1921, he had once again to attack the official involvement in recruiting. The decree No.40, like its predecessor in 1913, contained a trenchant statement of Norton's belief in free labour. In 1913 he had had a vision of a population of smallholders and artisans:

To make of the native of Africa an agriculturalist, an artisan independent and free, possessing a plot of land, with professional instruction and tools which will permit him to live in relative comfort and to produce more than is necessary for his food and sustenance, flooding the market with goods and artifacts of every kind; to create small proprietors or small manufacturers; these are the ends to which the administration and government of a colony such as Angola should look.[28]

This romantic image has a peculiar place in Portugal's colonial rhetoric, and was to reappear in the idea of the *colonato* of industrious white and black peasants, which the New State tried to realise in the 1950s and 1960s.

In his 1921 decree abolishing the administrative involvement in recruiting, Norton made an often-quoted declaration of faith in free labour:

The only way to attract the native to work is to pay him well, furnish him with abundant and healthy food, surround him with ease and comfort superior to that which he enjoys in his traditional way of life, and treat him with respect, sympathy, goodness and justice.[29]

However, the system of administrative coercion could not be simply abolished by decree when it had its roots so deep in the self-interest of employers and administrators. What happened was described for the British Foreign Office by the Consul-General in Luanda, A.B.Hutcheon:

On the issue of the decree, many of the district officials took the line that they should no longer do anything in the way of securing labourers, and made it their business to impress on the natives who came to be contracted that they were not compelled to work and that if they did not wish to, they could return to their homes. As a result, the supply of labour was almost completely cut off. On learning of this the High Commissioner. . . issued a lengthy circular. . . pointing out that the authorities, while refraining from taking an active part in the engagement of labourers and from employing force in any way, were to use their influence with the natives to encourage them to hire themselves out, making them see that it was in their own interest to do so.[30]

29. *Providencias tomadas* . . ., pp.103–6, Decreto 40.
30. PRO FO 371 7211 (1922), Hutcheon to FO, 12.8.1922.

By the use of this particular euphemism, the administrative direction of labour continued. It was banned again in the labour code of 1928, along with all residual forms of unpaid labour for the state, and this coincided with the fall in world prices and the consequent recession of the colonial economies. Demand for labour fell and, as a result, the 1930s saw conditions of relatively free labour. However, the system by which private employers went to the local administrator when they wanted labourers revived with the expansion of the economy during the Second World War.

South African mine labour

In the story of contract labour the South African mines have a unique importance. As we have seen, Africans from southern Mozambique began migrating to the mines before Portuguese colonial rule was established. The colonial authorities then moved to regulate this traffic, partly to make sure that the slave trade did not restart, and partly in order to profit themselves from the migration. According to the agreements with the Transvaal, the Portuguese received a capitation payment for every labourer as well as important railway and transit traffic concessions and a free trade agreement. They fought in vain for still further advantages, but in the end had to be content with obtaining large payments by doubling African hut tax and by insisting that it be paid in sterling. Eventually this tax was collected at source on the Rand. The motive of the authorities was to obtain as much financial return from African labour as possible, and throughout the colonial period Mozambique's budget and her balance of payments depended heavily on the income she derived from the South African contracts.

Labour for South Africa came principally from the districts south of the Sabi (the *Sul do Save*), but between 1903 and 1913, and again after 1935, recruitment also took place in Zambesia and the north. Throughout the twentieth century, a monopoly of recruitment was held by the W.N.L.A. (Witwatersrand Native Labour Association). The officers of the Association set up recruitment camps, and then toured the country areas enrolling workers. In new areas of recruitment great difficulties were experienced. A W.N.L.A. official, W.Shepherd, contrasted strongly the ease of recruitment in the south with the difficulties faced further north where the women, powerful figures in the matrilineal, uxorilocal Makua communities, did all they could to prevent the departure of their men.[31] By 1910, nearly two generations had passed since migration to the mines had

31. Shepherd.

begun, and one report suggested that 90 per cent of the males in the *Sul do Save* had had South African contracts. By this time the maintenance of the flow of workers depended as much on the reports of those returning as on the allurements of the recruiters.

Before the opening of the railway in 1895, migrant workers marched overland, and even after the rail connection was established, there were long marches to the railheads. Many workers were taken to Delagoa Bay by sea, and their route to the mines is described by Shepherd:

Although the natives took quite readily to transportation to Lourenço Marques by sea, they seldom had a very pleasant time, as the accommodation of several hundreds of natives on the smaller coastal vessels had little luxury, and frequent bad weather produced intense sea-sickness and great discomfort, the only point in its favour being that the voyage was generally short. Having arrived at the Ressano Garcia, the Frontier Emigration Post, they were vaccinated and again medically examined, and then, after resting for a few days, and if fit, they entrained for Johannesburg, and there again were looked after by the Association and distributed to the various mines in proportion to the requirements.[32]

Labourers were not given much choice by the Association as to which mine they would go to, and the mines anyway had wage agreements which successfully prevented wages finding their level in a competitive market. It was this denial of freedom of choice which probably led to the very high rate of clandestine emigration. No one knows how many workers crossed the borders illegally, but it may well have been as many as went through legal channels. Illegal emigration was cheaper for the employer, who evaded taxes and formalities and had some extra control over the workers, but it was apparently very attractive also to the Africans as they could choose their place of work and could themselves evade administrative supervision.

How many Africans went to work in South Africa, and to what extent did this number absorb the labour resources of Mozambique? Figures are hard to obtain and unreliable. Official statistics show that between 1909 and 1916 an average of 90,700 Mozambicans were working in South Africa in any one month.[33] Even before 1913 the overwhelming majority of these came from the south. In 1908, out of 79,543 Mozambicans on the Rand, 89.5 per cent came from the south, 6 per cent came from Mozambique district and 3 per cent from Zambesia.[34] These figures, of course, do not take into account

32. Shepherd, p.255.
33. *Anuário de Moçambique*, pp.159–60.
34. *A Manual of Portuguese East Africa*, p.177.

clandestine emigration. What percentage of the labour force of the south did this constitute? A competent observer, R.N.Lyne, writing in 1913, estimated that 7 per cent of the population of the Inhambane district was absent working on the Rand.[35] Government statistics confirm this view but sharpen the focus. In three *circunscrições* (administrative divisions) of Lourenço Marques district in 1915, the percentages of the active *male* population absent in South Africa were respectively 14, 26.5 and 23.7 per cent.[36] As most dispassionate observers at the time commented, there is no reason to suppose that figures of this magnitude had any serious adverse effect on the labour supply within Mozambique, or that they represent anything but a surplus to the requirements of African agriculture, which was traditionally carried on by women. In more recent times, although the mines have taken fewer Mozambicans, there has been a tendency for the total number seeking work in South Africa to increase. In his study of the Gwambe, Fuller estimated that half the men of working age were absent in South Africa at any one time, and that most men between the ages of seventeen and sixty have spent more than half their adult years in the Union of South Africa.[37]

Mortality among migrant workers was high. Between 1908 and 1916, an average of 3,080 died on the mines every year, most from illness. This constituted 4 per cent of the workforce.[38] Mortality was heaviest among those recruited from north of the Sabi, and after recruiting in the north was banned in 1913, the mortality rate dropped noticeably. Many miners, however, contracted progressive diseases like tuberculosis or phthisis, from which they later died unrecorded by the statisticians. Against these very real hazards was to be set the comparatively high pay. Up to the 1920s, a miner on the Rand could earn up to five times as much as a worker in Mozambique, and taking into account the fact that he received free food and lodging and did not have to support his family, his pay compared very favourably with that even of a skilled worker in Britain. Comparisons between wage rates in different countries and at different times can be almost meaningless, but for what they are worth, such comparisons show that up to 1940 the South African miners can be considered as an élite among the world's working class. In the 1920s, a black miner on the Rand might earn between £5 and £8 a month out of which he paid taxes.[39] In the same period,

35. Lyne, p.215.
36. Capela, pp.188–92.
37. Fuller, p.149.
38. *Anuário de Moçambique*, p.159.
39. Katzenellenbogen (1981).

wages in Britain for skilled workers ranged from £10 to £14 a month, out of which the full living expenses of themselves and their families had to be met.[40] An ordinary contract worker in the Inhambane district might have to work ninety-five days in 1917 to earn enough money to pay his tax; on the Rand the hut tax could be earned in less than a month.[41]

In general, then, the miners were a favoured group of workers whose position was protected by their value to the colonial exchequer. Besides being relatively highly paid, they had greater contacts with wider currents of religious and cultural experience. They had opportunities of acquiring some industrial skills beyond those of most Mozambicans. Yet the fact that these advantages were enjoyed through migration meant that change in their homeland was, if anything, held back. The *Sul do Save* became notorious for economic backwardness and for the slowness with which the change to cash-crop farming was made compared with other regions.

Labour within the colonies

Before the 1930s, there is little doubt that working conditions for African labourers in the Portuguese colonies fell far short of what was proscribed by the law and what was regarded as acceptable by contemporary opinion. The methods employed to extort labour, the physical violence frequently used on the workforce, cheating on pay, underpayment, forcible re-contracting and many other abuses are too widely and well attested to be seriously doubted. What is less well known is the way in which the African population reacted to labour for the Portuguese, and the extent to which they were affected by it.

The first point to remember is that until the last years of colonial rule the Portuguese administration in Africa was inefficient, arbitrary and very unequal in its effects. Demand for labour fluctuated greatly from place to place and from one year or one decade to the next. There were times and places where the demand became so intense that workers had to be rounded up by the police, and the population burnt their huts and fled *en masse*. In other areas, no Portuguese administrator was seen from one year to the next, and simple evasive devices allowed the African population to live almost undisturbed. In general, however, the picture is one of a very inefficient and partial mobilisation. Even though the Portuguese and their various concession companies saw labour resources as the principal asset of the colonies and the principal means of

40. Cole, p.643.
41. Quoted in Capela, p.167.

accumulating capital, it was not able to make very full use of them because of the successful evasion of contract labour by perhaps the majority of the African population.

Nothing resembling comprehensive figures for the labour force exist, and the only guides one has come from partial and fragmentary assessments. For instance, in the Inhambane district in 1913, according to R.N.Lyne, only 1,000 workers were contracted to private concerns. This would have amounted to about 0.2 per cent of the population.[42] In 1915, in five circumscriptions in the Lourenço Marques district, a total of 6,479 labourers were recruited by the administration, constituting 3.7 per cent of the population.[43] Of course, large numbers of workers were going to the Rand from these regions as well.

North of the Sabi in the Mozambique Company territory and in Zambesia were the areas of most intensive utilisation of labour. Between 1912 and 1916, an average of 86,000 Africans are recorded as being in employment in the Mozambique Company's territory, and this must have amounted to at least 25 per cent of the population. However, most of these workers were on contracts of two or three months only. In 1926, the labour force had risen to 108,000, and the average length of contract had increased from eighty to 108 days. However, 40 per cent of this labour (43,000) was recruited from outside the Company's territory. Thereafter, although numbers fluctuated, over half continued to be recruited 'abroad'.[44] Because the Mozambique Company did not allow Rhodesian or South African recruiters into its territory, this suggests that the level of utilisation of labour was much lower than the Company's claim that it was employing virtually the whole of its potential work force.

It was in Zambesia that the demand for labour was always highest after the successful expansion of sugar, copra and sisal estates and, in the 1930s, tea. In 1908 J.P. Hornung was employing 36,540 workers each year on his Caia estates. In 1928, the daily labour requirement of the whole Sena Sugar complex was 25,000. In 1930, the Boror Company's daily requirement was 12,000 workers. These are merely samples, and it is a hopeless task to try to assess fully the amount of labour employed in Zambesia. This labour was, however, recruited from a vast catchment area. Sena Sugar in 1912 controlled recruitment in 14,000 square miles of Zambesia, and the total area of the *prazos* in that year contained a population of over 600,000 people. Even so, workers were recruited from outside this region,

42. Lyne, p.215.
43. Quoted in Capela, pp.184-92.
44. Neil Tomlinson (1978).

from government-controlled territory to the north and from the Nyasaland Protectorate.[45]

Although always unpopular, the labour obligation did not at first fall very heavily on this, the most intensively developed region of Mozambique. According to the *prazo* law of 1892, only two weeks' labour a year was owed by each African adult. Although contracts could be pushed up to one month, it was found impossible to obtain more labour than that without provoking mass emigration. The most recent study of the subject comments on the 'discovery that all the companies made, that excessive demands upon the people resulted in mass emigration from their *prazos* and that it was essential to take account of African feelings.'[46] And . . . 'In practice, the people were successful in limiting the demands made upon them to a point at which the system itself broke down.'[47] And . . . 'In order to protect his labour supplies, Hornung was compelled to levy less labour than the plantations actually demanded and to experiment with a kind of paternalism whose ultimate source was the ideas held by the people themselves of what the *prazo* system was all about.'[48]

Mass evasion of labour led Africans to move from *prazo* to *prazo*, or across the borders into Nyasaland. This in turn forced the *prazo* companies to spread their recruitment net wider and wider, although the effect of this was to dilute the demand for labour on the population as a whole. Another effect was that wages were gradually forced up. Hornung recruited much of his labour simply by offering higher wages than were available elsewhere in Mozambique or in British Africa nearby.

The depression of the 1930s led to a slackening of demand for labour and to a brief experiment with the removal of administrative coercion in Zambesia. A labour census in 1941 revealed that at least one-third of the working population were not engaged in contract labour at all.[49]

Although mass resistance by the African population to labour demands tempered the behaviour of the *prazo* companies, the companies would resort to an extreme use of force when there was a sharp rise in labour requirements due to boom conditions in world markets or the need to carry out some large-scale capital project. Particularly affected were the years immediately following the First

45. These figures all come from Vail and White.
46. Vail and White, p.158.
47. Vail and White, p.167.
48. Vail and White, p.169.
49. Vail and White, p.281.

World War when, in order to expand production, the companies rounded up vast gangs of labourers to work in conditions, which often caused a high mortality rate. It was these black years which led to the inquiries of the League of Nations into conditions in the Portuguese colonies.[50]

In Angola the position also varied considerably from place to place, demand being high in the plantation areas and much lower elsewhere. Diamang employed 10,000 labourers, but recruited these throughout Angola; Robert Williams, on the other hand, could not obtain local labour, and had to import his railway construction gangs from West Africa and other sources. Apart from a few thousand *serviçaes* recruited in Angola for São Tomé, there was no export of labour on an official basis, and it was probably only in the extreme south before the First World War that appreciable numbers regularly left for work abroad. Referring to the 1930s, Henrique Galvão dramatically declared: 'Only the dead are really exempt from contract labour.'[51] This may, of course, have been true in some places at some periods, but it is not borne out by the figures that Galvão himself quotes. Between 1935 and 1939, the workforce of Angola was calculated at an annual average of 728,662 or 20.8 per cent of the population.[52] This figure clearly excludes women altogether. Of this number, 55.7 per cent were stated to be self-employed, 26.2 per cent were privately contracted, and 18.1 per cent were liable to be contracted by the state. Therefore as a percentage of the population as a whole only 3.7 per cent were liable to be forcibly contracted and less than 10 per cent *in toto* were doing contract labour.

Direct coercion was supplemented, and in theory superseded, by the use of the African hut tax to obtain labour. In 1928 the minimum agricultural wage had been set at such a level that an African would have to work between sixty-five and 100 days. However, those who could command other cash incomes could in effect free themselves from this form of coercion. The evidence is that taxation became a less and less effective means of forcing Africans into the labour market. René Pélissier, writing of Angola, has calculated that

in a population of 4,562,606 [in 1960] each one paid in theory 27 escudos a year, or the equivalent of three to four litres of wine or two dozen eggs. Even if one knows that in reality only certain male *indígenas* were liable. . . one cannot speak of a prohibitive rate since it corresponded on average to one month's cash payment for labour at the minimum rate.[53]

50. Ross.
51. Galvão, p 52.
52. Carreira (1977), p.120; Galvão, p.52.
53. Pélissier (1978), p.133.

In other words, wages had moved far ahead of the wage/tax ratio established at the beginning of the *Estado Novo*.

The transition from subsistance farming to cash crop growing and wage-earning was one which brought profound change to African society. Labour was recruited in an arbitrary and sometimes violent manner, and it was this, rather than the actual scale of the labour requirement, which was resisted.

At one end of the spectrum of resistance were the actual outbreaks of armed rebellion in which the labour issue is clearly a grievance — for instance the Barue rising of 1917 or the Kongo rebellion of 1913. However, armed resistance petered out after 1920, and from that time the commonest way in which opposition was expressed was for the population to migrate. For obvious reasons, emigration was most frequently found in the border regions. It seems that in the first two decades of the twentieth century, up to 300,000 Makua left Mozambique to settle across the border in Nyasaland. Migration also occurred from the northern border districts into Tanganyika. The British Acting Governor in that territory estimated in 1922 that 3–5,000 people were entering the territory each year, and he listed among the causes higher taxation, penal labour and the practice of detaining women if their menfolk did not turn up for work.[54] There was also steady emigration from the frontier regions of Angola. A British doctor, A.J.Board, writing to his family from the Northern Rhodesian frontier district of Balovale in 1935, recorded:

We are still being almost snowed under with immigrants from Portuguese territory; 75 reported today, and we average 200 a week. I take this as a tribute to the English methods of administration. The Portuguese officials are a pretty callous lot. Torture is still practised by their officials and forced labour, which after all is only another name for slavery — men and women are compelled to work on the roads for nothing and treated abominably.[55]

Henrique Galvão called this a 'demographic haemorrhage' and distinguished the situation in Angola from that in Mozambique by another of his vivid phrases: 'The inhabitants of Mozambique emigrate; those of Angola flee.'[56] The long-term result of emigration can perhaps most vividly be seen in the relative population densities. In the 1950 census, whereas Quelimane and Nampula (the coastal districts of central Mozambique) had 11.5 and 16.4 persons per

54. PRO FO 371 8377 (1922), enclosing Acting Governor of Tanganyika to CO, 27.5.1922 and 4.10.1922.
55. A.J.Board to family, 26.9.1935.
56. Galvão and Selvagem, vol. iv, p.132.

square kilometre, the frontier districts of Lago and Niassa had 2.2 and 6.2 persons.[57]

The difficulty of assessing the extent and significance of this emigration is considerable. First, it does not appear to have prevented Mozambique and Angola from experiencing a rise in population equivalent to other African countries. Secondly, it was at least partly offset by the immigration of people into Mozambique and Angola. This cannot be quantified at all, but it is clear that whereas Makua in large numbers were settling in Nyasaland, Africans from the Protectorate were coming into Portuguese East Africa in search of work. Thirdly, it is also clear that much of the emigration was in order to take advantage of cheaper goods in British territory or to enjoy lower rates of tax. Although the probability is that the Portuguese colonies experienced a net outflow of population, the phenomenon of African migration in the colonial era is multi-faceted, and is a complex kaleidoscopic rearrangement of peoples seeking the maximum freedom for themselves and new economic roles in the modern world.

57. Galvão and Selvagem. vol. iv, p.134.

6
THE AFRICAN POPULATION UNDER PORTUGUESE RULE, II

The régime of the crop-marketing companies
By the 1920s it was widely recognised that the attempt to develop the colonies through the system of concession companies had not been a success. With the exception of Diamang and Sena Sugar, few of them had achieved very tangible results. Meanwhile tens of thousands of labourers were annually going abroad to seek work, and many critics considered that this labour could and should be utilised at home. How was this to be done? Up to the 1920s, the colonial economies had been linked with that of the mother-country primarily through a tariff which discriminated in favour of Portuguese goods. This, however, had by no means led to a captive market for Portuguese industrialists, and it was far from clear that the Portuguese economy as a whole was deriving much benefit from the empire. What was lacking was any coherent approach to the development of the colonial economies or any clear idea of what their contribution to the metropolitan economy should be. An answer to these questions was to be attempted by the politicians of the New State, one of the principal objectives of which was to create an integrated Lusitanian world economy.

The aspect of this which most directly affected the African population was the setting-up of the so-called 'zones of influence'. This idea, which derived from German and Belgian practice, was initially set out in a decree of 1926, and is therefore very much part of the legacy of the Republic. The New State, however, eagerly adopted and elaborated it. The colonies were to be divided into sectors, to be granted to concessionaires who would have the right to buy and market certain items of African produce. Initially, the scheme was to cover cotton only, but it was later extended to cereal crops as well. Within the 'zones of influence', Africans were to be 'encouraged' to grow crops as a means of fulfilling their labour obligations. The scheme did not get off to a good start, and the market for cotton was soon hit by the great depression. However, in 1932 a minimum price for cotton was guaranteed to exporters, and from then on the system gathered momentum, leading to a decade of frenetic cotton production.[1]

1. Bravo.

In 1938 a government agency, the *Junta da Exportação de Algodão*, was set up to organise the cotton growing and to disseminate information and skills. Some of the concession companies were newcomers to the colonial scene, whereas others were already well-established. In this last category were Sena Sugar and the Zambesia Company, which had abandoned their *prazo* concessions in 1928 when they found that the collection of African tax and fiscal labour was no longer profitable. Once the government had agreed to a minimum price, the cotton concessions appeared attractive both for the profits to be made from the sale of cotton and because it allowed the Companies to continue, in effect, controlling the labour resources in their concessions.[2]

The concession companies did not leave the growing of cotton in their zones to chance, but organised cotton 'campaigns'. These were actively supported by the local administration and involved much activity by officials of the cotton companies and the *Junta*. First, suitable land in a locality was selected and all the local interests were consulted; the land was then cleared by hand and *machambas* marked out. *Machambas* were plots of cotton for each of which a specified individual was responsible. Their size was graded: for example, in Niassa in 1947 the largest *machamba* measured 1.2 hectares, and the smallest (to be worked by a woman over thirty-six years old) was 0.2 of a hectare. The cycle of cotton planting, weeding and picking was then gone through, often supervised stage by stage by an official. 'Unhappily', wrote Nelson Bravo, 'the intervention of every administrative authority would be solicited scores if not hundreds of times a year.'[3]

There are various estimates of the amount of labour required to work a *machamba*, but on average it seems to have absorbed 150 days in a year. To prevent shortfalls of food production, the cotton-grower would often have to mark out a *machamba* for food crops as well. At its height, cotton-growing employed a substantial part of the Mozambique population; in 1944, it was estimated that 791,000[4] people were involved. However, in the 1950s, when Portugal's demand for cotton was being fully met, the numbers employed fell and some of the worst land was abandoned. This trend was accompanied by greater expertness in the choice of land and in its preparation, so that productivity rose dramatically. In the Muchope area of southern Mozambique, for example, there were 2,796 growers in 1947-8, but ten years later this number had fallen to 1,768,

2. Vail and White, pp.277-8.
3. Bravo, p.121.
4. Bravo, p.79.

and cotton-growing in the highlands of the district, the *Serra*, had ceased. Yet cotton production had risen from 100,000 kg. to 171,000 kg.[5]

The amount earned by the cultivators also varied greatly according to local agricultural conditions, but it seldom exceeded the amount they were able to earn as paid labourers. No one attempted to disguise the fact that forced crop growing was intensely unpopular. Nelson Bravo referred to the clearing of the *machambas* as

hard and tedious work, which almost all the *indígenas* detested because of the effort which had to be expended over many days. And, because as a rule they do not feel the economic necessity to do it, the authorities were frequently forced to intervene with insistent and paternal advice.[6]

The 'insistent and paternal advice' was frequently administered by the police, and the active intervention of the administration was necessary right up to 1961 when the system was discontinued.

Unpopular or not, cotton-growing formed a major part of the lives of Mozambican Africans for almost thirty years. It began a transformation of rural life, for cotton campaigns brought into the rural areas agricultural experts, administrators and officials. Numerous studies of the land, soils, etc., were made, and in some areas technological change was promoted. For example, the use of ploughs and oxen on the cotton *machambas* of the south suggest the beginnings of an agricultural revolution that was later extended to food cultivation.[7] Many more African families were brought into growing cash crops, and the fact that the cotton companies tried to make use of traditional social and economic units of production was a change from plantation agriculture, where the labourer was taken away to work far from his home. On this account it may have been preferred to the older types of labour, although in Zambesia, at least, it existed alongside the labour on the plantations. Finally, it contributed to what was a very marked feature of European colonialism, namely the preservation of many of the pre-colonial social and even economic structures, while at the same time promoting the production of large surpluses for the world market.

The cotton campaigns also presented the opportunity for some social engineering. In the 1930s, the idea had been mooted that the dispersed African populations should be brought together into larger units — no doubt so that they could be more easily taxed and controlled, but also to promote economic co-operation. This idea

5. Marques, p.87.
6. Bravo, p.114.
7. Fuller, p.152.

was eagerly adopted by the *Junta*, which felt that, with only one official for every 5–10,000 producers,[8] it could not adequately supervise cotton production in scattered villages. In the 1940s, some amalgamation of settlements did take place under the watchful eye of the cotton company officials. These were the prototpyes of the *aldeamentos* set up during the war, and this sort of concentration and collectivisation of effort appears to have an appeal for the post-independence government of Mozambique as well.

Compulsory cotton-growing was also introduced into Angola, but on a much smaller scale, and production of cotton and cotton seed in Angola has averaged less than 20 per cent of the output of Mozambique. Nevertheless, the dominance of Cotonang in the Baixa de Cassange was as complete as that of any of the Mozambique concession companies within their zones, and the serfdom in which the company's peasants lived was a material factor in the outbreak of the *jacquerie* at the end of 1960.[9]

Mission and mission influence

It is not surprising to find that Christianity took root and grew in the Portuguese colonies — the religion of individualism establishing itself alongside the economic individualism of wage-earning and market production. If official statistics mean anything, they show a quite remarkable advance of the Christian churches, at least in Angola. In 1933, less than 10 per cent of the African population was estimated to be Christian, but in 1950 this figure had risen to 50 per cent and by 1960 to 66 per cent, 2.2 million being Catholics and 800,000 Protestants.[10] In Mozambique it was estimated that in 1960, 10 per cent of the population were Christian. The marked disparity between the two colonies clearly requires some explanation.

In Angola the advance of the missions was marked by considerable tensions with the state. English Baptists had established a mission in the Kongo region in 1878, and although this area was allotted to Portugal in 1885, the terms of the Berlin Act allowed for freedom of missionary activity. One Baptist mission station was established at the capital of the Kongo king, and its position there was such that it could scarcely help influencing political affairs. This influence was partly felt through the conversion of sections of the population who thus became more independent of their chiefs and the Portuguese authorities. The missionaries also established

8. J B F Lima, p.27.
9. Pélissier (1978),pp.402–8.
10. Pélissier (1978).

schools and hospitals, which again served to attract the loyalty of Africans away from the Portuguese, who had done neither. These missions were harassed; in 1903, the Portuguese forbade the use of English in teaching and questioned the right of the missionaries to practice medicine. The Baptists were also frequently called on to act as mediators between the population and the administration.[11]

In central Angola, on the Benguela plateau, missions of the American Board of Commissioners were set up after 1881, and rapidly expanded their activities after the end of the caravan trade. They had local rivals in the form of the Holy Ghost Fathers, who established themselves after 1896. The Plymouth Brethren started missions in 1890, initially in Bihe and then, after the destruction of Cokwe independence, in the eastern provinces of Lunda and Moxico which bordered on Zambia, where they were also active. The Methodists had a mission in the historic hinterland of Luanda, and there were a number of other Protestant missions including the *Liga Filafricana*, founded in 1896 by the remarkable Swiss linguist and missionary entrepreneur, Héli Châtelain.[12]

In southern Angola the field was occupied, almost unchallenged, by the Holy Ghost Fathers. The original mission had been founded by Duparquet in Damaraland in 1878, and had operated at first in areas east of the Cunene still outside white control. The Fathers specialised in mission stations which were economically powerful and well-organised, and some of them had their own armed force of converts. As Portuguese rule advanced, tensions rose. After 1887, the government tried to make use of them to help its expansion in the interior. The mission was to receive a subsidy, and in return was contracted to set up lines of mission stations to act throughout the country as a pacifying agent.[13]

. In Mozambique, Catholic missionary work had been virtually discontinued after the abolition of the religious orders in Portugal in 1834. The Jesuits, however, returned in 1880 and established a number of mission stations on the Zambesi *prazos*, themselves leasing *prazo* Boroma where they built a magnificent baroque palace for their headquarters. Later the White Fathers started work in the colony. In the *Sul do Save* region, a number of Protestant missions were established, Free Methodists and Episcopal Methodists round Inhambane and the Swiss Evangelical mission near Lourenço Marques.[14] An Anglican diocese, called Lebombo, was created in

11. Carson Graham.
12. Soremekun; Tucker, Santos.
13. Clarence-Smith (1975).
14. Helgesson.

1893, principally to minister to Mozambican Africans who had joined the Church of England during their stay on the Rand, and a small Anglican enclave found itself incorporated in northern Mozambique by the partition of 1891. In spite of its remoteness and the hostility of local Portuguese, it survived and modestly expanded its work right through to independence.[15] The only other Protestants north of the Zambesi were attached to a mission of the Dutch Reformed Church in Tete district.

In general, the spread of Christianity in northern Mozambique was strictly limited, for which the spread of Islam is probably the explanation. In three *concelhos* around the town of António Enes which he studied, Mello Machado found that in 1964, Catholics only made up 3 per cent of the population compared with 41 per cent who were Muslim.[16] In Angola, on the other hand, Christianity had no rival, for Angola is perhaps the only major African state with no Muslim population at all.

The Protestant missions found themselves caught up in the armed resistance to Portugal in the Ovimbundu heartland of Bailundu in 1902[17] and in the Kongo rising of 1913. In the widespread arson and violence that accompanied these wars, the mission stations generally escaped harm and in the Kongo the missionaries even tried their hand at mediation. In each case they suffered reprisals from the authorities which took the form of deportations. The suspicion and hostility which existed between the government and the missions at this time was very real. The missions often provided outspoken criticism of the régime, and fuelled the campaign against the continuation of the slave trade in the twentieth century with such works as C.A. Swan's *The Slavery of To-Day*. The Mozambique high commissioner, Joaquim Mouzinho de Albuquerque, explained the authorities' point of view:

> Even if the missionaries do not have the slightest notion of serving any interest hostile to our rule, the simple fact that they join the quality of being foreigners to a difference of religion is sufficient for them to appear, in the eyes of the natives, as rivals of the Portuguese and consequently as aids in any reaction against our authority.[18]

The Protestant missions were never closed down, but they did not receive any government subsidy, and in 1921 they were made to conform to stringent conditions which were aimed at cutting down their independence and their capacity to oppose the objectives of the

15. Paul (1978).
16. Mello Machado, p.351
17. Wheeler and Christensen.
18. Mouzinho d'Albuquerque, p.99.

régime. By decree 77 of that year, all missionaries in Angola had to be *bona fide* ministers of religion; they had to teach in Portuguese and not in any foreign language; they were not to take part in commerce of any kind and were not to print, write or teach any African language except at the level of catechism classes.[19] Most of the missions survived these controls, and when the first nationalist risings took place in 1961 they once again played a major part in alerting the world to the issues and to the nature of the struggle that was taking place.

The Catholic missions were also to be found opposing the régime. Particularly in the south of Angola, they spoke out against the bloody wars of pacification, thus precipitating a confrontation in 1906 when the Holy Ghost Fathers were forced to submit to Portuguese episcopal jurisdiction. The abolition of religious orders and the disestablishment of the Catholic church in Portugal in the early days of the Republic threatened the missions with dissolution, but the authorities had no way of filling the vacuum which they would have left in the interior, and they were allowed to survive. After 1919 they were restored to a modicum of favour, and the New State took them into partnership, giving them financial aid and even paying their catechists. Nevertheless, although one section of the Catholic hierarchy came to identify itself closely with the régime, the missionary orders became increasingly critical of the government during the 1960s and helped, at a crucial stage of the war of independence, to weaken the solidarity of the Portuguese colonial establishment.

In general, the penetration of missionary ideas corresponded with the extent to which the old communal social and economic relations had been broken down. As old authorities were destroyed or became irrelevant, the missions often provided the only alternative set of values and the only alternative organisation. The missionary, G.M. Childs, wrote in 1958;

The breakdown of traditional authority has been so rapid that the social life of the villages [among the Ovimbundu] is now very near to complete anarchy. [. . .] The missions and churches have been compelled to take over, Church leaders — catechists, deacons and pastors — have taken on judicial functions. Church meetings, both local and regional, have become courts and councils.[20]

Both Protestants and Catholics trained African catechists to man the outstations of missionary penetration. The catechist became an important local leader, one better able to identify with the interests

19. *Providencias tomadas. . .*, Decreto 77.
20. Quoted in Edwards, p 83.

of cash crop farmers and nuclear families. Moreover he was not tainted, as was the chief, by association with the government and its demands for tax and labour. Adrian Edwards wrote of his role among the Ovimbundu,

> The catechist's presence is a mark of the identity of the village. The catechetical school is the only institution which groups people of different domestic groups on a village-wide basis, and in which people participate in a wider set of social relations on a village and not on an individual basis.[21]

Among the Ovimbundu, the Protestant churches were locally independent. Their pastors and elders were elected, and they were financially independent, which increased their appeal for the new élite that was emerging. To quote Edwards again,

> Umbundu protestantism retains certain historical features of Congregationalism — democratic selection of officials with strict discipline binding members of the congregation, industriousness and zeal for education, and a certain consciousness of being a spiritual élite.[22]

This element of independence and local leadership was less apparent in the Catholic communities which experienced a traditional hierarchical structure and which laid more stress on sacrament than teaching. Moreover, the Catholic church was more closely associated with the government and received favour from it, again detracting from the possibility of its promoting a new African leadership.

Certainly, until the Second World War, the principal experience that most Africans had of European institutions and values came through the missions. Missionaries encouraged monogamy and introduced the ox-plough, both of which did much to transform the traditional social and work relations of the peasantry. Hygiene and sanitation were also stressed. As Alf Helgesson wrote,

> The message of digging latrines went literally along with the one of the Christian faith. It is still quite common to hear a report on how many latrines have been dug during the last quarter when the Methodist Quarterly Conference is in session.[23]

Missionaries introduced the first medical services and schools, and promoted the spread of new craft skills in the countryside. Henri Junod wrote in 1927, at the end of his great study of the Thonga of Mozambique, with a profound appreciation of the significance of the Christian 'revolution':

21. Edwards, p.83.
22. Edwards, p.89.
23. Helgesson, p.68.

Christian marriage is no longer a collective act, but has been individualised together with the many other acts of social life. It remains a social act indeed, but an act accomplished by two individuals on their own responsibility . . . This Christian or Western individualism will kill primitive collectivism and all its rites.[24]

Symbolic of this change was the replacement of the circle with the straight line:

The new Thonga village is no longer a well-defined family. It has become an agglomeration of families belonging to different clans, attracted to a particular spot by the European town or by the Church and the school. The straight line, with its capacity for infinite prolongation, has taken the place of the circular, with its necessarily restricted length. Considering that new ideas are now invading the Bantu tribe from all sides, it is certain that the old circle will disappear more and more and that regular streets will be more generally adopted.[25]

Syncretist religions and messianism

The African's response to Christianity has never been predictable. Why, for instance, was there such a markedly different response in Angola and Mozambique? One can do no more than guess at an answer, but clearly part of the explanation lies in the strong influence of Islam in Mozambique, a religion which inevitably attracted converts because of its overtly hostile relations with the colonial government. Christianity may well have been held back also by the slower rate at which the old communal society disintegrated. Migrant labour was widespread in central and southern Mozambique, but clearly this was less of a solvent for traditional African society than the cash crop farming and peasant production of Angola. Moreover, the concession companies seem to have been successful, whether deliberately or not, in keeping missions out of their sphere of activity, so that generally the level of missionary activity in Mozambique was much lower than in Angola.

The second major problem associated with the spread of Christianity in the Portuguese colonies is the comparative absence of messianism and African independent churches and religious movements, although there is always the possibility that this absence is no more than the result of a lack of information on such movements.

During the wars of pacification, there had often been strong backing from traditional religious cults for those who resisted the Portuguese. For instance, in Barue the activity of the spirit mediums

24. Junod(1927), vol.1, p.535.
25. Junod(1927), vol.1, p.525.

was essential to the organisation of opposition. The crushing of armed resistance, however, appears to have caused a crisis for traditional religions. On the one hand, many Africans were attracted to the Christian churches, while on the other, new forms of religious expression rose to prominence. In this connection the witchcraft and fetish eradication cults are of particular importance. The *mourimi* movement in southern Mozambique can be considered typical of the complexity of such cults. The movement was inspired in the first place by the serious famine of 1913–14, and was a search for renewed fertility of the soil. It attributed the disaster, however, partly to the defeat of Gungunhana the Gaza king, and partly to the activity of sorcerers.[26] Similar movements occurred in Zambesia. The Mcapi cult was strong in Northern Rhodesia and Nyasaland in 1934, and may also have touched Mozambique.[27] Then in 1947 the Bonjisi/Bwanali witch-finding movement, which originated in Nyasaland, established an independent centre in Mozambique. Bonjisi was a Mozambique Ngoni who had been to Johannesburg, and the name he used clearly reflected the current mission-inspired respect for the *Bom Jesus* and his resurrection. Pélissier has suggested that witchcraft eradication movements of this kind followed naturally on military defeat, and were a conscious rejection of the old religion that had failed.[28]

Healing and spirit possession cults also came to the fore. These were often closely related, and sometimes show clearly that they were a response to the penetration of European ideas into the world of traditional medicine. Charles Fuller has suggested that among the Gwambe of southern Mozambique possession cults had a particular attraction for women, and gradually came to be the repository of all surviving traditional beliefs and customs. Nevertheless, they were adapted to the new economic and social order, and there is a clear element of syncretism in some of their practices.

In the wardrobe of the medium, who changes costume to represent such characters as the housewife, the chief, the gold miner, the peddler, the lover, and others, are clothing and ornaments which these personalities wear. The equipment includes replicas of guns, bicycles, stethoscopes, thermometers, and other European articles, and bells, books, suitcases, and other products of foreign cultures. One medium claims that Indian merchants, Jewish storekeepers from Johannesburg, a Portuguese farmer, and a Roman Catholic priest, each with appropriate clothing, have been numbered among the spirits which possessed her in her trances.[29]

26. Junod.
27. Richards.
28. Marwick.
29. Fuller, p.204.

One would assume that, moving along the spectrum from traditional religion to orthodox Christianity, there would be a number of flourishing independent churches. It has, indeed, been claimed that in Mozambique there were some eighty such churches, mostly offshoots of similar movements in South Africa, but in general Mozambique appears not to have seen the immense mushroom growth of independency which occurred in countries to the south.

North of the Zambesi there are tantalising references to Islamic revivalism. The British Consul-General, Long, wrote from Lourenço Marques in 1922:

An Arab Mahomedan priest, apparently a British subject from Palestine, is travelling down this coast from the north, by easy stages, holding meetings of his co-religionists at which he is reported as having referred to the recapture by Mohammedans of Constantinople and of 'lands stolen from the Turks by the British'.

At Quelimane, I understand, this man interviewed the local Portuguese authorities and protested against the low rates of pay which were received by Mahommedans in this district and I am informed he was placed in the local jail for a brief period for having shown disrespect to the authorities.[30]

In Angola, religious movements during the height of the colonial era are better documented,[31] though still surprisingly few in number. The overwhelming majority of such movements flourished among the BaKongo of the north. Across the border in the Belgian Congo, over 500 separatist religious movements are known, and inevitably a number of these spread into Angola, often using Angolan exiles as a medium. Among the BaKongo, spirit cults were influential, and there was a tradition of religious and cultural centralisation which was a relic of the former political importance of the Kongo king. The Kongo region was also one where the Baptist missions were teaching a type of Christianity favourable to messianic interpretation. The religious movements among the BaKongo have been more or less continuous, but their emphasis changed as the colonial era progressed. Some of the earlier ones, like Ngwila and Mafulo in 1916-18, reflected the frustrations of the final military pacification and promise the coming of a messiah and the overthrow of the Portuguese. In the 1930s the syncretism of one of these movements reached highly original, and topical, proportions. Mpadi's followers in 1939-43 wore uniforms taken from the Salvation Army, and formed paramilitary units. Mpadi himself promised the coming of Hitler, 'the protector of the blacks'.[32]

30. PRO FO 371 9480 (1923), Lang to FO, 13.12.1922.
31. Santos.
32. Pélissier(1978), p.168.

Some of the movements occurred among Kongo Baptists. That of Simon Kimbangu, which began in the Belgian Congo in 1921, apparently had a strong appeal among Baptist catechists, while the founder of what was probably the most important of the movements, Simon Toco, was educated by the Baptists, had been to the *liceu* in Luanda, and had worked for the mission for five years. However, as many ideas appear to have originated with Catholicism as with Protestantism, and both were mingled with elements from African religion. In the 1920s and 1930s the stress lay on the finding out and destruction of fetishes — similar to the witch-finding cults already mentioned. There were also a number of movements which called for the killing of cattle, or of cattle with particular markings, another feature which has clear links with the religious and political self-expression of the Xhosa in South Africa.[33]

Most of these movements were implicitly hostile to the missions or the colonial government, although their opposition was seldom directly articulated. One of the most overtly hostile was the movement led by Simon Lassy in Cabinda in 1953, which featured prophesies that those who continued to attend Catholic sacraments would die. Simon Toco apparently preached that Jesus was a black man, but that this fact had been deliberately suppressed by Europeans who had torn the relevant page from the Bible.[34] René Pélissier has justly described these movements as 'the search for an anti-colonialist God'.[35]

Outside the Kongo region there are very few African revivalist movements of which records survive. The Lunda area was touched by some of the developments in Northern Rhodesia and by outbreaks of ritual cattle killing; the Mbundu people produced at least two syncretic religions in the 1930s and 1940s, the movements known as Moise Noir and Kazonzola. The latter may conceivably be a faint echo of the cult of the same name which spread Garveyism in Africa in the 1920s. Among the Ovimbundu and Ovambo, there are virtually no known movements of this kind at all.

Only one cult, that of Simon Toco, spread throughout Angola and became of significance for more than one ethnic group. Tocoism was originally a movement of the BaKongo, and only spread because of the action taken against it by the Portuguese who exiled its leaders to different parts of Angola where they continued their preaching. It was also partly infiltrated by elements of the Watch Tower which gave it tenuous links with wider African protest movements.

33. Santos, chap.5; Pélissier (1978), p.181.
34. Santos, p.471.
35. Pélissier (1978), chap.4.

Pélissier estimates that, at the most, these movements can never have claimed more than 50,000 adherents at any one time. Compared with the popularity of similar movements in other colonies, this number is tiny. In the modern history of African religion, Angola and Mozambique appear altogether exceptional in the small number and overall weakness of their independent churches and messianic religious cults.

Credible explanations of this phenomenon are not easy to discover. The most obvious is to attribute it to the hostility of the Portuguese authorities, who were frequently active in their persecution of independent religious movements. However, this cannot be the whole explanation, for until the last years of the régime the Portuguese administration was not uniformly effective at village level, and in many areas scarcely had any presence at all. As late as 1958 John Paul could describe a nineteen day journey through northern Mozambique from Lake Nyasa to the Tanganyika border in which he saw no other white man nor any motor vehicle.[36]

Other hypotheses offer themselves. For example, Pélissier has suggested that the Ovimbundu lacked any tradition of centralised authority, and that therefore messianic cults took no root because in some way messianism, with its belief in a single saviour, is linked to absolutist institutions. It is also possible that many 'Portuguese' Africans lacked the pre-conditions for independency. For instance the spread of the vernacular Bible in Angola appears to have been very slow compared with other colonies.[37] However, this argument has been decisively rejected by those who have examined comparatively the cultural development of the peoples of central Africa.

A more likely explanation can be found in the independent nature of the Protestant missions themselves and their relationship with the colonial authorities. Many of the Protestant missions in Angola and Mozambique were not part of an elaborate ecclesiastic hierarchy. Some, like Châtelain's *Liga Filafricana*, virtually had the status of independent churches themselves; others, like the Methodists round Inhambane, functioned for years through their African catechists and had no resident white missionaries.[38] All of them encouraged the activities of their African catechists, and allowed them to establish independent congregations. Indeed, one of the features of the spread of Protestantism in Angola was the work of the independent African preachers.

To this is linked a second factor, namely that the missions

36. Paul (1975), p.51.
37. Tucker, p.146.
38. Helgesson, pp.59-60.

themselves stood between their flocks and the demands of the local *chefe do posto* for tax and labour. The protection they had to offer may not have been very effective: what matters is how they were viewed by the population. As Edwards wrote of the Ovimbundu,

> The missionaries are the Europeans who appear in the most favourable light, and even among the pagans the attitude to the missions is without the fear accorded to the post . . .[39]

However, it went further than this;

> The establishment of new types of grouping and leadership at the local level has been the work of the missions, and it is through the missions that these new groupings are articulated onto the total Angolan social system. The missionaries who provided this articulation between the 'civilised' society and the local organisation of the natives, are the section of the 'civilised' population which most satisfies, in its relations with the people, the expectations of the Africans.[40]

The lack of independent church activity is paralleled by an apparent lack of other forms of African protest or organisation during the period between the end of pacification and the outbreak of insurgency in 1961; and this lack extends to metropolitan Portugal. The régime's policy of muzzling organisations by infiltrating them and making them work for the state proved far more effective than outright repression in eliminating expressions of dissent.

Wage-earning, towns and the survival of the peasant farmer after 1945

After the Second World War the economies of both Angola and Mozambique began to grow, and it might be supposed that this would have increased the demand for African labour, and hastened the integration of the population into the capitalist economy as wage-earners. What happened was not so simple.

In Angola agricultural production grew by 146 per cent between 1950 and 1964, but there was a steady overall *decline* in the demand for rural labour. In 1950, the rural wage-earners of Angola numbered 314,543; in 1964 they numbered only 241,351. Moreover, this decline was greater than it appears, for over the same period the African population actually increased by 15 per cent. An analysis of the figures shows that, whereas the number of migrant workers with contracts remained fairly constant, there was a steady fall in the

---

39. Edwards, p.86.
40. Edwards, p.87.

employment of local labour on a casual basis.[41]

From the point of view of the employers, the explanation appears to be that, faced with a rising wage bill, more investment went into mechanisation and more care into the utilisation of labour. From the African point of view the story appears to be this. In the areas of agricultural expansion, for instance in the coffee-growing regions, the African population took the opportunity to expand their own production of cash crops, so that, for example, in 1964 Africans were producing 26 per cent of Angola's coffee. There was, therefore, a fall in the numbers of local workers available for employment, with the result that migrants had to be brought in. Approximately 50 per cent of all migrant labourers in 1964 worked in the two coffee districts of Cuanza Norte and Uige, and the coffee industry employed 43 per cent of all rural labour. The main exception to this pattern was in Lunda district, where the mining and agricultural activities of Diamang were now largely worked by local labour.[42]

The overwhelming majority of migrant workers were Ovimbundu from the districts of Huambo and Bihe, which in 1964 supplied 67 per cent of the migrant labour force. In the 1920s and 1930s, the Ovimbundu had led the way as cash crop farmers, expanding their territory and growing maize and coffee for the market. What had happened to drive so many of them to become contract workers? It appears that after the war they began to suffer from the twin problems of a growing population and declining agricultural yields. Their agriculture had depended on continually breaking virgin land, and they had paid little attention to restoring its fertility. Now, with a growing population and with no new areas of land to open up, many of them were forced to migrate in search of work. However, wage labour was still viewed chiefly as a supplement to agriculture and the numbers who migrated varied considerably between good years and bad.

The situation of the Ovimbundu was not, however, typical. In post-war Angola, the African farmer generally prospered. Of the economically active population in the early 1960s, 87 per cent worked on their own account, and the number involved in wage labour was the smallest in Africa.[43] The African peasant had not only survived the imposition of colonial rule and the attempt to introduce a capitalist economy; he had adapted himself to it and his produce formed an important part of Angola's agricultural production.

41. Mendes, pp.55–6.
42. Mendes, p.61.
43. Mendes, p.56.

In Mozambique, the labour pattern was different. After the war, between 70,000 and 80,000 workers were regularly employed on the Zambesi plantations, and the total agricultural labour force was estimated in the early 1960s to be 129,000 per cent or 3.8 per cent[44] of the economically active population. This workforce was mostly recruited from local sources. Compulsion gradually disappeared, working conditions improved, and a new generation — born to plantation labour — proved more acquiescent than its parents. Working for the plantation companies became an accepted way of life, so that in 1961 the manager of Chá Oriental could write:

The labour situation remains embarrassing to me due to the difficulties I am having in refusing employment to all those asking voluntarily for it.[45]

However, a large part of the population, possibly as many as three-quarters of a million, were employed in the 1940s in compulsory crop growing, and at least another quarter of a million were migrants working abroad. If the cotton workers are included, then about a million and a quarter Africans (rather less than half the economically active population) were wage-earners; exclude the cotton-growers, and the proportions are more than halved.

During the post-war period, there was a steady decline in the numbers involved in cotton and rice growing, and after 1961 all compulsion ceased. At the same time, however, there was a steady rise in the numbers of those seeking work abroad. Why was this? After 1945, the population of the colony grew rapidly, but there was not sufficient expansion of the capitalist economy to employ it. Peasant cash crop farming continued to dominate the domestic economy of much of northern Mozambique and of the area round Inhambane,[46] and this continued to expand with the growing importance of cashew sales. With the end of compulsory labour in 1961, many plantation companies were forced to relinquish to African peasant farmers land which could no longer be worked. The alternative, where poor land or lack of transport prevented cash crop farming, was emigration. The expanding economies of Rhodesia and South Africa, where wages were higher and opportunities greater than at home, proved a great attraction, so that by 1966 as many as half a million Mozambicans may have been working abroad.[47] It is interesting to note that exactly the same trend can be detected among the white population, which also emigrated in large numbers.

44. Abshire and Samuel, p.268.
45. Vail and White, p.372.
46. Wield.
47. Herrick, p.43.

There was considerable growth of the towns after the Second World War, though urbanisation took place slower than elsewhere in Africa. The population of Luanda grew from 61,000 in 1940 to 240,000 in 1960, when it had become easily the largest city in either colony. Four other Angolan towns — Benguela, Lobito, Nova Lisboa and Sá da Bandeira — also had over 20,000 inhabitants in 1960. In that year, about 12 per cent of the population was considered urbanised, possibly a quarter of these being white.[48] In Mozambique, Lourenço Marques had a population of 120,000 (45,000 whites) in 1960, Beira 25,000 and Quelimane 20,000.[49]

Although the numbers attracted to the towns were relatively small, there were already signs in both colonies of the emergence of a genuine urban proletariat. The railway workers and stevedores of Lourenço Marques were not only fairly well paid by the standards that applied to African workers, but they showed signs of solidarity and organisation. There were a number of strikes in the 1940s and 1950s, though little is at present known about these. In general, however, no workers' organisations were allowed to form except those promoted by the government — a possible exception being the farming co-operatives that emerged among the Makonde and other cash crop growers, and which survived the sometimes active hostility of the administration. Lourenço Marques also developed a rather specialised form of proletariat in the large number of prostitutes who served the tourist trade — although many of these operated from their own homes in the suburbs where they lived with their families.

In both Mozambique and Angola, certain ethnic groups acquired traditions of working in certain types of employment, and built up a level of basic skills which was often reflected in higher wages. In general, however, a skilled labour force was slow to evolve; this was because white immigrants met much of the demand for skilled labour. An estimate for the skilled labour force of Angola in the early 1960s suggests that it numbered about 126,500 (102,400 of whom worked in towns and 84,000 of whom were African or *mestiço*).[50] Even among this group, industrial skills had scarcely begun to form. Half the skilled workforce were employed either in construction or in service industries, and less than 10 per cent in manufacturing. Africans also did not enter the commercial sector in significant numbers. The retail trade in Angola was largely in the hands of whites; in Mozambique, despite sometimes active

48. Pélissier (1978), p.29.
49. Herrick, p.15.
50. Mendes, pp.67,70.

persecution, it was dominated by Indians and in Guiné by Lebanese.

The cities naturally attracted people from all over the colonies, but the extent of ethnic mixing was much less than that which occurred in the mining towns of Rhodesia and South Africa. Luanda was overwhelmingly a Mbundu city — in 1960, 86 per cent of its population were Mbundu, with only the Ovimbundu (8 per cent) and the BaKongo (5 per cent) forming considerable minorities.[51] Lourenço Marques was equally the capital of the *Sul do Save*, 90 per cent of its African population coming from the Thonga, Shangaan and Chopi peoples.[52] Although many urban workers were migrant contract workers, there was never any ban on women settling in the towns. In Lourenço Marques, many workers arrived with their families and reproduced village settlement patterns around the city, which was in vivid contrast to the regimented townships of South Africa or the tin shanty towns of many other parts of Africa.

Rapid urbanisation, and the slums which grow up with it, are often seen only in terms of the problems they cause — poverty, crime, the destruction of communal and social values, and exploitation. For those who flock from the countryside to the cities, however, the journey is no descent into hell but one into what is seen as a land of opportunity. Luanda and Lourenço Marques were the places where the lines of social mobility were most open and where a large mediating class of *mestiços* and *civilisados* was to be found. It is necessary, therefore, to ask what opportunities Portuguese rule had given the African population to acquire the skills and values of European civilisation.

The road to assimilation

The last census to record 'civilised' Africans as a separate category was held in 1950. In that year there were about 30,000 Angolan and 5,000 Mozambican black *civilisados*. Although these figures may not be entirely accurate, it is clear that few Africans had availed themselves of the opportunity to enter the 'civilised' community of the whites. There were two reasons for this. First, very few Africans wanted to become 'civilised'; secondly for those who did want to, it proved very difficult to achieve the status.

If an African was recognised as 'civilised', he was exempt from African taxation and from the labour laws, he had freedom of movement and, in theory, access to government office; and he was able to participate fully in the European community. Yet none of this, not even exemption from contract labour, proved attractive — perhaps another indication that by the 1950s, contract labour was no longer the burden which it had been. Moreover, there were disadvantages. An African *civilisado* had no rights in communally-held land; he could not become a chief or enjoy rights under African law; he had to pay European taxes, which could weigh more heavily on him and were less easy to evade than was native tax; and he did not qualify for free medical attention or free schooling. Moreover, he found himself competing for employment with poor whites and *mestiços* and was not usually in a favourable position to make his way in the individualistic society of the whites. It is fairly certain that many more Africans qualified, in terms of education, wealth, and so on, to be considered 'civilised' than ever attained that status. This latter group, called by Pélissier *évolués*, possibly formed a more important sector of emerging African leadership than those who became formally recognised as *civilisados*.[53]

The other reason why there were so few 'civilised' Africans was the difficulty of attaining the status. Until 1954 the qualifications were not clearly defined, and an aspiring *civilisado* had to apply to the administration. There were long delays and considerable expense before success was possible, and the authorities appear to have made few efforts to see that the policy succeeded. Probably the administration also used a process of political selection. In spite of their emphasis on the education of an élite, comparatively few Protestants were accepted as 'civilised'. In 1950 only 21 per cent of Angolan *civilisados* were Protestant — the 79 per cent who were Catholic no doubt being considered more favourably disposed towards the régime.[54]

Before an African could even contemplate acquiring 'civilised' status, he had to obtain a certain level of education. For the vast majority of Africans, this meant attending a mission school in a rural area. It is very difficult to discover how widespread mission education really was, for the available statistics tend to record a paper educational enrolment which probably bears little relationship to the reality, and which gives no idea of how much further education may have gone than the simple registration in a primary class.

Apart from ineffective nineteenth-century liberal legislation which provided for the ends but not for the means,[55] it was the Republic that devised the first education programme for Africans when in 1913 it decided to set up 'lay missions' to take over from the missions of the religious orders in the colonies. In 1921, mission

51. Pélissier (1978), p.357.
52. Mitchell, p.46.
53. Pélissier (1978), p.72.
54. Pélissier (1978), p.70.
55. Samuels.

education was brought firmly under state regulation but it was only in 1929 and 1930 that a coherent educational system for the colonies began to be implemented. The system was to consist of three tiers, providing rudimentary, primary and secondary education.

How many Africans received education? Figures do not always distinguish African pupils from those of other racial categories, but in 1929 there were supposed to be 30,613 pupils in rudimentary (pre-primary) schools in Mozambique, most of whom would have been African;[56] in 1936, there were supposed to have been 59,949 children in school altogether — 9 per cent of the school age group. A detailed census of mission education in Angola in 1933 showed 46,000 pupils attending primary schools, of whom 86 per cent were at 'bush' schools.[57] After the Second World War, a strange discrepancy begins to appear in the educational statistics: primary school attendance in Mozambique increases to three or four times the figure for Angola (for example, in 1956 there were 68,759 in Angola compared with 264,233 in Mozambique).[58] There is no easy explanation for this discrepancy, since mission activity was much greater in Angola than in Mozambique. At the end of the 1950s, the percentages of the school age group who were attending school were Angola 8 per cent, Mozambique 24 per cent and Guiné 7.3 per cent.

Secondary education was far more limited even than primary education. In 1957, there were only 23,600 secondary school pupils registered in the whole of Portuguese Africa, and most of these were attending technical schools, with a mere handful following academic courses at one of the city *liceus*. The government had left education to the missions, and after 1935 had paid a subsidy to the Catholic but not the Protestant ones. In its official pronouncements, the government had expressed an interest only in moral and Catholic education, which would help preserve traditional Portuguese values. It showed no interest in education 'for its own sake', and was little concerned with increasing the levels of literate or industrial skills.

The figures quoted above suggest that educational opportunity was very limited, particularly at the secondary level. Whether it was perceived by the African population as being limited is another matter. Those who have written about education in Africa have concerned themselves almost exclusively with European-style education in European-style schools — as though before the coming of Europeans no African received education. The contrary is, of course, the case. African societies have their own educational

56. Pires, pp.7–8
57. Tucker, p.141.
58. Abshire and Samuels, p.183.

institutions and traditional ways of bringing up children and imparting knowledge. These continued to function during the colonial era, though frequently modified by the changes taking place in society. The majority of the African population of the Portuguese colonies were, by the 1950s, still only very incompletely integrated into the new economic and social order, and it is doubtful whether a European style of education had any relevance for a man who was still a subsistence farmer and who still preserved many of the family and lineage ties of the pre-colonial era. It is another example of the tunnel-vision of Europeans that the process by which children are alienated from their community by a European-style education is still invariably seen as progress.

These statistics understate the variety of educational opportunity. It is not clear whether they include catechetical schools and koran schools, and they certainly understate the education obtained abroad by contract workers. The channels of educational opportunity may well have appeared more open to the ordinary working population than they do now to westernised intellectuals.

African societies also had their own traditions of medicine and their own medical practitioners, and these have remained vigorous and active until the present. European-style health facilities were available in the big cities, and some hospitals and dispensaries were set up in rural areas by the missions. In 1933, for example, there were sixteen mission hospitals in Angola and sixty-seven dispensaries, but their care was little more than a token contribution.[59]

The government was chiefly concerned with public health and the control of epidemics, and this is a wise choice of priorities in any country whose resources do not permit a high level of personal medicine. Epidemic disease appears to have been one of the by-products of the opening up of the country and the movement of the people consequent on contract labour. Through contract labour people were often brought into a different climate and a different disease environment, and there were severe outbreaks of tuberculosis, influenza, smallpox, sleeping sickness and leprosy. It has been alleged that in the 1920s as many as 50 per cent of a contract labour force might die during the course of a contract, and it is well known that mortality rates were exceptionally high among miners from northern Mozambique and cocoa workers in São Tomé. Preventive measures were taken to control sleeping sickness in Angola and the islands, apparently with some success. Similar campaigns were undertaken against smallpox, tuberculosis and leprosy. In the Lunda district the public health functions were undertaken by

59. Tucker, p.141.

Diamang, and in Guiné the government concentrated its resources on the provision of fresh water supplies.

Whatever the success of such measures as were taken, the African population of the territories recovered, after the 1930s, from the sharp demographic crisis which appears to have occurred at the beginning of the century. In the population figures one can see, symbolically expressed, an eloquent tale of survival. In the sixteenth century the Indians of Central America, faced with disease, social disruption and forced labour, had virtually died out — the African populations in the early twentieth century, in many ways facing a similar challenge, survived and, after a decade or so, began to experience a population explosion. Between 1900 and 1930 Angola's population rose by about 600,000 or 22 per cent but between 1930 and 1960 it grew by 1,300,000 or 39 per cent.[60] In Mozambique, the population rise between 1930 and 1960 was 2.6 million or 65 per cent.[62] In each case the rise took place while there was heavy emigration, which suggests that the underlying growth rate was higher still. Clearly whatever cultural or environmental barriers had stood in the way of population increase in early colonial and pre-colonial Africa had now been removed.

The mestiços and the world

Those Africans who did become 'civilised' formed part of the world of the *mestiços*. It was a small world. The 1950 census listed the numbers of *mestiços* as follows:

Angola	29,648
Mozambique	25,149
São Tomé	4,300
Guiné	4,568
Cape Verde	103,251[63]

Although their numbers had increased since the beginning of the century, relatively the *mestiços* had undergone a massive decline. In the nineteenth century they had outnumbered the tiny white population, and had held important positions in commerce and the administration. In 1900 they still equalled the number of whites; by 1950 they were outnumbered 2:1 in Mozambique and 3:1 in Angola. Only in the smaller colonies did they retain something of their former importance.

60. For Angola's population, see discussion in Pélissier (1978), pp.26–30.
62. For Mozambique's population see F. Santos; Herrick.
63. Bender, p.32.

This relative decline in the *mestiço* population is especially striking because there were never any laws forbidding inter-racial marriages or liaisons, and the Portuguese often claimed to make a positive virtue of miscegenation and the multi-racial society. It is all the more extraordinary when compared with the growth and vigour of the Coloured population of South Africa, where sexual relations across the colour line were always frowned on and were ultimately made illegal. The explanation of the decline of the *mestiços* lies in the very absence of strict racial segregation. The *mestiço* group tended to disintegrate, and become absorbed at each end of the colour spectrum. Many *mestiços* passed successfully as whites and married with them, while still more sunk from the status of being *civilisados* and were reabsorbed into the African community. This trend is clear when the pattern of marriages is examined. Marriages between white and *mestiço* took place and between *mestiço* and black, in each case enabling the offspring to move out of the half-caste group, while marriages between black and white were rare, which meant that the *mestiço* group was not replenished.

In the nineteenth century, the *mestiços* had formed the largest part of the Portuguese community. They had dominated commerce and had provided military commanders and civil governors. Many of them were men of education, and the birth of journalism and democratic politics owes much to their efforts. During the twentieth century, their position was continually depressed as they were displaced by white officials from Portugal and their wealth was displaced by white immigrant capital. As the capitalist economy grew, they were to be found occupying skilled jobs but seldom any longer owning their own businesses. For example, truck driving was an occupation which in Angola became a preserve of *mestiços*. Most were city-dwellers — they formed a community of 13,000 in Luanda in 1960 — and some held posts in the lower ranks of the administration. Although their economic and social position was declining, relatively if not absolutely, many had a level of education very much higher than that of the white immigrants who poured into the colonies in the 1950s and 1960s. This was to make them potentially a dangerous source of discontent, and once they had come to identify with the African population, they provided much of the leadership for the nationalist movements.

A peculiarly important role was played by the *mestiços* from Cape Verde, which had never been subject to the laws governing *indígenas* and *civilisados*. Her inhabitants were almost all classified as *mestiços* and they continued to dominate the life of the archipelago. Traditionally, Cape Verdians had played an important part in the commerce and administration of Guiné, and the government knew that they could be attracted into the civil service because of the extreme poverty of the islands. In the 1950s, therefore, large numbers of Cape Verdians took jobs in the mainland African colonies, and this led to a considerable increase in the size of the *mestiço* population and to a significant injection of new ideas and cosmopolitanism into the half-caste community of Mozambique and Angola.

Much attention has been attracted by the intellectual and political activities of the *mestiços* in the days before effective metropolitan rule was established.[64] Under the monarchy and the Republic, there was considerable political and press freedom, and the *mestiço* communities of Luanda and Lourenço Marques took advantage of it to express their opposition to the colonial government. This journalism had its birth at a time when the *mestiços*, at least in Angola, dominated the colonial society of the capital and played a prominent part in government, commerce and law. As Douglas Wheeler has shown, nineteenth-century Angola saw *mestiços* as generals, lawyers, parliamentary deputies, town councillors and mayors. Their press was radical, republican and anti-colonial in the sense that it expressed the interests of their class against the policies of Lisbon.

The most famous of the *mestiço* journalists was Fontes Pereira, who was active between 1881 and 1891. He had worthy successors in A.J. Miranda (active 1913-14) and António de Assis Júnior (active 1917-21). These *mestiço* leaders had contacts with some white republican groups and with black *civilisados* and they occasionally spoke up on issues of wide concern to the generality of Angolan Africans, like forced labour. However, their main orientation was always the interests of their own group, and their associations were social as much as political. What political significance they had was derived principally from the persecution they suffered from the authorities. In 1912 the *Liga Angolana* had been formed; it was a recreational and social club in Luanda, and in no way a political party. However, it achieved a standing among Luanda *mestiços* since some of the politically active, like Miranda, were members. Its importance as an organisation was seen in the growing hostility of the whites to it, and in the attempts made to link it with rural rebellion in the Kongo region in 1914 and 1917. In 1921, however, together with its offshoot the *Grêmio Africana*, it was granted the right to elect delegates to the new Angolan *Concelho Legislativo*. But a year later, in a major drive against opposition organisations, the *Liga* was suppressed.[65]

64. Wheeler and Pélissier; Henriksen.
65. Wheeler and Pélissier, chaps.4 and 5; Pélissier (1978), chap.6.

The *mestiço* and *assimilado* press in Lourenço Marques appears to have had close associations with Angola. One of the earliest journalists, Alfredo de Aguiar, was a *mestiço* officer from Angola and later a *Grêmio Africana* was also founded in Mozambique. The degree of contact between the coloured intellectuals of the two colonies has not really yet been investigated. Again, Mozambican journalism was aimed at the specific concerns of the *mestiços*, in particular the poor education facilities, but it also catered for the market of African migrant labourers en route for the Rand. Prominent here was the Albasini family whose founder had been settler, trader and ultimately Portuguese consul in the Transvaal Republic.[66]

There were some *mestiço* and *assimilado* associations in Lisbon at this period. In 1912, a *Junta de Defesa dos Direitos de Africa* was formed in Lisbon with a newspaper, *A Voz d'Africa*. This was shortlived, however, and at the first Pan-African Congress held in 1919, Portuguese Africans were represented by a former governor-general of Mozambique, Freire de Andrade. In 1921, a body called the *Liga Africana* was formed to which were affiliated *mestiço* and African bodies in all the colonies. Its leader was José de Magalhães, a senator representing São Tomé in the Portuguese parliament. The *Junta* then reorganised as the *Partido Nacional Africana* under another São Tomé deputy, João de Castro. The two parties came to form a right and a left wing, each with its own news-sheet. In 1923, a session of the third Pan-African Congress met in Lisbon, but when the fourth Congress met in 1927 no Portuguese delegates were present at all.

By 1927, *mestiço* and *assimilado* associations had ceased to be politically active in Lisbon or in the colonies. They had been persecuted by the police and infiltrated by the authorities, so that they became harmless social clubs which avoided controversial statements or objectives. However, in 1938 the *Liga Nacional Africana* (formerly *Liga Angolana*) did present the visiting President of Portugal with a list of grievances and a demand to represent Angolan Africans to the government.

There are signs of vestigial and transient movements during the 1930s, and during the 1940s the first stirrings of a new nationalism occurred in Lisbon, but Pélissier is undoubtedly right to refer to the period between 1926 and 1950 as the *génération silencieuse*.[67]

Historians in search of the origins of modern nationalism have naturally looked hard at these early movements and have found in them echoes of the ideas of Marcus Garvey, signs that some of the

66. Henriksen, pp.155-60.
67. Pélissier (1978), p.235.

writers had a broad, 'national' viewpoint and a consciousness of the evils of colonialism. All these things can indeed be found, but the real nature of these movements was an expression of the interests of an urban class, once influential and even dominant, which was now in decline. The *mestiços* denounced Portuguese corruption and the discriminatory economic policies of the mother-country, and they were anxious for improved educational facilities — a bourgeois preoccupation which features prominently in their writings. However, their general political stance was much closer to radical Portuguese republicanism than to any African nationalism or even proto-nationalism. Faced with foreign criticism of Portugal's colonial rule, the *mestiços* closed ranks with their rulers. Pélissier again —

Assis Junior et ses camarades de la Liga angolana durent apprécier à leur façon le talent diplomatique de Magalhães, dont la réaction typique est celle d'un patriote portugais face à l'étranger plus que celle d'un défenseur des *contratados* travaillant dans les plantations bien portugaises d'Angola et de São Tomé.[68]

The 'silent generation' of the *mestiços* coincides with a period of almost total quiet among the *indígenas* in the rural parts of the colonies. Next to nothing is heard of protest movements or of *indígena* movements of any kind during the 1930s and 1940s. This apparent passivity has already been noted in the discussion of religious movements, and one final attempt must be made to assemble an explanation.

First, there is the isolation of many Africans from all external influences. The lack of capital development and the persistence of peasant and communal agricultural systems were possibly greater in Portuguese Africa than in any other colonies. Contract labour may not have been as all pervasive as is sometimes implied and *serviçais* anyway frequently served in areas near to their homes. Even in the cities and mining compounds, there appears to have been relatively little tribal mixing.

Secondly, the *mestiços* and *civilisados* who might have provided some leadership were to be found principally in the towns where they were under police and administrative supervision. Anyway, members of these groups had access to government jobs and skilled occupations, and for the most part identified with the régime.

Thirdly, the principal means by which Africans could acquire a 'political' consciousness was through the church. For reasons already suggested, the church appears to have retained the loyalties of its members and to have bred dissidence to a lesser extent than in other colonies.

68. Pélissier (1978), p.228.

Fourth is the factor of emigration. This took place on a large scale — both temporary and long-term — and it is likely that dissidence and opposition were most often expressed by the people with their feet.

Fifth is the fact that, in spite of the systematic destruction of the prestige of the chiefs, in spite of forced crop-growing and contract labour, the peasant economy — both the old communal agriculture and the cash crop farming by individuals — survived better in the Portuguese colonies than with most of their neighbours. It is not often from peasant groups that organised opposition is sustained.

Finally there is the fact that the phases of development through which other colonies passed were delayed in Portuguese Africa. The era of pacification lasted a generation longer than in most other parts of Africa; the chartered companies ruled longer than their German and English counterparts, and a centralised administration was not fully established until the 1930s. Large-scale capital development came late, and urbanisation and inter-tribal contacts were less widespread. The Portuguese colonies had evolved out of step with those of the English and French, and were largely unprepared for the nationalist revolution, which had to be organised abroad, and which broke on them in 1961.

7
THE WHITE COMMUNITY IN THE PORTUGUESE COLONIES

The old white community

Europeans had been settling in Angola, Mozambique and Guiné since the end of the fifteenth century, but their numbers always remained very small. In 1875 they would only have numbered a few hundred in all. The small size of the European community was partly the result of an unfavourable climate which led to a high death-rate, particularly among children, and partly a consequence of the type of economic activity pursued. The whites had always been divided into three classes — officials, convicts and traders. The first usually only stayed for a short time and did not bring their families with them. The other two groups came expecting to stay for long periods or permanently, but they also seldom brought European families with them, and formed liaisons with African or *mestiço* women. The European community, therefore, was continually being absorbed into the half-caste population, and within two generations was frequently indistinguishable from the local Africans.

Many whites lived as traders in African villages in the interior, or set themselves up as chiefs or war's lords over a subject African population. A number of the seaports, however, did develop as small towns of the European type. These towns were built around the fort, the church, the customs house and the governor's residence, and frequently these buildings were the only substantial structures in the place. Over the centuries, however, some of the ports had been endowed with fine public buildings and private mansions, which often crumbled away in the generation after they were built, exhibiting the state of decaying grandeur typical of so many Portuguese towns. Foremost of these was Luanda with its fort of São Miguel, its churches with their blue-tiled interiors, and its rich merchant houses built on the hill above the port. Mozambique Island also reflected something of the importance it had once possessed in international commerce. The island was guarded by three forts, including the massive sixteenth-century São Sebastião, and displayed numerous churches built in elegant eighteenth-century baroque style. The Jesuit College had been turned into the governor's residence, and the island was crossed with streets of town houses and commercial buildings. Ibo reflected a similar prosperity, which had come to it with the boom in the slave trade. A star-shaped fort commanded the narrow navigation channel, backed by an elegantly laid-out town with soft, ochre-washed traders' houses with deep verandahs and a classical church overlooking the dhow harbour.

In 1875 Cameron passed through Benguela, then the second town of Angola, and gave a sketch of what he saw.

The town is laid out in wide streets, and, the houses being white-washed and the doors and windows painted in bright colours, had a very clean appearance. In a central position in the town is a tastefully arranged public garden, where a band performs on Sunday evenings. The only public buildings are a well-constructed customs house, a very good hospital, the house of the governor, a court house, and a church which is never opened except for baptisms and burials . . . A few horses are kept there and the place boasts of one carriage; but the usual means of locomotion, as no white man ever walked during the daytime, is the maxilla, which is slung from long poles over which awnings are spread and carried by two men.[1]

The small size of the European colony and the close relations which it had with African and *mestiço* traders led to the growth of a very mixed community in which men of African descent held important positions and in which social mixing was common, reflecting the lack of any coincidence of skin colour with economic class. In 1854 Livingstone, then on the first leg of his famous journey across Africa, arrived at the ancient fair of Kasanje which was then nearing the end of its days.

The village of Cassange is composed of thirty or forty traders' houses, scattered about without any regularity, on an elevated, flat spot in the great Quango or Cassange valley. They are built of wattle and daub, and are surrounded by plantations of manioc, maize, etc.

The anniversary of the Resurrection of our Saviour was observed on the 16th April as a day of rejoicing, though the Portuguese have no priests at Cassange. The coloured population dressed up a figure intended to represent Judas Iscariot, and paraded him on a riding-ox about the village; sneers and maledictions were freely bestowed on the poor wretch thus represented. The slaves and free coloured population, dressed in their gayest clothing, made visits to all the principal merchants, and wishing them 'good feast' expected a present in return.[2]

The Portuguese for their part performed some civic ceremonies, and the captain then invited all the local dignitaries to a dinner. Livingstone concludes his portrait of the old colonial trading fair with this comment:

1. Cameron, vol.2, p.269.
2. Livingstone, p.344.

None of these gentlemen had Portuguese wives. . .It is common for them to have families by native women. It was particularly gratifying to me, who had been familiar with stupid prejudice against colour. . .to view the liberality with which people of colour were treated by the Portuguese. Instances, so common in the south, in which half-caste children are abandoned, are here extremely rare. They are acknowledged at table, and provided for by their fathers as if European.[3]

Convicts

Commerce had always been the *raison d'être* of the Portuguese colonies in Africa, but the Lisbon authorities had continued to dream of creating another Brazil, of establishing a permanent European population which would create plantations and industries. Many settlement schemes had been tried, but the oldest of them all was the policy of sending convicts to Africa. The presence of exiles in the colonies was a feature of the African empire from the fifteenth century to 1974. The exiles left Portugal as undesirables, but it was believed that out in the colonies they would usefully serve national interests by spreading Portuguese influence. Exiles were of three kinds. The largest group were those condemned for crimes against property or the person; next came political exiles, men who had fallen foul of the government of the day and were thought to be safer in exile where they would probably die of fever; the third group were orphans and prostitutes who were sometimes sent out to increase the number of female Portuguese in the colonies. By the nineteenth century, this last group no longer featured among the exiles, who were now made up of criminals and political prisoners exclusively.

Not all the convicts sent to Africa came from Europe. Some came from Goa or the other colonies, and there were even gradations in the place of exile within Africa itself, so that a convict sent to Luanda or Mozambique Island might, as a result of further offences, be sent to some station in the interior. Although most of the convicts were white, some were Indian or African, and a fair proportion were soldiers sentenced for military offences.

All the African colonies were used as places of exile, but from 1881 until the 1930s none were sent to the islands. Angola was by far the most important convict settlement, and between 1883 and 1914 an average of 240 convicts a year arrived.[4] Mozambique took far fewer, only 365 serving sentences in the eleven years 1905–1916.[5] Of these,

3. Livingstone, p.346.
4. Bender, pp.86–8.
5. *Anuário de Moçambique*, pp.546–9.

ninety-five were convicts sent from Angola. Until the end of the nineteenth century, most convicts were enlisted in the colonial forces unless completely unsuitable. Others would be taken on as employees by the state or private businesses. Some redeemed themselves sufficiently to hold important colonial offices, and one ex-convict became a district governor in Mozambique. However, for many there was no suitable employment, and the government was forced to try to make productive use of their labour in internal settlement schemes.

Clearing houses were set up for newly-arrived convicts (in Mozambique the old fort of São Sebastião was used), after which they were sent to agricultural settlements in the interior or to man frontier posts. Convicts were officially encouraged to marry or to bring their families with them at state expense. In time, it was hoped, they would form industrious and settled Portuguese communities similar to the British convict settlements in Australia. The reality was far from these hopes.

Conditions for the convicts were appalling, and the settlements were inefficiently run, and totally lacked organisation. Prisoners who reached them died of disease or starvation, and many deserted and took to the bush as bandits or mercenaries, fighting for African chiefs in their resistance to colonisation. Others drifted into the towns, where they formed a shiftless white criminal class or set up as liquor sellers. In the early part of the twentieth century, a quarter of the white population of Luanda were ex-convicts, and one of the city's African suburbs boasted twenty-one grog shops, eleven of which were run by ex-convicts. Paiva Couceiro was only one of the governors who raised publicly the deplorable state of the exiles;

> In Luanda there are many criminals who have been driven on to the pavements of the public square through penury of various kinds. We speak of Luanda in particular because there is found the criminal depot which provides, from among those who have finished their sentences, a large body of people suffering the most pitiful moral and material misery. In addition to this the hospital (in other respects equipped and directed in such a way as to be a considerable credit to us) does not possess enough accommodation to provide shelter and treatment for the different manifestations of tuberculosis and the frequent cases of mental illness.[6]

The convicts were not very satisfactory as soldiers either, and were liable to display every form of indiscipline and mutiny. Cameron commented on the convict garrison of Benguela;

> The loyalty of the soldiers to their flag I did not expect to find very marked,

6. Paiva de Couceiro, p.162.

but I was scarcely prepared for the proposal made to me by a white non-commissioned officer, that if I desired to take the town he would place himself and his comrades at my disposal and would give up the fort to me on condition that I should give them meat three times a week instead of only once...[7]

Most of the convicts (possibly 80 per cent) were illiterate, and the overwhelming majority were male. It is difficult not to conclude that they contributed next to nothing to the establishment of a stable white community. This was at last recognised officially when in 1932 Salazar discontinued the practice of exiling criminals from Portugal.

The political exiles were rather different. They were much fewer in number and tended to be better educated. They came out as a result of the political upheavals in Portugal or in Portuguese India, and frequently took an active part in the white politics of the colonies. It was probably this group which was responsible for the attempted coup in Luanda in 1930, and which fed the incipient white radicalism which occasionally revealed itself in the colonies. In 1936 a concentration camp was opened at Tarrafal in the Cape Verde Islands and many political dissidents continued to undergo exile right up to 1974, among them Mario Soares (socialist prime minister of Portugal 1976-8) who was sent to São Tomé in 1968.[8]

Free white immigration up to 1940

In 1940 there were 27,400 whites in Mozambique, 44,000 in Angola and 1,400 in Guiné. This figure, which includes officials, military personnel and convicts, reflects the comparative failure of a century of continuous effort to establish a European population in the colonies. Apart from the convict shipments, immigrants had come to Africa in three ways. Some had come out as soldiers and officials and had stayed on after their term of service was over. This group scarcely achieved numerical importance before the end of the wars of pacification in Angola around 1920. Secondly, they came out as private individuals to undertake some economic or missionary enterprise. Thirdly, they arrived as part of government-sponsored immigration schemes. But, however they came out, their role in the colonies ultimately came to depend on the evolution of the economy and the part they could play in it.

The encouragement of emigration to the colonies was official policy throughout the last century of Portuguese rule. It was seen as an essential pre-requisite for the fulfillment of Portugal's 'civilising'

7. Cameron, vol.2, p.270.
8. Soares, pp.218–23.

mission, but it was also a response to the persistent loss of population from mainland Portugal and the islands to Brazil and the United States. Between 1850 and 1950, 1.5 million Portuguese emigrated to Brazil alone, and in the early twentieth century the annual rate was running at about 35,000 a year and was a major source of concern to the authorities.[9] It was widely felt that if this flow of population could be diverted to the colonies, good Portuguese would not be lost to the motherland. A greater Portugal—a second Brazil—would then soon take shape in Africa. Mouzinho de Albuquerque wrote:

It is of the first importance to open up a field where the worker, the small trader, the clerk and the great mass of those who seek government jobs shall find lucrative application for their skills and energies, without any burden for the impoverished treasury and with evident advantage for the economic equilibrium of the metropole.[10]

If politicians at the end of the nineteenth century were not always clear how the colonies might benefit Portugal, here at any rate was one answer for them. The colonies could provide employment for the 'demographic excess which the lack of development allows to exist in the metropole' as the colonial minister, Viera Machado, put it.[11] The fact that most of the emigrants were poor and illiterate peasants was moulded to fit the colonial ideology, for it was claimed that they would bring the traditional peasant virtues, such as thrift and industry, to the task of developing Africa.

In order to attract immigrants, various colonisation schemes were devised between 1850 and 1926. Immigrants were offered assisted passages, free grants of land, remission of taxation, and frequently government aid in the form of subsidies and free issues of tools and food. Schemes of this kind were devised for Pemba Bay in the 1850s and for Moçamedes and Huila in 1849 and the 1880s. In the 1890s, Mozambique operated a scheme which provided free passages for immigrants, and further colonisation schemes were proposed in 1899, 1902, 1907 and 1910. In 1911 a major project was designed to take place around an urban centre in Angola, and in 1916 there were suggestions that Jews might be encouraged to establish a settlement, also in Angola.[12] In the 1920s, investigations began into a proposal for a barrage on the Limpopo which would provide irrigation for a colonisation scheme,[13] while many immigrants were attracted to Angola during the boom years of Norton de Matos' government of

9. Castro, p.58.
10. Mouzinho d'Albuquerque, p.113.
11. Rodrigues Júnior, pp.29-30.
12. Gaspar.
13. Rodrigues Júnior, p.21.

the colony. One estimate, indeed, suggests that between 1920 and 1924, the white population of Angola rose from 20,700 to 36,192.[14] Parallel with these colonisation schemes there existed the penal settlements and a number of private projects as well.

Most of these planned colonies ran into problems. Gerald Bender estimates that between 1900 and 1940, whereas a million Portuguese left for Brazil, only about 35,000 emigrated to Angola.[15] Why did Africa prove so unattractive to settlers? The planned colonisation schemes all suffered from insufficient preparation; land was inadequately surveyed, and not enough attention was given to transport infrastructure and the needs of the settlers in the early days after their arrival. In 1902, for example, when Robert Williams was granted his railway concession, a scheme was proposed to counter British influence by establishing 200 families in the Benguela highlands. Four years later the surveys had not been completed. In 1907, under the vigorous leadership of the Governor-General, Paiva Couceiro, the plan was pushed ahead, and a small experimental agricultural station was set up. A few settlers began to arrive, but in 1909 the railway ran out of money and the line halted 80 kilometres short of the settlement area.[16]

There were other problems, however, for the first two decades of the twentieth century mosquito-borne diseases were very common even in the cities, and the traditional high mortality among white immigrants continued.[17] The settlers who came, illiterate and unskilled, as they often were, could neither survive on their own nor compete with Africans in the labour market. Mouzinho de Albuquerque, commenting on a newly arrived batch of 100 immigrants in 1897, wrote: 'This is not colonising, populating or nationalising, it is merely an extending of misery.'[18] Where subsidies were provided, immigrants frequently preferred to live on these, as they represented a real improvement on the poverty from which they had fled in Portugal. Then, even when settlers did start farms, they soon discovered more congenial ways of life as hunters, transport riders and traders, or they drifted to the towns in search of work offering a steady wage. Many moved on from Angola and Mozambique to seek a future in the more prosperous cities of South Africa.

By 1930 there was only one area of the Portuguese colonies where the schemes of the previous fifty years had succeeded in establishing

14. Pélissier (1978), p.35.
15. Bender, p.98.
16. Paiva Couceiro, p.152.
17. Neto, p.52.
18. Mouzinho de Albuquerque, p.114.

a white rural community. This was on the Huila plateau behind the port of Moçamedes in southern Angola.

The whites of Southern Angola[19]

During the era of the slave trade, the Portuguese had largely neglected the extreme south of Angola, and it was only in 1840 that the port of Moçamedes was founded, the region being established as a full province in 1849. Between 1849 and 1851, some 500 settlers were brought in, mostly from Brazil, and a number of successful economic enterprises began. Cotton was grown for a world market which experienced sensational price rises during the American civil war; fish was caught and salted; sugar-cane was grown to make rum to exchange for ivory in the now booming trade in the latter commodity. Not all the immigrants made good, and in 1877 the white population was still estimated at only 508 (200 of whom were women). Some of these had penetrated inland, however, and had settled among the Nyaneka of the Huila plateau.

After 1879, Boer trekkers began to cross the Cunene in considerable numbers, and in 1881 a colony of Boers was allowed to settle in the Huila highlands where it was hoped they would establish a community of pastoral farmers. Boer dominance in the Huila highlands soon, however, threatened to bring its own problems, and in 1884-5 the Portuguese authorities acted to bring in large numbers of settlers from Madeira, some 600 arriving in response to government advertisements. As well as the Madeirans, there was a steady immigration of Portuguese fishermen, some of whom sailed their own boats from Portugal, so that by 1900 there were 367 white fishermen earning a living on the Moçamedes coast.

The development of this white community in southern Angola has been studied by Gervase Clarence Smith, who has shown how precarious was its economic survival. The fishermen who worked the rich fishing grounds off Angola had to struggle against African rivals, against debt and climatic conditions that required them to import their water supplies and filled their drying fish with blown sand. The industry was gradually taken over by a few large companies, and the small-scale enterprises went out of business. The Madeiran peasants who went to the Huila highlands were inexperienced and found their crops ruined by frost, drought and disease. Many of them left and went to other parts of Angola, although a few did succeed in becoming permanently settled on some of the

19. For this section see Clarence-Smith (1975); Clarence-Smith (1979); Medeiros.

favoured land with rich alluvial soil. The Boers flourished better than either of the other groups. New arrivals in the 1890s swelled their numbers to 900 by 1900 and to nearly 2,000 by 1910. However, although their farms were thickly established round Humpata in the highlands, their prosperity came increasingly to depend on more nomadic pursuits. In the early days, they raided their African neighbours for cattle and then took to hunting, pursuing the game deep into the basin of the Okavango. Others used their skill with oxen and wagons to establish communications with the coast and provide transport for the Portuguese.

Most striking of all was the extent to which this white community came to depend on government expenditure. With the exception of fish and, for a few years, cotton, export crops failed, and the prosperity of the community became tied to supplying government forts and military expeditions. Many of the settlers went along with the military campaigns as irregulars, receiving a daily wage and a share of captured cattle. Others supplied food or wagons for the armies. However, campaigning came to an end after 1915, and the subsequent growth of rail and motor transport took away the economic basis on which the whites had survived. During the 1920s the Boers began to leave Angola, lured by the Union government to South West Africa, and by 1928 almost all of them had left, enabling many of the Nyaneka to return to the lands from which they had been expelled in the previous century.

White peasants and small-scale white economic enterprise had, therefore, succumbed to the climate and to the inability to survive hard times. They were drawn inexorably by high government expenditure to become economically dependent on military campaigns and state purchases, or they were bought out by large-scale capital enterprises. A few individuals had, however, acquired or accumulated sufficient money to form a class of planters operating with their own capital. Although very few in numbers, this class became possibly the most influential sector of the white population.

The independent planter class

Although the odd Portuguese, *mestiço* or Luso-Indian might be found anywhere in the colonies running a business, there were, by 1940, only three areas where the planter class can be said to have established itself. These areas were, southern Angola, the Cazengo highlands of northern Angola and the Manica highlands in the territory of the Mozambique Company. Zambesia had many plantations, but most of them were company-owned. The same is true of many of the plantations of São Tomé and Principe.

The origins of the Angolan planter class go back to the 1840s, when the authorities were anxious to suppress the slave trade and to find other exportable commodities to sustain the commerce of the colony. Active encouragement was given to African and Portuguese farmers who would produce exportable colonial crops. As a result, sugar-cane began to be grown on the alluvial lands of the lower reaches of the Dande, Bengo and Catumbela rivers and on the coastal oases near Moçamedes. By the mid-nineteenth century, each of the major Angolan ports had a hinterland of plantations. One particularly favourable region was the Cazengo highlands, which proved to have land ideal for coffee-growing. Land grants were made there in areas nominally under Portuguese control, and both white and black landowners registered farms.[20]

Much of the capital used to establish these plantations was accumulated locally. Some of it had originally been invested in the slave trade, part of which came from Brazil, but the rest appears either to have been derived from legitimate trading profits or to have been accumulated by officials in the course of the tax-collecting activities. This local origin of plantation capital is a marked feature of Angolan development at this period, and the close links of the planters with trading activities was to remain. Much of the sugar produced, for example, was destined to supply internal African markets with rum and was not for export. Many of the planters continued to run trading enterprises or reverted to trade when times were hard.

The planters were always few in number, and this reflected the precariousness of their economic position. Their main problems focused on the costs of their labour and transport. Servile labour, whether slave or contract, was difficult to control, and continually deserted, while transport costs from the highlands to the coast absorbed all profits except when world prices were exceptionally high. Under these pressures the plantation economy eroded at the edges. In bad years many of the planters reverted to trade, becoming middlemen who bought from the African producer, while their bankrupt estates were sold to banks and land companies, which were unwilling to invest much themselves, but which took the opportunity to acquire landed assets when these were cheaply available.

Nevertheless, the planter class never disappeared. Its life was prolonged by periodic injections from high world commodity prices or by marketing opportunities within Africa itself. Cotton boomed in the early 1860s; in 1873 and again in 1893, world coffee prices

20. For the nineteenth century history of Cazengo, see Birmingham (1978); Jill Dias.

reached record heights; sugar went through a profitable period at the turn of the century when, following the high tariffs imposed on imported spirits, the trade in locally-produced rum experienced boom conditions. By 1910, however, the sugar-growers were again in trouble as the government increasingly clamped down on the liquor trade. The fortunes of the planters are written in the feeble tally of Angola's exports. At the height of the boom in the 1890s, 10,000 tons of coffee had been exported, but this fell steadily to a mere 4,000 tons by 1907, with no significant recovery until 1922. Sugar exports in 1914 amounted to barely 6,000 tons, and cotton to just 165 tons. Moreover, sugar apart, much of this production was the result of African enterprise. It creates a very false impression to write of the Angolan planter class as though it consisted only of white Portuguese; African-owned plantations were always of significance, and the considerable growth of coffee production in the 1920s was almost all due to the increase in the number of African growers.[21]

The planters dominated settler politics, and were able to exert considerable pressure on the colonial authorities. They were strident in their demands for a tough labour policy, and opposed all measures designed to eliminate servile labour. Their concern for their own labour supply led them into the anomalous position of becoming the allies of the humanitarian lobby, for they were articulate opponents of the practice of sending contract labourers to São Tomé. Their opposition helped materially to get the system altered after 1910. In the early days of the Republic, they fought a sometimes violent battle against the colonial authorities, who were determined to root out surviving forms of slavery. They successfully resisted implementation of the decrees allowing Africans freedom of contract, and on a number of occasions they were able to bring about the withdrawal of measures and even the resignation of officials.

During the twentieth century, despite increased white immigration and the gradual improvement of transport infrastructure, the white planter class did not prosper. Plant diseases, fluctuating world prices, labour problems, the vagaries of the climate and high transport costs made their position hopelessly insecure, and it was not till the 1930s that the Portuguese government began to develop policies to protect colonial agriculture. The few who made good devoured the less successful in bad years, and there was a distinct tendency for Angolan capitalism to become locally monopolistic, capital becoming concentrated in the hands of one or two major operators

21. Salgado, p.230; Carreira (1977).

who would dominate whole districts of the colony.[22] The remainder tended always to sink towards the petty bourgeoisie, or revert to bush trading. This process was observed by Alexander Barns who travelled in Angola in 1926.

> ...Several small farms were passed growing wheat and potatoes but only in a very small way. The largest of them, although doing a certain amount of cultivation has, I was told, 'degenerated' into a mere maize buying establishment from the native grower. The owner had many wagons and teams which we met on the road loaded with sacks of traded maize en route for the railway.[23]

The 1940 census showed that no less than a quarter of Angola's whites listed their occupation as 'trader', while less than 10 per cent were agriculturalists.

The planter class in Mozambique is much more difficult to describe. During the last quarter of the nineteenth century, Mozambique witnessed the activities of various entrepreneurs who subleased *prazo* concessions, or worked stills producing spirit from cashew or sugar-cane. Those who attempted agricultural production themselves were, however, few and far between, and as late as the 1920s the high commissioner, Brito Camacho, commented on the lack of agriculture round Lourenço Marques so that the city had to import even basic foodstuffs which could have been locally grown.

It was in the territory of the Mozambique Company that something resembling the Angolan planter class did begin to emerge. From the beginning the Company was active in promoting white immigration; it also allowed its officials to acquire land concessions. By 1927, it could boast 1,045 white farmers. The most successful farms were set up in the Manica highlands in the circumscriptions of Chimoio and Macequece, where conditions were not dissimilar from those of the Rhodesian plateau, and where the existence of the railway provided a solution to the transport difficulties.[25] There cattle could be raised, and in 1927 32,000 hectares were planted with maize. Some of the estates were owned by land companies, and at least one third of them were worked by non-Portuguese concession-holders, so that the existence of a permanent Portuguese planter class was not as assured as the figures might suggest. Moreover, their position was somewhat precarious because of labour problems and fluctuating prices and production. Like their Angolan counterparts, the Mozambique Company planters formed a vigorous political

22. Clarence-Smith (1979), p.53.
23. Barns (1928), p.113.
24. *Portuguese West Africa* (1949), p.21.
25. Nunes, p.218.

lobby which harried the Company's administration into keeping up the labour supply and, in the 1930s when prices for maize began to fall, into setting up a maize-marketing organisation which would give preference to their crops over African-grown maize.[26]

In the Niassa Company's territory, a number of plantations were established in the coastal regions. Many of these were taken up by German planters after the First World War, but many also were operated by Company officials who frequently showed greater interest in their commercial profits than in administering the territory. The numbers of planters in the north, however, was always small.

The white official

The government official has always been an important, and frequently dominant, element in the Portuguese population in the colonies. Before the 1890s, there existed a basic three-tiered administrative structure. Each colony had a governor-general beneath whom were the governors of the districts. In the third tier were the municipal councils (where these still survived), Portuguese land concessionaires (like the *prazo* holders of Mozambique), captains of forts or trading fairs with a purely local authority, vassal chiefs and *capitaes-mores*. The *capitão-mor* might be an African, *mestiço* or Portuguese; he was granted a commission to represent the authority of the government in a certain region where he would be empowered to maintain 'order', administer justice and collect hut tax, etc.

Although most of the governor-generals were senior members of the Portuguese establishment, frequently army officers or even aristocrats, the lower echelons of the service were drawn from an astonishing range. Although service officers probably predominated, it was not uncommon for there to be district governors of African, Indian or convict origin, while in the third tier, local dignitaries on the town councils, or *capitaes-mores*, were drawn from those who had acquired sufficient local influence to secure a commission. Pay and living conditions generally were appalling, and service in the colonies held few attractions for Portuguese of ability. Many of the government officials were in fact 'doing their bit of time', as Wallis Mackay put it, and he unflatteringly continued to describe

the emaciated representatives of the Government, who, in their offices at the Customs... seemed scarcely able to hold their heads up over their writing-tables, and who lay listlessly on couches and on the ground during the day, [but] were here to a man during the night, eager, wide-eyed,

26. Neil Tomlinson (1979).

gamblers, bending their backs to the work till the early hours of the morning, as though their lives depended on chance. Perhaps to a large extent their lives do depend upon casts of the die, for I have been informed that the parent government at Lisbon leaves these wretched outcasts to live on what they can glean from passports and more nefarious forms of commercial enterprise...[27]

From the 1890s a new administrative structure was evolved. It was set out in formal decrees for Mozambique in 1907 and for Angola in 1914, and was finally fully implemented in the 1920s. This made provision for a four-tiered system. At the top was still the governor-general, advised by a *Conselho do Governo*, and served by an increasingly complex system of government departments. Below him were the district governors. The third tier was now to be made up of circumscriptions (*circunscrições*), *concelhos*, military districts (*distritos militares*) and municipalities. There was to be an evolutionary relationship between these. Before an area was fully pacified, it was made a military district; the next stage was for it to be declared a circumscription and placed under an administrator (*administrador*); when the 'civilised' population had grown sufficiently, it acquired the status of a *concelho*, which meant that the *civilisados* (of all colours) sat on various advisory boards; finally, when a town of sufficient size had grown up, it was allowed to have its own municipal commission (*commissão municipal*) or full-scale municipal council (*camara*). The fourth tier was made up of the district officer (*chefe do posto*), who dealt with the African population at village level, on a day-to-day basis.

During the early part of the twentieth century, the general trend was for military and naval personnel to be replaced by civilians, although the complete 'demilitarisation' of the colonial civil service was only achieved under the New State. The office of governor-general was always viewed as a major political appointment, and during the 1890s and again in the 1920s the post was held by men who were granted the special title of high commissioner and who held ministerial rank. Occasionally a man of major importance in the world of Portuguese politics, like Brito Camacho, would be given the office, but it was more common for a man's career to move the other way and for a successful period in the colonies to be made the launching-pad for a political career at home. Norton de Matos and Freire de Andrade, for example, became important and successful politicians, while Paiva Couceiro tried, unsuccessfully, to lead a monarchist revival and was at the head of numerous plots against the Republic. Some governor-generals worked their way up in the

27. Mackay, pp.134-6

colonial service and were appointed essentially for their colonial experience — such men as Alves Roçadas or J.J.Machado — but only one, Pedro Massano de Amorim, served as governor-general both in Angola and Mozambique. During the last years of the monarchy and the first years of the Republic, colonial governors proved very transient. There were nineteen changes of governor-general in Angola between 1886 and 1920, and twenty-eight in Mozambique. Under the New State there was to be much more stability, and senior officials were chosen essentially for their loyalty to the régime.

In 1906, in a move to break away from dependence on service personnel, the *Escola Colonial* was founded in Lisbon to train colonial officials. It functioned in the premises of the Lisbon Geographical Society, and was run by that august and imperialist body. Courses were available in colonial administration, public health, economics, geography, commerce and a few of the African languages, and the training lasted two years. In 1927 it was renamed the *Escola Superior Colonial* and later became the *Instituto Superior de Estudos Ultramarinos*, awarding diplomas at university level. It seems, however, that it took a long time for this training to have any great influence on the colonial cadres. In 1955 only between one-third and a half of senior officials in Angola had diplomas, while among the *chefes do posto* only fifty-one out of 268 were qualified.[28]

The colonies were always short of administrators, and the administrators tended to be short of experience. As late as 1959, there were only 682 career civil servants in Angola, manning eighty-one *concelhos* and circumscriptions, and 267 *postos*. Moreover, these officials seldom acquired deep experience of the peoples over whom they ruled. According to Galvão, in 1947 only two administrators and ten *chefes do posto* had held their posts for more than six years, while the overwhelming majority in all grades except administrator had spent one year or less at their posts.[29]

This inexperience is all the more significant because the officials held very wide powers in the absence of any real form of indirect rule. For much of the early twentieth century, the colonial civil service was underpaid, its resources were stretched to the limit and the calibre of those who occupied the posts was not high. The *chefe do posto* was often isolated from all regular contact with his superiors, and held semi-autocratic powers over the African population. In view of his low pay and meagre prospects, the temptation to abuse his position was considerable. Mouzinho de Albuquerque thought

28. Pélissier (1978), p.126.
29. Quoted in Pélissier (1978), p.122.

that few of those holding the job were really up to the task . . .

. . .some through excessive indolence, others with their spirit embittered through loneliness to the point of losing their head at the smallest obstacle, others through lack of imagination to overcome deficiencies and surmount difficulties which are to be found every day in the bush.[30]

Many of them took payments for the supply of labour, or used contract labourers to work their gardens. Galvão referred to their struggle

with a humiliating pauperism which fetters the free movement of their faculties or leads them to undesireable solutions which damage the morality of the Province. Corruption spreads in the class whose low level of income is also the cause of its intellectual and functional mediocrity.[31]

The inefficiency of the bureaucracy before the 1940s was proverbial, and the inability of the Portuguese to organise a consistently effective administration must always be borne in mind when considering the impact of their colonial policies. Brito Camacho wrote scathingly of the lack of expertise:

The agricultural establishments of the province, almost without the customary exceptions, are managed by navy or army officers, bureaucrats of some kind or species who have had no preparation for the direction of such services. If I am not mistaken, a bachelor of theology was the director of an important northern company when I went there, and a poet from the administrative department was sent to study the cultivation of cotton in Egypt on behalf of an agricultural enterprise over whose destinies he presided.[32]

Under the Salazar régime, this particular complaint was increasingly remedied with the building up of technical cadres to run cotton and cereal *Juntas* and to promote the government's development plans. By the 1940s and 1950s the bad days were over, and the civil service, its morale raised by the importance attached to it and its views by the régime, was achieving a commendable and sometimes impressive efficiency. At the same time it seems that Africans and *mestiços* were increasingly being excluded from the more senior administrative posts (although a Cape Verdian was governor of Malange at the time of the outbreak of the revolt in 1961).

White immigration under the New State

Salazar began by looking very sceptically at expenditure on colonial

30. Mouzinho de Albuquerque, p.84.
31. Galvão and Selvagem, vol.iii, p.230.
32. Brito Camacho, p.56.

immigration schemes. Bounties to new immigrants were stopped, and this, together with the general cuts in government expenditure, probably led to a decrease in the white colonial population during the first decade of the New State. After the Second World War, however, white settlement in the colonies began again, this time on a massive scale, as can be seen from the accompanying table.[33]

WHITE POPULATION OF ANGOLA AND MOZAMBIQUE

Year	Mozambique		Angola	
1940	27,400	(100)	44,083	(100)
1950	48,200	(176)	78,826	(179)
1960	97,200	(355)	172,529	(391)
1970	150,000	(547)	290,000	(658)
1973	200,000	(730)	335,000	(760)

From these figures it is clear that the long-standing reluctance of metropolitan Portuguese to emigrate to the colonies had been overcome. During the late 1940s and 1950s, Africa was attracting 50 per cent of all emigrants from Portugal, nearly twice as many as Brazil.[34] This compares with scarcely 3 per cent of emigrants in the first part of the century. During the 1960s, however, the situation altered again. Emigration to Africa continued at an even rate and even slightly increased, but the impact of the European Economic Community led to a spectacular growth in the exodus of Portuguese workers to France and the other EEC countries. By 1965, nearly 71 per cent of Portuguese migrants were going to Europe. The emigrants were responding, as one might expect, to perceived economic opportunity, and this Africa was now offering. The most obvious, and best publicised, of these opportunities were the government-sponsored *colonatos*.

After the war, the New State once again favoured planned settlement schemes designed to fulfil a number of objectives. They were to divert emigration to Portuguese territory; they were to increase agricultural production in the colonies; and they were to serve the ideological needs of the New State by becoming model peasant communities and, in addition, models of multi-racialism where black and white would be seen to live and work together in harmony. A massive amount of effort was invested in these *colonatos*, and they are an interesting experiment in social engineering.

Four major white settlement schemes were got underway in the

33. Bender, p.20; Henriksen, p.135.
34. Robinson, pp.154-6.

1950s, together with a rather larger number of schemes designed for Africans alone.[35] Two were in Angola and two in Mozambique, and three of the four were associated with major dam projects and with railway extensions, so that they formed part of a broadly-based investment programme. Cela in central Angola was the most ambitious, the earliest and the most costly of the schemes, and it seems that some of the mistakes made there were avoided in the case of Matala, built to profit by the Cunene dam in southern Angola, and the Limpopo valley project in Mozambique. At Cela, the idea orginally had been to settle Portuguese families in communities where they would reproduce the patterns of peasant agriculture familiar in Portugal. Holdings were small, and it was intended that the immigrants would perform their own labour, the hiring of African workers being banned. The Matala scheme was significantly different. African labour could be hired and larger amounts of land were made available, so making possible agriculture of the plantation type. Moreover, at Matala African farmers were settled alongside Europeans, and this policy was followed also in the Limpopo valley project. By the early 1960s, there were about 600 families settled in the Angolan *colonatos*, and perhaps twice this number in Mozambique (including Africans). Owing to the high turn-over among immigrants, however, the *colonatos* were responsible for considerably more than this number of immigrants reaching the colonies. Pélissier estimates that perhaps 6,000 Portuguese were brought to Angola in connection with these schemes.

The *colonatos* were a strange mixture of realism and fantasy. The chief engineer of the Limpopo scheme, Trigo de Morais, wrote:

Barrages, irrigation canals and *colonatos* are to be found everywhere in the world, but perfect inter-racial brotherhood, which can be observed in the mixed *colonatos* of Mozambique and Angola, can only be found in Portuguese territory.[36]

In the context of the politics of Africa in the 1950s and 1960s, they were little more than sandcastles built to stem the tide of nationalism, but as a solution to chronic rural poverty and underdevelopment both in Portugal and Africa, they were a sign that the government meant action and not just words. They must be seen against the background of many similar schemes which had been tried in the twentieth century in the Iberian peninsula, where massive government investment in irrigation and communications had been

---

35. The discussion on the *colonatos* is derived from Bender; Pélissier (1978); Abshire and Samuels; Kimble.
36. Faria, p.47.

a way of anchoring rural workers to the land and reviving rural prosperity.[37] Moreover the concern of the authorities that white and black should mix on economically equal terms, that whites should not simply become small employers of black labour, and that marketing and purchasing co-operatives should be established, all deserve sympathetic consideration.

However, like their counterparts in Spain, the rural settlement schemes proved expensive and were largely failures. In Spain the attempt to revive rural agriculture took place at the same time as the industrial labour force in the north was rapidly expanding. The towns were quite simply able to outbid rural agriculture by offering better employment prospects, higher wages and more attractive living and working conditions. In a society where, whatever the restrictions on political freedom, the population enjoyed a large measure of personal freedom, it was impossible to retain active and enterprising people on the land. Exactly the same problem was encountered in Africa. Free to leave the *colonatos* once their obligations to the state had been performed, the immigrants were inexorably attracted to the cities and to the expanding job opportunities in the Rhodesias and South Africa. Recreating peasant Portugal simply could not compete as an attraction with the booming industry and bright lights of Luanda and Lourenço Marques.

The majority of the immigrants, however, were never destined for the *colonatos* in the first place. They came over on assisted passages to fill jobs created by the expanding economy and government services. A large part of them were poor and sometimes illiterate workers from northern Portugal. In 1960, of the whites in Angola who had been born in Portugal, 65 per cent came from the north and 12 per cent were illiterate. For them the arrival in Africa was not primarily a change from Europe to Africa but was seen as a movement from country to town. Instead of moving to Lisbon or Oporto, they were coming in from rural districts to Luanda and Lourenço Marques. There many of them settled in the slums (*muceques*) alongside African rural immigrants, and sought unskilled town work driving taxis, polishing shoes, and acting as waiters, bartenders or household servants. By 1960 55,000 Angolan whites (32 per cent of the white population) lived in Luanda, where they made up 24 per cent of the city. In the same year, 50 per cent of the white population of Mozambique were living in the capital, Lourenço Marques.

During the war against the nationalists in the 1960s and 1970s,

37. Naylon.
38. Pélissier (1978), pp.48,39.

Portuguese immigrants continued to pour into Africa. As late as the autumn of 1973, the huge, rusting liners of the Companhia Nacional de Navegação were sailing to Africa full to overflowing with peasant settlers. These sat huddled in subdued crowds on the decks, the women crocheting, the men playing cards or smoking apathetically as they awaited their future in the colonies. In the second class would be families coming out to join men in the forces or young people contracted to work for banks or businesses in the up-country towns. The first class, preserving the full splendour of the Edwardian period, was reserved for governors, generals, heads of state corporations — in one ship the whole spectrum of Portugal's ambitions in Africa about to be extinguished in the coming revolution.

Race relations

In the constant interaction of different groups which forms the basis of the history of any country, race is only one of the ways in which people establish their identity and define their interests. Racial, ethnic and religious differences can certainly appear to dominate class differences, but they seldom entirely supersede them. The various chapters in this book are concerned with group interaction in the economic, religious and political fields, and this section merely draws attention to two questions to supplement the general discussion. First, to what extent did the whites in the Portuguese colonies adopt an ideology based on racial distinction (race here used solely to indicate skin colour)? And secondly, to what extent were the racial attitudes of the settlers translated into a legislative framework?

First, it is necessary to point out that consciousness of race, and racial attitudes generally, are not immutable in a culture, or even in an individual, and any suggestion that a culture, a people or an individual may be inherently race-conscious or not race-conscious is quite unhistorical. Race (skin colour), nationality, family, religion, class, age, sex and locality are the eight principal ways in which human beings establish their identity, and circumstances may cause any one of these, or any combination of them, to gain as ascendancy at any one time. All communities in which people of different racial origin have mixed have on occasion revealed conflict based on racial distinction; but they have also experienced periods when consciousness of skin colour appears not to have been important.

In the nineteenth century and earlier, the white population of the Portuguese colonies was too small to man all the colonial posts, and did not have enough white women to enable it to form a self-contained white society. Portuguese men intermarried with women of other racial groups, acknowledged the children of these unions, frequently arranged for their education back in Portugal, and saw that they obtained jobs in the colonial administration. The strong position of the father in the Portuguese family, and the pride taken in paternity, helps to explain this readiness to accept half-castes into the white community. Many of the leading figures in colonial society, including governors, military commanders, parliamentary deputies and mayors, were of mixed descent. However, the influence of this *mestiço* class ultimately rested on its importance in trade and business and on the indispensable role it played in sustaining Portugal's presence in Africa.

In the early twentieth century, because of increasing numbers of whites — for instance, in southern Angola — a purely white society could sustain itself, and the acceptance of African customs, beliefs and values declined as fewer mixed households and mixed families were established. Economic change also brought African and Portuguese into open conflict over labour and the occupation of fertile land. Competition for land might be very severe locally, but generally it was not a great source of conflict in the colonies. Labour, however, was different. It was among the planters, whose precarious economic situation made them focus all their anxieties and frustrations on the alleged shortages and shortcomings of their labour force, that the most strongly articulated racial feelings emerged and the strongest demands for racially based legislation were made. They were tacitly encouraged in this by the generation of colonial administrators of the 1890–1910 period. Men like Mouzinho de Albuquerque were avowed admirers of British imperialism, and adopted many of the racial attitudes common in British colonies at this time. Their desire to see Portuguese Africa reawaken from what they thought of as anarchy, poverty and degradation led them, like the planters, to focus their frustrations on the African population and its 'barbarism'. The writings of these administrators and colonial governors are quite explicitly racialist in their values and assumptions.

One result of these trends was to be a great decline in the importance of individual Africans and *mestiços* in public life. They were eased out of administrative and military posts, and gradually had to confine their role to the lower ranks of the administration, although it is worth observing that at no time were Africans and *mestiços* totally excluded from the establishment, and there were, for example, coloured deputies to the Cortes in the 1920s. In the economic sphere, the relative importance of African and mulatto businessmen and entrepreneurs declined with the growth of white capitalism, while a strongly differentiated wage system emerged in which white workers were paid a higher rate than blacks for similar work. This in practice formed a solid protection for the poor white worker, who came to form a substantial majority of the white community.

Thus far, the conditions seem to have been ideal for the emergence of a racial ideology and a racially-based system of legislation similar to that of British Africa. However, this never occurred, for the official ideology became one of multi-racialism. It therefore becomes a question of importance why the burgeoning racial ideology of the colonial administrators, the planters and the poor whites did not dictate the form and tone of colonial legislation.

The answer lies in the relationship of the settlers with the home government, and of Lisbon with its colonial civil servants. For the most part, this was a relationship of extreme suspicion and often of mutual contempt. The contempt of metropolitan politicians for the colonials was matched only by the resentment of the settlers for the Lisbon bureaucrat. However, this was not just mistrust and dislike, it was also a basic conflict of interest: a conflict over labour, over tariffs, over economic legislation and ultimately over political power in Africa. It was a battle that was decisively won in the early days of the New State by the central government, which was able to reduce the colonies — officials and settlers alike — to complete subjection.

It did not serve the interests of metropolitan Portugal to support racial attitudes for two basic reasons. Throughout the nineteenth century, Portugal had had to face hostile criticism from English and Germans who wanted to deprive her of her colonies or gain economic privileges within them. To achieve this, they sought continually to disparage Portugal's ability to rule in Africa. Portugal was indeed very weak, and could not establish an administration in her colonies to rival those of Britain or Germany. Where she could not rival her critics, or meet their criticisms directly, she had to turn the argument and claim that she was attempting to carry out a totally different sort of policy to theirs — one in which intangible benefits of 'civilisation' were to be conferred in place of the more tangible objectives of British policy like capitalist economic development. Likewise, once African nationalism began to pose a threat in the 1950s, Portugal sought to counter this by once again emphasising the difference of her régime from those of other colonial powers. As she could not meet the criticisms of nationalists in any other way, she had to do so by denying them the 'racialist' stick which had proved the most effective in beating the other colonial régimes. It should be observed here that non-racialism was one of the central propositions of the African nationalists themselves.

In their attempt to convince the world of the reality of their mission to create a multi-racial community, the metropolitan politicians were prepared to ignore totally the prejudices of the local settlers who did not have the power or influence to combat them.

Nevertheless it was not all a propaganda exercise. In the 1940s and 1950s, there was never the close correspondence between class and race that existed in British Africa. Although coloured people were seldom to be found in the top jobs, no hard and fast colour line could be found lower down in the hierarchies of business and the professions. In Angola, whites and *mestiços* dominated the retail sector, ran country stores and drove trucks; in Mozambique Indians, and in Guiné Lebanese, successfully defended their position in trade against white rivals. In the coffee country of Angola, some African planters survived alongside their white counterparts, even into the period of intense capitalisation after the Second World War. In São Tomé there were even coloured owners of cocoa *roças*.

In other sectors of the economy, black and white were to be found doing similar jobs even down to the level of domestic servant and farm labourer, for some Portuguese immigrants worked in this capacity for other whites. The massive influx of poor and uneducated Portuguese not only created a 'poor white' community but one which the state was unwilling to support with the same props that were provided for its counterpart in South Africa. No laws enforced ratios of black and white workers and there was no legal job reservation. Business was free to appoint or promote cheaper black labour if and when it could. As a result the poor whites were forced to mingle much more with Africans of their own class. Many lived in the African slums, and this was not prevented by law; a housewife shopping for a kilo of onions or tomatoes in the market of Lourenço Marques would try the wares of black, mulatto or white stallholders, while at football matches mixed teams would be cheered fanatically by mixed crowds. Racial mixing of this kind was the inevitable result of the continued immigration of uneducated Portuguese peasants into the colonies. Although their whiteness was a massive advantage for them, it could not always overcome their lack of education, skills or capital. The realities of class were frequently greater than the prejudice of colour. The revolt of 1961 undoubtedly injected a strong strain of racial hatred. After the attacks by MPLA on the prison in Luanda in February of that year, armed gangs of whites roamed the African townships and a number of lynchings took place. These found their counterpart in the systematic attempt by UPA guerrillas to exterminate whites in northern Angola after the March rising. The settlers retaliated with a policy which came simply to be described as *preto visto preto morto*

(a black seen is a black dead).[39]
Yet the war of liberation never became a straightforward racial struggle. Tribal hatred of the BaKongo for Ovimbundu seems to have been as much a feature of the early massacres as the hatred of black for white. After the initial violence, overt manifestations of racialism were stamped out by the government. In other colonial societies, 'poor whites' might have secured legislation to protect themselves as the price of their loyalty to the régime, but for ideological reasons the Portuguese authorities would not accede to this, and the settlers were powerless to enforce it. Indeed the régime officially outlawed any colour bar and gave the seal of official approval to public manifestations of racial mixing like mixed football matches, mixed school classes or mixed reception committees for visiting politicians.

Representative institutions for the whites

Although individual concession-holders might be granted wide administrative power, at no time was the white population of the colonies as a whole self-governing, and no régime in Lisbon ever intended that it should be. Such an idea ran counter to the prevailing belief that colonies and mother-country should form part of a single political whole. However, representative institutions can serve other functions than that of wielding power. They can be a means whereby local interest groups can make known their views, and they are a way in which the government of even the most authoritarian state can acquaint itself with what is being said and thought. In other words, they are a vital channel for communication even when they possess little formal power.

The administrative reform of 1868–70 established a number of checks on the power of the governors. There was first the *Junta do Governo* (later *Conselho do Governo*) which formally advised the governor-general and was, at first, made up exclusively of senior officials. Later it came to have elected members (seven in 1917 when there was no Legislative Council, and two in 1960 after one had been set up). This body continued right through the modern history of the colonies, but its role was chiefly executive, and it scarcely performed the functions of an advisory body at all. Separate *juntas* had charge of the courts and and the treasury, but although these acted as checks on the powers of the governors, they hardly amounted to representative institutions.[40]

39. Pélissier (1978), p.536.
40. Lobo Bulhões.

In a different category was the *Junta Geral* set up in 1869 for Angola alone. This was definitely a consultative body, and although its members were appointed, they included a slightly broader spectrum of local opinion — teachers and municipal representatives, for example, having seats. An expanded role was envisaged for this body in the Organic Law for Angola published in 1914, but only in 1921 did the new body, the *Conselho Legislativo*, take shape. Apart from senior officials, the council had members representing the municipalities of Luanda, Benguela and Moçamedes, a representative of each district elected by the local commercial and agricultural associations and a 'representative of the natives of the province, chosen by election from among them, for which purpose the identity card is sufficient qualification.[41]

This Legislative Council may originally have been intended as a first step towards self-government, but it never had independent powers of legislation, and disappeared in the early days of the New State. It was re-established in 1953, but even in its final phase it never had more than a consultative role, although the governor-general was bound to seek its advice. The name of this body is, therefore, quite misleading, and it never acquired the importance of the Legislative Council of the British colonies.

Participation was slightly more real lower in the administrative hierarchy. After 1907, every community with 100 or more whites established a municipal commission, and this was expanded into a municipal council when the number reached 2,000. In addition, every *concelho* (district) would establish a partly elected council to run its affairs. In addition to these formal bodies, there was very often a *Commissão de Melhoramentos* (an improvements commission) or some other body set up to handle specific problems — a number of districts in Mozambique, for example, having hunting commissions.[42] The chairmen of all these local councils were always appointed by the governor-general, and it was they who acted as spokesmen for their region on the higher bodies. Municipal government was suspended in 1932 in Angola, and in 1940 in the other colonies. In Angola it was restored in 1942, but elsewhere not till 1961.

Finally there was direct participation in metropolitan Portuguese politics. In 1869 the colonies had a total of eight deputies, and this number was increased until there were in all twenty-three at the end of the New State. Although elections took place, there was seldom a

---

41. *Providencias tomadas*. . . ., Decree (no.4) promulgating the *Carta orgânica* of Angola.
42. E.g. *Anuário de Moçambique*, p.561.

rival to the governor's nominee, and the electoral process was closely controlled by the governor's right to draw up the lists of voters. The franchise was always restricted, but it never excluded people on the grounds of colour. One of the seriously contested elections was the presidential election of 1958 when General Delgado challenged the official candidate Admiral Tomás. In spite of massive manipulation of the voting by the authorities, Delgado polled heavily in the colonies, and this has usually been taken as some kind of measure of the frustrations of the settler community with direction of their affairs from Lisbon.

It is difficult to avoid the conclusion that the story of these institutions is scarcely one of a vigorous democratic tradition. At best they were a shop window, a pretence at consultation and co-operation, for no government, either of the Monarchy, the Republic or the New State, had any intention of sharing power with the settlers or of allowing them any say in affairs.

Where settler influence was felt, it was through unofficial pressure groups which came together to fight on specific issues. Such pressure groups organised effectively and with some success over the questions of contract labour and alcohol, and in the early days of the Republic there was a vigorous settler press which could seriously embarrass the government. The one consistent theme was hostility to Lisbon, but after 1910 an undercurrent of republicanism surfaced with the formation of settler parties like the Partido Reformista de Angola and the Partido Republicano Colonial. The activities of the press and the parties were curbed in the final days of the Republic, and although there was a minor insurrection in Luanda in 1930,[43] the New State established its authority with ease. In Mozambique, settler pressure groups like Acção Nacional de Moçambique were formed, but their weakness was seen when they failed in their campaign to oppose the 'Hornung Contract' in 1921.[44] The maize farmers of Manica were more effective, adopting tactics of violent demonstration in Beira and causing the resignation of at least one governor.[45] The New State organised the pressure groups as it organised everything else. Corporate associations (*grêmios*) were established for the major economic interests, and it was these which were supposed to negotiate with the government. They were as weak and ineffective as they were no doubt supposed to be.

In general, therefore, the settlers had remarkably little say in the affairs of the colonies. In the long run they seldom succeeded in their

43. Wheeler and Pélissier, chap. 5.
44. Vail and White, p.201.
45. Neil Tomlinson (1979), p.9.

political campaigns, and they were never able to impose a political or a racial ideology to their liking. Their lack of any local power, or control of arms and resources, was seen only too clearly during the wars of independence. The strings of power lay in the hands of Lisbon, and the whites were powerless to organise themselves as a political force once Lisbon had decided to capitulate.

8
SALAZAR, AFRICA AND THE NEW STATE

Colonial policies of the Monarchy and the Republic

During the days of the slave trade, the colonies had in practice enjoyed a high degree of independence. Such autonomy was an affront to the liberal constitutionalists in Portugal, and the administrative reforms of 1869 had begun to dismantle the powers of the governors-general. In that year, a separate *junta* was set up to handle the colonial treasuries and the process of the division of authority in the colonies had begun. As the century advanced, the division grew steadily wider. In 1888, inspectors of the treasury were appointed who were directly responsible to Lisbon and who could by-pass the governor-general. The colonial budgets were now handled entirely from Lisbon, and the extraordinary device was adopted whereby there was held to be a single colonial budget in which the expenses and revenues of all the territories were pooled.

Meanwhile, other independent authorities were created. In Mozambique, the chartered companies and the *prazo* concessions, with their own systems of taxation and labour recruitment, effectively removed much of the country from the direct control of the governor-general. Even within the truncated area that he did administer, his powers were circumscribed. The director of Public Works, the Manager of the Lourenço Marques railway, the *intendente-geral* of the military district of Gaza and the *commissário-geral das minas* were all ministerial appointments and effectively outside local control.[1] Funds for development, for railways and for pacification campaigns had to come from Lisbon and be authorised there; tariffs, tax laws, labour regulations and, above all, concessions all tended to be made in Lisbon. Concessions, in particular, were often granted through backdoor intrigue without the interests of the colonies being consulted at all. The Banco Nacional Ultramarino, for example, received a concession which enabled it to control colonial currency without, apparently, being responsible to anyone.

Economic policy was not much more coherent. Although the tariff of 1892 had established a generally favourable preference for Portuguese goods imported into the colonies, this scarcely amounted to a well-worked-out imperial trade policy. It was shot

1. Mouzinho de Albuquerque, p.55.

through with anomalies and was administered solely in the interests of the mother-country, making no pretence of favouring colonial goods. Where the interests of the colonies clashed with those of metropolitan Portugal, for example in the case of alcohol production, it was Lisbon interests which triumphed. The chaos in currency was even more striking. In 1890 the Banco Nacional Ultramarino had received its concession. Its general policy was to link the currency to sterling and to make it fully convertible into gold. The result was an extreme shortage of specie and the circulation of numerous other currencies, notably Indian rupees and South African sterling. This was actively connived at by the government which in southern Mozambique collected taxes in sterling in order to encourage South African labour contracts. In the Mozambique Company, territory sterling notes were actually issued.

To this muddled situation has to be added the fact that the colonies were only partly pacified, and that until after the First World War many areas were outside effective Portuguese administration altogether.

It was against this humiliating chaos and inefficiency that the very able administrators who served in the colonies at the turn of the century campaigned. Their leader and most coherent publicist was Eduardo da Costa, but the writings of António Enes, Ayres d'Ornellas and Mouzinho de Albuquerque all speak with the same voice. Mouzinho was perhaps the most vivid personality and most trenchant critic of the system. He was an open and avowed admirer of Cecil Rhodes and of Anglo-Saxon vigour and efficiency. In 1898 he wrote:

Compare these administrations [in British colonies], so simple and independent, so little bureaucratised, these countries so little administered, with any Portuguese colony, bound with an infinite number of laws, *portarias*, regulations and orders sent from the metropole at random; clogged up by a plethora of functionaries, in general badly paid and worse selected in Lisbon, occupied in minuting, copying, registering, sending out numberless *officios*, duplicates, triplicates, circulars, etc., almost all of them dispensable.

He went on to outline a plan to save the colonies. It involved pacification, for without that there could be no general and effective administration; the establishment of independent authorities in the colonies with financial responsibility; economic development and the realisation of the economic potential of the colonies. Pacification, autonomy and development — these were the watchwords of this school and in the later years of the monarchy their ideas began to

2. Mouzinho de Albuquerque, p.68.

take effect. They were able to commit Lisbon to the campaigns of pacification and to heavy investment in railways before the First World War. More important, the first steps were taken towards unifying the colonial administrations and re-establishing their autonomy. Crucial in this respect was the labour law of 1899 drawn up by Enes, and the administrative reorganisation of Mozambique begun by Ayres d'Ornellas' law of 1907, which outlined for the first time a coherent governmental structure under civil as opposed to military control.

Although most of the colonial reformers were convinced monarchists, the Republican leaders who took power in Portugal in 1910 adopted their view of the colonies and determined to press ahead with decentralisation and the granting of administrative autonomy to Angola and Mozambique. The reforms begun in Mozambique in 1907 were taken up in Angola in 1914 and an organic charter for the colonies was prepared, only to be postponed during the years of the war. The Republican leaders were also genuinely keen to end the labour scandals in the colonies, and took action to regularise the contracts of workers going to São Tomé. They also pressed ahead with expenditure on communications infrastructure, adopting Paiva Couceiro's strongly-held belief that there could be no pacification without roads, steamers and railways.

The rule of the high commissioners

After the First World War, the long-delayed plans for devolving power on the colonies were put into practice. In 1920, two high commissioners were appointed, Brito Camacho to Mozambique and Norton de Matos to Angola. The post of high commissioner had existed before, being created for António Enes and Mouzinho de Albuquerque in Mozambique between 1894 and 1898. The high commissioners of the 1920s held ministerial rank, controlled the armed forces, could rule by decree, and for the first time had financial autonomy which included responsibility for their own budgets and the ability to raise loans.[3]

In 1921 Angola remained a country of great potential, but singularly little fulfilment. The arrival of Norton de Matos in that year with wide financial powers was to coincide with a marked change in the country's fortunes. Norton drew up plans for the government to spend the equivalent of £13 million on infrastructure projects, and turned first to the London money market and then to the great concession companies for loans.[4] The largest sums were

3. *Providencias tomadas. . .*, Decree no.1.
4. PRO FO 371 7110 (1921), Bringes to FO, 16.4.1921.

earmarked for ports, railways, white colonisation and a mysterious item called 'native assistance'. In the event, Norton's policy proved a textbook illustration of the consequences of deficit finance. By 1926 the road network on the plateau had doubled, and the 21,251 miles of motor road open in 1937 gave Angola a system which the British Consul called 'among the best in Africa'.[5] Connections between the plateau and the coast still relied on the railways, but these also doubled in extent. Two new branches were opened on the Luanda line, which had been nationalised in 1918, and the Benguela railway reached the Katanga border in 1928 and Elizabethville in 1931. A fourth line running inland from Amboim was begun in 1921 and had 106 kilometres completed by 1923. Harbour works undertaken at Lobito and Luanda, and a virtual rebuilding of the latter city, were further signs of high spending. A start was also made with an Angolan air service with a base at Huambo. Government assistance to Portuguese immigrants was stepped up, and the numbers of whites entering the colony rose dramatically.

As this policy of high spending unfolded, restrictions on the issue of government paper were lifted. An Angolan State Bank was created to counter the all-pervasive influence of the Banco Nacional Ultramarino, and the colony adopted its own currency unit — the *angolar*. Extensive credits were made available, and bankers and businessmen took advantage of Angola's paper prosperity. The latter included the notorious Alves Reis, whose Banco de Angola e Metropole invested heavily in Angolan stocks with false banknotes unwittingly printed for it by the government's own printers.[6] To some extent this spending was supported by favourable commodity prices, and by a genuine expansion of African and settler agriculture, which in turn led to temporary increases in customs and hut tax returns. However, this was not enough to prevent rapid inflation as the *angolar* spiralled downwards, first in the wake of and then ahead of the *escudo*. Foreign exchange discounted at more and more preposterous rates, and shortages of imports began to hit the economy.

Government deficits grew steadily, and borrowing threatened to outstrip Angola's capacity to service its debt. In 1921 the debt had stood at 9,000 *contos*; by 1931 it amounted to 800,000 *contos*,[7] and annual debt charges were consuming half the colony's income,

---

5. *Report on Economic and Commercial Conditions in Angola* (1937), p.30.
6. Bloom.
7. *Report on Economic and Commercial Conditions in Angola* (1937), p.2.

which had scarcely risen at all in real terms as a result of Norton's speculations. Norton indeed failed to raise all of his £13 million loan, and as a result Lisbon had to step in as early as 1925 to honour Angola's commitments. Lisbon's traditional distrust of colonial autonomy appeared amply justified. The politicians of the New State were to point an accusing finger at this republican profligacy, and were to introduce a régime of stultifying financial puritanism, but they were destined in the long run to reap the benefits of this high spending. Already by 1926, diamond mining was rapidly expanding, and the first successful results of oil prospecting were being announced. The foundation had been laid for what was to become one of Africa's strongest economies.

The rule of the republican high commissioners in Mozambique marked less of a break and failed to lift the colony from its administrative and financial chaos. Brito Camacho, who became high commissioner in 1921, was faced by a complex series of questions which in eighteen months had overwhelmed him and his régime. He had to renegotiate the Mozambique-Transvaal convention in the full knowledge that South Africa wanted to gain control either of Mozambique itself or of the port of Lourenço Marques; he was faced with the scandals of the Niassa Company and the *prazo* concessions and with a bitter internal wrangle between the settler organisations and the concession companies and W.N.L.A. over labour. His efforts to raise loans became hopelessly involved with international rivalries and with the politics of labour and land concessions.[8] Meanwhile, the local economy was thrown into chaos by the decision of the Banco Nacional Ultramarino to withdraw the gold backing to its notes issue — a move which immediately crippled foreign trade and put a premium on foreign exchange earnings.

Although none of the fundamental problems of Mozambique was solved, the decade was not wholly disastrous, and world market conditions led to a temporary boom in plantation agriculture. The Mozambique Company went ahead with the Trans-Zambesia Railway, which was connected in the 1930s with the Zambesi sugar plantations and later with the Tete coalfields, creating for the first time an important internal transport network. Moreover the strong economic ties with South Africa survived the temporary lapse of the convention, and the sterling earned by migrant labour and the transit traffic of Lourenço Marques kept the Mozambique economy fiscally sound.

This republican interlude needs to be placed in a context of the

8. Vail and White, chap.5.

overall evolution of the empire, and of the shifting relationships between the different sectors of its economy. These can be summarised as follows: 1. an autonomous African peasant economy largely based on communal agriculture, which was predominatly subsistence but which was ready to produce or collect commodities for the market and to provide for their transport to the coast; 2. a plantation sector made up of small Portuguese farmers with little capital, or large, predominantly foreign-owned, companies — the former more common in Angola, the latter in Mozambique; 3. government spending, which can be subdivided into military and civil expenditure; and 4. invisible earnings from migrant labour and port and transit dues. Shortage of capital in the second and third sectors led to extensive use of cheap labour as a substitute and to the reliance on African taxation as a source of funds.

The republican period showed that the relations between these different sectors could change. Military expenditure, which had sustained local markets, especially in southern Angola, and which had amounted to a large interest-free subsidy to the colonial economies, was greatly reduced after 1918 and was temporarily replaced by the infrastructure expenditure initiated by Norton de Matos. When this ran into trouble in 1925, the republican period was almost at an end and with it the era of Portuguese subventions to the colonies. The great expansion of road and rail transport led to a reduction in the use of human carriers both by the government and by African traders — capital investment had here come to replace cheap labour. At the same time, due partly to changing world markets, but also to the improvement in transport, there was a great shift in the African economies to cash crop production by peasant family units in Angola, and in Mozambique an expansion of plantation production which competed strongly for labour supplies with South African mines and the government. Finally, the invisible earnings of the Mozambique economy threatened to falter with the expiry of the South African agreements, but in the end they recovered.

To summarise, real attempts were made to maintain government expenditure in the colonies at a high level, but to shift from military to infrastructure expenditure and to replace the use of cheap labour in the field of transport by capital investment.

The New State — fact and fiction

In March 1926, a military coup in Portugal toppled the last republican administration. The military leaders were unable to deal with the many problems facing the country, and failed to negotiate a loan from the League of Nations. In a new internal reshuffle in April 1928, General Oscar Carmona came to power, and appointed Professor António Salazar of Coimbra University to be finance minister.[9] By 1930 Salazar was the dominant voice in the government, and had obtained what was in effect a veto over the budgets, and hence policies, of all departments. In 1932 he became prime minister, and held the post continuously until his retirement following a stroke in 1968. Salazar's Portugal has been little studied, and a number of largely fictitious portraits of it are still current.[10] One of these, which is popular with those of right-wing persuasion, is that Salazar's régime re-established Christian and family values in a country torn by irreligion, cynicism and violence; that it restored stability to the most politically unstable country of Europe; that it sought to tame the excesses of organised capital and organised labour; and that it fought the racial dogmas of the twentieth century with a deliberate espousal of the ideal of multi-racialism.

Another fiction, more simply stated, is held by those of left-wing persuasion. This is that Salazar's government was just another fascist régime built on the twin models of Mussolini's Italy and Franco's Spain; that this fascism was little more than an ideological front for big business; and that it promoted an élitism more extreme than that in avowedly racial societies. Like all theories that are widely believed, both these views of Salazar's régime can be substantiated by a considerable depth of argument. Neither, however, has proved wholly adequate to account for its behaviour, and perhaps now a new portrait should be drawn.

The first and most striking characteristic of the régime is its longevity and its stability. From 1928 onwards, it was seldom seriously challenged by internal dissent. There was an attempted coup in 1933, and perhaps another in 1961, and the presidential elections of 1958, when Humberto Delgado challenged the official candidate, concentrated opposition forces dangerously. However, these are the only moments when the position of the régime appeared at all difficult. This stability was achieved partly by a successful use of propaganda and the control of news, and partly by the activities of the secret police — but both of these functioned in a very low-profile manner. Portugal never became a closed society like eastern Europe; people were free to travel if they could afford to, foreign books and journals could be bought in Portugal, and many surprisingly outspoken things could be published in Portuguese. The

9. Kay, chap.3; Robinson, pp.43-50.
10. However, three important recent books are Kay; Robinson; Graham and Makler.

secret police indulged in periodic purges, and silenced, or tried to silence, some of the régime's most outspoken critics, but its activity was perhaps most effective where it simply prevented opposition organisations from becoming established and winning recruits. The authoritarianism of the régime was concerned in general much more with gaining control of institutions than with repressing individuals.

In practice, the régime gained wide support and still wider acquiescence. Salazar was careful to avoid indentification with the extreme groups on the right — the monarchy was not restored or the church re-established — yet the general orientation of the régime was such that these right-wing factions lost support and dwindled to insignificance. The régime made a point of gaining and keeping the support of the armed forces and the bureaucracy. Both did well under Salazar; the army's budget was the one sector of public expenditure that was allowed to expand during the 1930s as Salazar adopted a rearmament programme,[11] while the bureaucracy was accorded a role of growing importance in the planning of the economy. Although Salazar made few concessions to wage-earners and peasants, one should not underestimate the support he gained even from this group. In particular, the Catholic ideology, which was so much to the fore in Salazar's public pronouncements, was an ideology widely shared by what was perhaps a majority of the Portuguese people.

However, the phenomenon of the support for the régime can best be understood by studying the large body of the uncommitted whose self-interest and desire for a quiet life lead them to identify with whatever régime establishes itself firmly. This phenomenon in Portugal has been described by Richard Robinson:

Situationism concerns the individual. It signifies at worst his survival and at best his advancement. 'The Situation' is the term given in Portugal to the prevailing political régime or government and, just as an individual needs a patron, so patron and client need to be 'on the side of the situation', at any rate in times of political stability.[12]

An interesting aspect of Salazar's régime is its exceptionally low public profile. Public speeches by the leader, public ceremonial parades, personality cults — all these existed but to a much lesser extent than in many liberal democracies. However, it might reasonably be claimed that the sobriety, puritanism and simplicity of lifestyle adopted by Salazar in the end made a greater impression on people than the flamboyance of a demagogic dictator.

11. Kay, chap. 6.
12. Robinson, p.33.

Salazar was a classical economist who believed in balanced budgets, limiting government expenditure and maintaining a strong currency, but he was no believer in laissez-faire. He and his advisers sought to plan the economy of Portugal and her empire, and created institutions to this end as thorough and all-embracing as those of any socialist régime.[13] Moreover, his attitude to foreign capital was one of extreme caution and his chief objective was for Portugal — an under-developed country — to develop herself from her own resources. In spite of the obvious differences in scale, it is relevant to make comparisons with the Russia of Stalin which also sought industrialisation and development from internally-generated resources. To achieve this, consumption had to be cut and resources diverted to investment — and where investment was inadequate, cheap labour and even forced labour had to be used. In Russia the rural population was made to pay for much of the industrialisation, and this can be closely paralleled in Portugal and her colonies where industrialisation was fed by cheaply-produced raw materials like cotton, by rural taxation, and by the provision of a steady supply of migrant rural workers. In Portugal, as in Russia, a disproportionate amount of the investment went on building up the armed forces and never found its way directly back to the people who had had to pay for its creation.

Salazar tried to impose on private business a series of controls which ranged from semi-compulsory membership of corporate associations (*grêmios*) to price controls and production quotas. Small employers were indeed whipped into line, but, with the connivance of the régime, a few great corporations and banks acquired what amounted to monopoly control of whole sectors of the economy. These great corporations worked closely with government, and there was considerable interchange between their senior management and the higher echelons of politics.[14] If Salazar's objective was a planned economy it was one with which the great monopoly corporations had no reason to quarrel.

The real clue to the ideology of the régime is not that it was Catholic, fascist or multi-racial, but that it was intensely nationalist. Salazar appears to have been deeply conscious of the contempt in which Portugal was held by the rest of Europe, of her diplomatic weakness and of the continued humiliating threats to the integrity of the mother-country and the empire. He and his propaganda department sought to boost the pride of Portuguese in their country and to assert Portugal's independence and importance in the world. It was

13. Oliveira Marques.
14. Graham and Makler, chaps. 1-4.

inevitable that to do this he should make play with the imperial tradition, the great navigators playing the role of founding-fathers rather in the way that the Elizabethans are so considered by many Americans and British. In the assertion of Portugal's independence, there was a subtle change of emphasis from the petulant non-cooperation alternating with bombast, which had been the hallmark of monarchist and republican diplomacy, to a less strong assertion of Portugal's rights while at the same time seeking to make Portugal indispensable to the great powers. Multi-racialism and the idea that Portugal alone was able to make the races work together only became a feature of the régime's propaganda towards the end of its life when it was faced by the threat of African nationalism — it was never central to the ideology of the régime and had little or no popular appeal in Portugal. Certainly it played little part in the 1930s when such views found scant favour in the rest of Europe.

There is a final feature of the régime which has been much misunderstood. The Salazar régime functioned without an elaborately organised body of support in the country. The *União Nacional* was little more than an electoral organisation to field candidates favourable to the régime at election time. A youth organisation called *Mocidade Portuguesa* and the so-called Portuguese Legion enlisted activists loyal to the régime. Yet these organisations had little influence and less power, and although they no doubt organised support to a limited extent, they probably failed to perform the vital function of a political party — that of enabling the government to listen to what was being said and thought in the country. In Salazar's Portugal the bureaucracy took the place of a party. The bureaucracy was full of the régime's supporters, prepared its policy documents, organised its propaganda, and gave advice. It appears to have been to the bureaucracy alone that Salazar listened, for he had the habit of moving even his closest political associates from their offices after only short tenures. Ultimately this was to be the fatal flaw of the régime as the lack of a party organisation caused a gap to grow between the rulers and the country which was fatal to the continued survival of the former.

The New State in Africa — continuity and change

To the fundamentals of colonial policy, the New State brought little or no change. The spate of colonial legislation which followed the fall of the Republic was principally a recodification of colonial laws rather than a statement of new policy. The first colonial minister of the military government was João Belo, who had made his name as a provincial administrator in Mozambique. Under his auspices a series of measures was adopted, the *Basas Orgânicas da Administração Colónial*, the *Estatuto Político, Civil e Criminal dos Indígenas*, the law setting up the 'zones of influence' and the cotton concessions, and the re-opening of negotiations with South Africa for a new labour convention. In these moves there was a mixture of the old and the new. The South African convention, which was eventually concluded after Belo's death in 1928, continued the previous arrangements for contract labour nearly unchanged, so that southern Mozambique remained an economic colony — a Bantustan, almost — of South Africa. The native statute also was a reaffirmation of the long-established principles by which Africans, before becoming 'civilised', lived under native law and enjoyed specific rights and duties as *indígenas*. Both these policies were to be continued under the rule of Salazar.[15]

The other two measures certainly involved a change of course. In the first, Belo began once again to assert metropolitan control over colonial finances. In the second, he took a major step towards integrating the economies of Portugal and the colonies for the first time.

Belo's period as colonial minister was transitional. After 1928 the colonies were gradually absorbed into the whole policy fabric of the New State. In 1928 came the important *Codigo do Trabalho Indígena*; in 1930 the *Acto Colónial*, and then in 1933 the new Portuguese constitution, the *Carta Orgânica* and the Administrative Overseas Reform Act. These measures reiterated the basic principles by which the empire was supposed to be held together, and made specific constitutional arrangements for their government. As far as the first were concerned, the African territories were seen as an integral part of the Portuguese state, not as territories in some sort of trusteeship. The aim of colonial policy was to integrate the colonies with the mother-country and this was to involve, on the one hand, building a common economy, and on the other pursuing the task of 'civilising' the African population and ultimately of turning them all into Portuguese citizens:

All this is to be achieved by following the Portuguese colonial policy of the assimilation of the natives, which means their integration into the body of the nation as soon as their way of life is sufficiently evolved to permit it.

This is how it was put by Professor Silva Cunha who became Caetano's minister for the overseas territories.[16] Once again, labour was to play a most important role in this process — or, as might be said today, the relationship of the people to the means of production

15. Vail and White, pp.234–6; Silva Cunha.
16. Silva Cunha, p.277.

was seen as the crucial factor. There was to be an obligation on all to work, but there was to be freedom of choice and an end to all unpaid forced labour.

It was in the formal relationship of the colonies with the Lisbon government that Salazar most clearly departed from the practice of the Republic and the preaching of the colonial writers of the Monarchy. There was to be an end to any sort of colonial autonomy. The post of high commissioner was abolished, and legislative and financial power was concentrated in the hands of the minister of the colonies. The minister was given the power to legislate for the colonies by decree, was to be responsible for all major appointments and for ratifying concessions. He alone could authorise loans and through government economic and commercial agencies he took an increasingly active part in the internal affairs of the territories. The governor-generals were reduced to the role of being heads of the executive, with very little initiative of their own in policy-making.

However, this assertion of central government control was not confined to the powers of the governors. The surviving concession companies had their privileges terminated, and administrative uniformity was imposed for the first time. Once again, however, Salazar was taking over from the Republic more than he cared to admit. The republican ministers had already made the crucial decisions not to extend the Niassa Company's charter, and to bring the *prazo* concessions to an end. The Mozambique Company's concession ran until 1941, and no steps were taken to terminate it prematurely. Diamang, however, continued to hold its virtually sovereign position in eastern Angola; the Company's investment, the taxes it paid and the loans it offered to the colonial government were all too valuable for the latter to risk interfering with its privileges.

This legislation was continually refined and amended. In 1951 the *Acto Colonial* was repealed and a new constitution produced. In fact, this again merely underlined the basic principles of the original settlement, except that the colonies were now declared to be Overseas Provinces of Portugal. The legal distinction between *civilisado* and *indígena* continued to 1961, when it was abolished and all Portugese Africans were in theory accorded equal status with metropolitan Portuguese.[17]

As has been emphasised repeatedly in this study, it is always more revealing to look at the actual implementation of policies than at the policies themselves. First, there was a steady increase in the scope and penetration of the administration. The hunger of the New State

17. For the régime's version of this legislation, see Wilensky; Silva Cunha. A critical discussion is in Duffy (1961).

for statistics, reports and plans was no less than that of its predecessors, but now the lone labour of over-worked *chefes* was supplemented by a growing number of government agencies and departments directing, monitoring, planning and regulating every aspect of colonial life. Henrique Galvão, in his study of Angola published in 1952, listed nine general administrative departments, two finance departments, eight economic departments (public works, geology, forestry, veterinary, etc.), three service departments and five departments concerned with marine affairs. There were also *juntas* organising coffee, cotton and cereal production, and others dealing with imports and exports.[18]

Even this did not begin to cover the agencies through which the New State sought to operate. By the new constitution, the Catholic missions were absorbed into the system as 'civilising agencies'. The *mestiço* organisations, which had begun to evolve into active political parties under the Republic, were tamed and made into quasi-governmental agencies. The hand of the bureaucracy was everywhere: there was a form for everything and a decree governed every form of activity. It was in the nature of the régime to absorb all national life into the bureaucracy. It was not a régime that ruled essentially through a party, an ethnic élite, or the military. All these played their part but to stress them is to misunderstand the nature of the system. It was in essence a régime of bureaucrats.

Henrique Galvão, himself a leading administrator in Angola in the 1930s, lashed the inefficiency of the system unmercifully. Referring to the economic departments he wrote:

The variety and multiplicity of the organs; their dispersal; their constitution as monopolistic compartments; the confusion which from the beginning has reigned between these bodies and the old organs of economic organisation [*sic*], especially in the technical field; the plethora of bureaucracy which is a traditional tendancy of corporate organisations; the inadequacies of badly trained management personnel, and also the cost of the services paid for by new burdens placed on production and on imports — all subvert the intentions of the legislators.[19]

The style and panache of Galvão's denunciations, his knack of hitting on the vivid phrase, the fact that he was so well placed to know exactly the situation in the colonies, made him for long the most often-quoted writer on Portuguese Africa. However, as the first tentative researches are carried out into the original archives, a slightly more flattering picture is beginning to emerge.

18. Galvão and Selvagem, vol.iii, p.236.
19. Galvão and Selvagem, vol.iii, p.350.

Salazar, it is true, inherited a corrupt and untrained colonial service, and had few resources with which to improve it. Indeed, his economic policies involved the cutting of government expenditure in the first decade of his régime. By the 1940s, however, the efficiency of the colonial service and the all-pervasive nature of its activities was rapidly improving. The *chefe do posto*'s duties now involved a detailed and paternalistic supervision of almost every aspect of daily life in the villages. In Guiné he was supposed to promote the use of pitch-forks, ploughs and ox-carts, encourage women to start sewing classes, maintain demonstration ploughed fields planted with cashew and groundnuts; he was to plant trees along the road, control the burning of the forest, see that all wells had concrete covers, encourage the use of latrines and the baking of maize bread; he was to encourage the use of Portuguese place-names and send objects in to the provincial museum — these tasks were in addition to his routine duties connected with public health, maintaining the roads and bridges, and collecting the hut tax. Such a régime is curiously reminiscent of the kind of enlightened despotism which Emperor Joseph II of Austria envisaged for the newly-emancipated peasants of Austria and Bohemia in the 1780s.[20]

Although, as so often happens with bureaucracies, numbers and skills were concentrated at the top at the expense of the cadres in the field, the efficiency of the administration steadily improved until it was actually able to operate a planned economy more thoroughly and in greater depth than any other colonial régime.

Economic policy

It would be a great mistake to see an economic policy for the empire springing fully armed from Salazar's brain as soon as he was established in power. There is evidence that at first he looked on the colonies simply as an economic liability. Portugal's trade with her empire had not grown as a proportion of her foreign trade since the beginning of the century, and the financial chaos of Mozambique and Angola were once again becoming a drain on the metropolitan resources. The immediate task was to make the colonies conform to the basic economic strategy he had adopted for Portugal. This may be defined as the reduction of government deficits, the elimination of floating debt, and the payment of all current expenditure from revenue — all this with the object of reducing interest rates, stabilising the exchange rate and halting inflation.

As far as the colonies were concerned, the initial target was to

20. *Anuário da Guiné*, pp.133–46.

produce balanced budgets and to make the colonies self-financing. Drastic economies were introduced, wages were cut, government-assisted immigration schemes were stopped, and taxation and customs duties were increased. The balanced budget became for the régime both a hallmark and a test of its virility. By 1939 the budget surpluses of Portugal amounted to 2 million *contos* (c. £18 million)[21] and Angola's surplus was running at over 40,000 *contos* a year. Sceptics would point to the significant item of 'extraordinary expenditure' in the budgets, which was still funded by borrowing, but by the end of the decade most of the surplus was genuine enough. The surpluses had been achieved at the expense of consumption and investment, and for much of the decade, while the world suffered from depression, there was no increase in production.

By the end of the 1930s, however, plans were being formulated for major state investment which would plough back the surplus into the economy. In 1937 a colonial development fund was set up which was to derive its finance from the budget surpluses with small additions from current budgets and from the profits of state-owned ports and railways. The first development plan drawn up for Mozambique included the building of branch-lines to Nacala and to the Moatize coalfields and an extension of the Mozambique railway to the Lurio river. There were to be road and port works and a cattle-breeding station, and work was to start on two major irrigation and settlement projects, the Limpopo valley and Umbeluzi schemes.[22] Transport and irrigation were seen as the keys to the colony's development, although it should be pointed out that these schemes had mostly been planned in the days of the Republic, and their realisation had been held back a decade by the financial discipline of Salazar's early years. A similar development programme was set on foot for Portugal itself, although a large and increasing part of the investment was set aside for rearmament.

In the event, much of this programme had to be postponed because of the war, but already by 1939 the régime's economic policy had taken a new and more sophisticated direction. The economies of Portugal and her colonies suffered from a series of interrelated weaknesses. There was a large deficit in the balance of trade, with exports concentrated in a few commodities in which Portugal enjoyed a near-monopoly, like fortified wines, cork and sardines;[23]

21. *Spain and Portugal* (Admiralty publication), vol.ii, p.217; Kay, p.44; *Portuguese West Africa* (1949). p.3.
22. *Report on Economic and Commercial Conditions in Portuguese East Africa* (1938), p.8.
23. *Spain and Portugal*, vol.ii, pp.213-15.

there was a low level of industrialisation and of food production, and the level of industrial skills was equally low. These problems were exacerbated by the decline of world commodity prices which severely hit Portugal, along with her colonies, as a producer of primary commodities. From the experience of the early 1930s Salazar and his advisers began to evolve the idea of a unified escudo economy — an economic counterpart to the political ideology whereby Portugal and her colonies formed a single unitary state.

This policy has been described with some accuracy as neo-mercantilism, but it should be seen more in terms of other development strategies of the twentieth century. Portugal and her colonies were to form a protected trading area in which there would be heavy tariff and quota preferences for imperial products. Rural areas were to achieve self-sufficiency in food, produce raw materials, and maintain a steady supply of cheap labour, all of which would enable urban Portugal to industrialise. Foreign capital was to be largely excluded, and where private Portuguese capital was not available, the state would finance investment. In this scheme the colonies were viewed essentially as parts of rural Portugal. Their role was to feed the economy with industrial raw materials and essential foodstuffs and to achieve import substitution in as wide a range of products as possible. They were also to provide the labour whose cheapness would keep the Portuguese economy competitive. The industrialisation was all to take place in metropolitan Portugal — at least that was the initial concept.

The crisis in foreign exchange which at the outset underlay this policy was caused by a heavy adverse trade balance. In 1928 the total foreign trade of the colonies amounted to 2.2 million *contos*;[24] in this figure imports stood in relation to exports at 42:58. The situation differed markedly from colony to colony. São Tomé remained as ever strongly in surplus, Cape Verde even more strongly in deficit. Guiné's foreign trade was roughly in balance, as it had been for most of the century. Portuguese India ran a very large deficit. Of the two large colonies, however, Angola had since 1920 consistently been able to cover its imports better than Mozambique, almost solely due to the growth of diamond mining. Mozambique was the great culprit, accounting for a third of the total deficit of the empire.

The trade deficit of Portugal and her colonies had traditionally been made up by invisible earnings, not by foreign borrowing. In fact, Portugal's national debt was one of the lowest of any country in Europe at the time of Salazar's take-over. The invisible earnings came from the remittances of emigrants, earnings on capital invested

24. Salgado, p.201.

abroad, tourism, services to international shipping (like the bunkering facilities in Cape Verde) and in Mozambique from migrant labour and transit traffic. Nevertheless, to service the high level of imports there had to be a satisfactory system for remitting payments, and it was that which had been reduced to chaos by the monetary adventures of the republican high commissioners and the cowboy activities of the Banco Nacional Ultramarino. By 1928 there was already a chronic shortage of foreign exchange, which reduced imports to a trickle and which was severely handicapping the productive side of the colonial economies.

In 1931 a pool system for foreign exchange was established with the government issuing import licenses on a basis of politically-established priorities. It was a determined effort to bring the whole commercial economy under state control and, aided as it was by the crisis situation in the colonies, it was largely successful.[25]

A second strand of the policy was to embark on a deliberate programme of import substitution. At one level this led to the wheat- and rice-growing campaigns in Portugal and the colonies, and to the gradual establishment in Africa of small-scale consumer industries making such items as soap, furniture and matches, and canning and processing food. Principally, however, it meant systematic promotion of trade between Portugal and the colonies. This indeed is one of the most striking features of the decade. Portugal in 1930 took 39.5 per cent of Angola's exports — in 1940 she took 63.23 per cent — while Angola's imports from Portugal rose from 37.4 per cent of her total in 1930 to 47.6 per cent in 1935.[26] Mozambique's imports from Portugal rose between 1931 and 1937 from 15.75 to 30.5 per cent.[27] Such broad figures, however, hide the specific thrust and purport of the policy. The New State sought to make the Portuguese empire entirely self-sufficient in certain basic commodities, and through a system of quotas and fixed prices to cushion the industries from the vagaries of world prices. Sugar and cotton were the two colonial crops most affected.

Portugal's textile industry had grown up in the late nineteenth century, making full use of the semi-protected colonial markets. However, almost all the raw cotton had to come from foreign sources. Cotton had been grown by planters both in Angola and Mozambique in the nineteenth century, and in parts of Zambesia it grew wild and had been the basis for the local African cloth industry.

25. *Report on Economic and Commercial Conditions in Angola* (1937), p.10.
26. *Report. . .Angola* (1937), p.3; *Portuguese West Africa* (1949), p.15.
27. *Economic Conditions in Portuguese East Africa* (1935), p.6.

However, in the early part of the twentieth century it showed no signs of establishing itself successfully as an export crop. The Mozambique Company had experimented with distributing cotton seed and marketing the crops, but again without success. In 1925, although Portugal was consuming 17,000 tonnes of cotton a year, the colonies were supplying her with only 800 tonnes. It was against this background that the cotton concession scheme was started in 1926. In 1932 a minimum price was guaranteed, and in 1938 the cotton export *junta* was set up.[28]

It now became official policy to lead the drive for cotton production, and this was done with all the blinkered determination of bureaucrats whose political masters had set them production targets. Heedless of cost or of the productivity of the enterprise, the cotton campaigns went ahead. By the outbreak of the war, 30 per cent of Portugal's requirements were being met from colonial sources, and the figure reached 95 per cent in 1950. Portugal took 100 per cent of all cotton produced, and paid a guaranteed price which has been estimated to have averaged 30 per cent below world prices.[29] In return, the colonies took large consignments of Portuguese cotton cloth. Not until 1944 was the first textile mill established in Angola.

Sugar was the other main crop to get this imperial preferential treatment. Apart from African peasant crops like groundnuts, sugar had been easily the most important of Mozambique's exports. However, the largest of the sugar companies, Sena Sugar, was foreign-owned, and the Portuguese-owned sugar companies in both Angola and Mozambique limped along far behind J.P. Hornung's empire. The power and influence of Sena Sugar in Zambesia made it the centre of controversy and of a political battle of national proportions when the high commissioner, Brito Camacho, granted Hornung a contract in 1921 by which he would be supplied with 3,000 labourers in return for expanding Mozambique's sugar production.

Sugar was riding high on the world markets in the early 1920s, and the Mozambique producers greatly expanded output. In 1928 the colony was producing 80,000 tonnes, more than twice the figure for 1919. However, up to 1927 at least 50 per cent of the Portuguese domestic market was supplied from foreign sources. With the price of sugar falling rapidly after 1925, and with Portugal suffering a widening balance of trade deficit, there was an ideal opportunity to support the colonial sugar industry and Portugal's foreign exchange position with an imperial sugar agreement. It took some years for

28. Bravo.
29. Bravo, p.186.

this to emerge, however. The first tactic tried was to tax foreign sugar, but this had little effect, and in 1927 a quota was applied, 77,000 tonnes (or 90 per cent) of Portugal's imports being reserved for colonial sugar. The quota system was temporarily abandoned when Salazar came to power, but it was reintroduced in 1930 with a fifty-fifty split between Angola and Mozambique. This appears to have been a deliberate policy to encourage the wholly Portuguese-owned Angolan sugar industry at the expense of foreign-dominated Mozambique sugar, and was a significant example of Salazar's economic nationalism at work. It was a policy that in the long run proved successful. From producing only 20 per cent as much sugar as Mozambique in 1930, Angola's production was 64 per cent of that of her rival by 1940.[30]

Gradually other colonial commodities received the same treatment. During the early 1940s, Portugal started to take fixed quotas of coffee (initially 25 per cent) and palm oil (40 per cent). Tea was different.[31] Mozambique's tea industry had grown rapidly in the 1930s, but was threatened by the International Tea Agreements. Portugal refused to sign these, and the Mozambique industry was able to reach the peak of its production just as the outbreak of the Second World War, in which Portugal was a neutral, presented it with a large-scale and virtually captive world market.[32]

Granted the specific and limited objectives of Salazar's economic policy, it must be concluded that it was a success. The Portuguese empire had made itself all but self-sufficient in cotton and cotton cloth, sugar, tea, vegetable oils, coffee and rice. In metropolitan Portugal, the 1930s saw wheat campaigns, reminiscent of the colonial cotton campaigns in that wheat was grown extensively in unsuitable areas but with the bureaucratic objective of self-sufficiency being achieved as early as 1932. Later there was to be a government timber policy which was to clothe the mountains of Portugal with millions of acres of conifers. Each of these major commodities was controlled by government boards set up to arrange prices, exports, quotas, etc., and to plan for the expansion of the industries. All of this made them, for all their private capital, more or less state-run enterprises.

The colonies after the war

The war brought great opportunities for change to the colonies.

30. Vail and White, pp.257-60.
31. *Portuguese West Africa* (1949), p.13.
32. Vail and White, pp.267-72.

Prices for colonial products soared, and there was a great expansion of their economies, much of which was maintained after the war had ended. The war also brought other changes. Independence movements flourished, and starting with the European colonies in Asia, one by one the empires were dismantled. In Europe there was pressure in favour of political liberalisation, and an increasingly critical approach towards colonial policies. Governments hastily devised development plans, and there was a rapid growth of investment in the colonies and of the industrial and service sectors of the colonial economies.

Portugal and her colonies were by no means isolated from these trends and responded to them, but the changes that took place were principally economic and social. There was little political response, and the growing tension between expanding economies and a static political system became more serious as the 1950s wore on.

The wartime rise in the prices of agricultural products affected the crops grown both by Africans and by plantation companies. The most spectacular increase was in coffee. Before the war, Angola exported only about 18,000 tonnes; by the end of the war it was exporting 40,000 tonnes, with African farmers still producing one-third of the crop. Sisal was another crop which enjoyed boom conditions. At the beginning of the war, Angola's exports were less than 4,000 tonnes, but by the end this had tripled. The same story could be told of palm oil, beans and other commodities.

A similar rise in prices had been experienced during and just after the First World War, but the growth had not been sustained. In the 1950s, however, most of the success story of the war years continued, as is to be seen in the accompanying table.

This expansion was not brought about, as it had been during and after the First World War, by a crude application of more cheap labour. Characteristic of much of this expansion was increasing yields from acreage and from a static or declining labour force. In addition there was an accompanying expansion in services and of processing industries, so that more and more of the primary treatment (crushing, decorticating, cleaning, etc.) was done in the colonies. The resultant demand for skilled and semi-skilled manpower helped to suck in immigrants.

The government looked upon this growth in agricultural production and in the economy generally as proof of the success of its policies, and made few changes in the basic strategy it had pursued since the 1930s. Each of the major export crops continued to be administered by an export board, and the producers were encouraged to join *grêmios* or producers' associations. This bureaucratic structure eliminated most of the elements of the free market from the

OUTPUT OF COLONIAL AGRICULTURE
(x 1,000 tons)

Commodity	Country	1950	1957
Copra	Moz.	46	58
Cotton	Ang.	6	6
	Moz.	28	32
Cotton seed	Ang.	10	13
	Moz.	56	64
Coffee	Ang.	47	57
Palm kernels	Ang.	12	12
Tea	Moz.	3	6
Bananas	Moz.	7	20
Sugar	Ang.	52	63
	Moz.	94	164
Sisal	Ang.	21	46
	Moz.	18	31

Source: *Economic Survey of Africa since 1950* (New York: United Nations, 1959), table 2-i.

development of Angolan and Mozambican capitalism, and the quota system continued to guarantee a share of the market in Portugal for colonial producers. The objective of the government still continued to be the integration of the economies of the '*escudo* zone'. The colonial currencies were linked with the Portuguese *escudo*, and Portugal's deficit in foreign trade was increasingly compensated by a favourable trade balance with the empire. From 1950 onwards, with the exception of 1957-60 when a small deficit was incurred, Angola's foreign trade was in surplus, sometimes considerably so. Mozambique's trade remained firmly in deficit, but this was more than made up by invisible earnings. Altogether the colonies operated in surplus, and much of this was transferred to the benefit of Portugal by the large favourable trade balance that Portugal had with her empire.[33]

The 1950s also saw the Portuguese government embark on systematic development plans. There had been government investment programmes before; Norton de Matos' scheme to spend £13 million in Angola in the 1920s being the most dramatic. Just

33. Abshire and Samuels, chap. 11.

before the war, another major development scheme had been drawn up, only to be delayed by the hostilities. After the war almost every colony in Africa was given its own development plan, and these became increasingly sophisticated, involving careful planning and research. The first two Portuguese development plans covered the years 1953–8 and 1959–64. The plans included metropolitan Portugal, which received 70 per cent of the investment.[34] Even so, the amounts invested in the colonies were broadly comparable with those invested by other colonial powers. For example, very approximately, £20 million were apportioned to Mozambique in the first plan and £41 million in the second. This compares with £16 and £30 million spent in Uganda over the same period and £17 million and £18 million in Tanganyika.[35]

The distribution of the funds is striking. In the first plan, 70 per cent of the funds for Angola and 74 per cent of those for Mozambique were to be devoted to basic infrastructure, the rest to dams and irrigation. No funds were earmarked for education or social services. In the second plan, social services and education were allocated 6 per cent in Angola and 14 per cent in Mozambique. This contrasts with the Belgian Congo, which allocated 20 per cent to social services during 1950–9, and Uganda which allocated 22.5 and 25.8 per cent in her two plans during this period. A large part of the investment in these two plans was in fact set aside for the white immigration schemes.[36] In the second plan, it appears that 71 per cent of all agricultural investment in Angola and 84 per cent in Mozambique was linked to the *colonatos*.

The first two plans were mostly to be financed from internal sources, Portugal herself providing some loans but no grants. Although loans financed 58 per cent of Mozambique's first plan, 95 per cent of Angola's investment had to be found internally. This can be compared with the following percentages financed from internal resources in other colonies — 21 per cent in Sierre Leone, 14 per cent in Kenya, 11 per cent in Tanganyika and 57.3 per cent in Uganda.[37] It is clear from this that the régime was still sticking closely to its basic economic philosophy that investment had to be generated from savings, that extensive deficit financing was to be avoided and that foreign capital was only to be used under stringent conditions. The

---

34. For the development plans see Kuder; Pössinger (1968); *Economic Survey* (U.N); Abshire and Samuels.
35. *Economic Survey* (U.N.), table 4-xxii.
36. *Economic Survey* (U.N.), table 4-xxii.
37. *Economic Survey* (U.N.), table 4-xxiv.

lack of resources devoted to 'social services' is certainly noteworthy. It can, of course, be explained in terms of the régime's priorities, which were to divert funds from consumption and from 'unproductive' social expenditure to investment. However, there are perhaps other explanations. The authoritarian nature of the régime clearly did not favour the promotion of education, which might breed discontent. Nevertheless, as the expanding economy clearly required skilled and educated people to service it, it might be thought that the self-interest of the régime would have led to more resources being devoted to education. However, the régime was still acting as though it really believed Portugal and her colonies to be a single state. Portugal could not employ her own workforce and was still losing large numbers of emigrants; the government hoped to be able to divert this emigration to Africa and so provide the educated, skilled and semi-skilled manpower which the colonies required.

This explains also the extent to which the régime concentrated its investment on irrigation projects. Although these could be justified in terms of the needs of Angola and Mozambique for irrigated crops, drainage and hydro-electric power, they were also the type of development in which Portugal possessed expertise, and they were intimately associated with white immigration schemes. The Limpopo and Cunene projects were seen as the complete model of colonial development. The dams would store water for irrigation; they would provide hydro-electric power; they would carry communications and increase the economic self-sufficiency of the colonies by promoting agricultural production; they would lead to the settlement of white farmers alongside black in ideal racial harmony; and finally they would be schemes that Portugal could design and finance herself. The dams, however, were also to power the first stages of industrialisation in the colonies, for already in the 1950s the first significant steps had been taken to broaden the purely agricultural base of the colonial economies.

In other respects, the post-war colonial policy of the Portuguese represented no significant change at all. The provision of services for Central and South Africa remained a high priority. Lourenço Marques continued to be of crucial importance to South Africa, and its port and railway operated with increasing efficiency and provided Mozambique with a growing income. The supply of labour to the South African mines gradually began to decline in importance, but this was more than made up for by the increase in labour migration to the Rhodesias and Nyasaland. In 1956-7, Angola and Mozambique between them were supplying 9,200 labourers to Northern Rhodesia, 7,700 to Nyasaland, 12,600 to Tanganyika, 99,300 to South Africa and an astonishing 125,000 to Southern Rhodesia — a grand total of 254,000.[38] Southern Rhodesian agriculture had become nearly as dependent on Mozambican labour as the gold mines of South Africa had been at the turn of the century. Transit traffic to Rhodesia also increased in importance, for the rapid expansion of the Southern Rhodesian economy put a premium on the value of the Umtali-Beira railway and on the port of Beira. In 1955, a second line linking Rhodesia to Lourenço Marques was completed. Transit traffic was also increased by the completion in 1935 of the Zambesi bridge, which connected Nyasaland directly with Beira, and by the final completion of the Benguela railway, which made Angola for the first time an important transit route for central African minerals. At the outbreak of the Second World War, the Benguela line had only been carrying 42,000 tons of minerals with net receipts of 8,000 *contos*; by 1947 the railway carried 119,455 tons, and by 1960 it carried 580,752 tons with net receipts of 267,210 *contos*.[39]

Increasingly, the economic links between the territories of southern Africa were also becoming political links. Portugal joined South Africa and Spain in a tiny minority in United Nations votes, and although Portugal was wary of her big neighbour in Africa, being mindful of previous threats to the integrity of Mozambique and wanting to dissociate herself from the apartheid policies of the Afrikaner nationalists, there was increasing political co-operation between them.

Political adaptation

Salazar was well aware that the nature of his régime was not in tune with the political ideas of the West in the 1950s and 1960s. Ideologically he refused to make concessions to liberalism, and even took pride in the isolation of Portugal which he chose to represent as the maintenance of the purity of her ideals. He did, however, make some changes. The aspects of his régime which were most reminiscent of fascism were played down, and more prominence was given to the electoral process. According to the Portuguese constitution, the president was to be elected by direct suffrage and the presidential elections provided a big opportunity for the opponents of the régime to mount some sort of public campaign — and incidentally to identify themselves to the secret police. Salazar was also anxious to enter the United Nations and to seek protection in membership of NATO, so ending Portugal's isolationism, which in the 1930s had

38. *Economic Survey* (U.N.), p.49.
39. Hutchinson and Martelli, appendix.

led her to reject the world commodity agreements and the International Labour Organisation conventions. Membership of these bodies did force Portugal to pay some attention to the susceptibilities of her associates. In 1955 she signed the International Labour Code, and in 1957 acceded to the Abolition of Forced Labour convention.

The legislative itch of the New State bureaucrats being as great as ever, almost all the colonial legislation of the 1930s was revised and some changes were made. Municipal government was revived in the colonies, and legislative councils were set up to advise the governors, and the status of the colonies was changed to that of Overseas Provinces of Portugal, a technical device by which Portugal tried to evade United Nations campaigns against colonialism. The most striking thing about the legislation of this period, however, is that it revealed no sign of the regime altering its stance or the basic principles of its colonial policies, and these continued at every turn to show their lineal descent from the ideas of the 1930s and even the 1900s.

The implementation of the legislation did, however, alter. During the 1940s, the administration had aided the great expansion of colonial agriculture by 'encouraging' the Africans to contract themselves as labourers. However, with the war over, there was much greater emphasis placed on seeing that the spirit as well as the letter of the labour laws was observed. The administration withdrew from direct involvement in labour recruitment, and assumed its rightful function as inspectors of the labour contracts. Employers increasingly found that they had to obey the law, and that the minimum legal conditions under which workers could be employed were being enforced.[40]

Very little was done to make the régime more flexible or more responsive to the opinions and aspirations of different sections of the population. During the 1930s, the settler and *mestiço* organisations had had their teeth drawn and been reduced to the status of official collaborators with the régime. The church was largely acquiescent, and the immigrant white community was unorganised. The African population was beginning to respond to the political ferment in neighbouring countries, particularly the Congo, but political activity was easily suppressed by the police and there was no armed opposition. What manifestations there were could be easily isolated and dealt with by the authorities. Industrial action by the Lourenço Marques stevedores was crushed and the movement of Simon Toco was dispersed, if not exactly killed off, by the

40. Vail and White, pp.299-303.

authorities. On the plantations of Mozambique and Angola, compulsion was no longer used to recruit labour, because it was no longer necessary as a new generation had been brought up to wage-earning, and came unbidden to seek employment.

It is clear that the régime was lulled by the apparent quiet in the colonies into believing its own propaganda — that Portugal had a singular genius for creating new, multi-racial communities, and that these would prevent unrest and the growth of independence movements in their territories. In fact the very success of its bureaucratic methods, which had enabled it to dispense with any party organisation, also deprived it of the means of listening and responding to what was happening beneath the surface. In 1958, however, subterranean tremors began to be felt which soon became surface eruptions and threatened to bring Salazar's whole world down in ruins.

9
PORTUGAL'S ISLANDS

The characteristics of island culture

In the fifteenth century Portugal took possession of four of the five principal groups of islands in the eastern Atlantic. Madeira and Porto Santo were settled from 1418 onwards, the Azores from the 1440s, the Cape Verde Islands after 1462, and the four Guinea Islands (São Tomé, Principe, Fernando Po and Anno Bom) after 1480. Portugal was forced to relinquish the Canary Islands to Castile in 1479.[1] These island groups are the peaks of submarine volcanoes and one of them, Fogo in the Cape Verde Islands, is still active. They all have, therefore, potentially rich volcanic soil. With the exception of the Canary Islands, all the islands were uninhabited when the Portuguese arrived, and the kings of Portugal tried to settle them by making them into 'captaincies'. The 'captains' were to be hereditary rulers of the islands with wide judicial, fiscal and manorial privileges, in exchange for which they were to divide their islands into individual holdings and bring in settlers who would undertake to cultivate them.

Although these island groups had much in common, they were to develop in entirely different ways, the principal influence on their history being rainfall. Madeira and the Azores lie in the belt of the Atlantic trade winds and receive plentiful and even rainfall. When the Portuguese discovered them, they were heavily wooded. São Tomé and the other Guinea Islands, however, lie on the Equator and experience heavy and persistent rain which covered the islands in tropical rain forest. The Cape Verde Islands lie in the latitude of the Sahara and receive generally light rainfall, which would be just adequate for agriculture if it were consistent. The main characteristic of the climate, however, is its inconstancy, and the islands suffer long periods of drought which may last for years in succession.

Madeira and the Azores lie nearest to Europe, and their climates favoured a Mediterranean type of agriculture. They were quickly and profitably settled by peasant farmers from Portugal, and already during the fifteenth century developed an export trade in sugar, wine and wheat. Although slaves were imported, the pre-

---

1. For the early history of the islands see Bentley Duncan; Diffie and Winius.

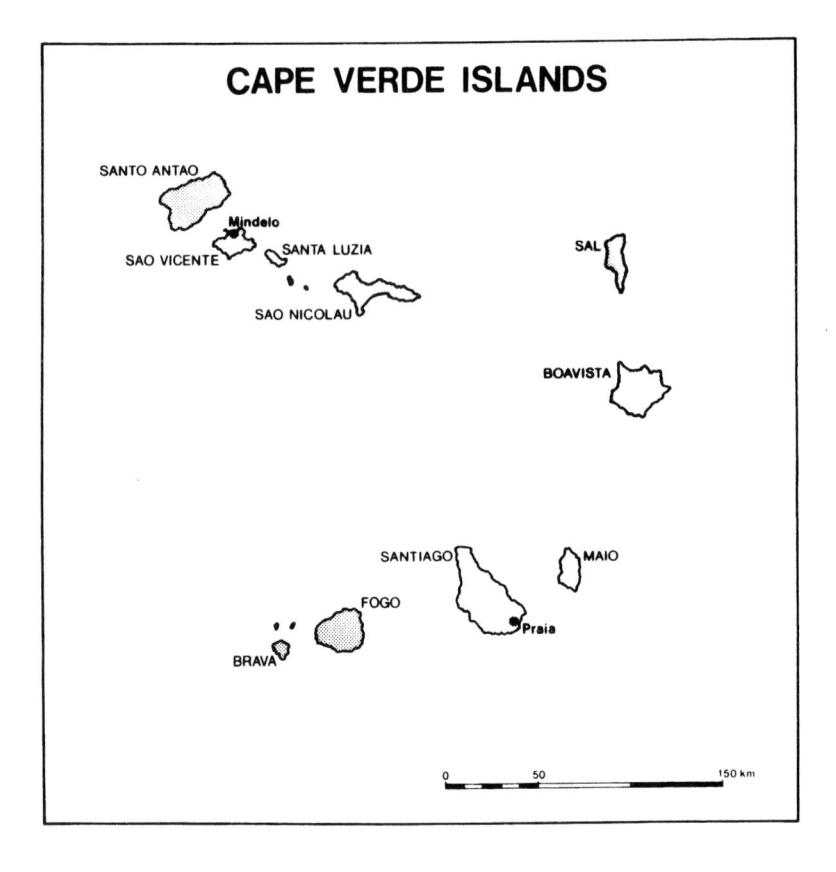

CAPE VERDE ISLANDS

dominant social pattern was that of Portuguese peasant farms.

The Cape Verde Islands attracted far fewer settlers. Their agriculture was poor and the distance from Europe discouraged peasant settlement and agricultural exports. However, the islands lay conveniently near the mainland of Upper Guinea, and they became a useful base for Portuguese traders operating in the Guinea rivers. The trade of Guinea brought some early prosperity to the islands, which was reflected in the town of Ribeira Grande with its town houses and cathedral. The demand for cloth in Guinea also encouraged the Cape Verde islanders to try their hand at growing cotton, and a weaving industry existed in the islands until the nineteenth century. When the slave trade became a large-scale enterprise at the end of the sixteenth century, slaves were collected in the islands for sale and dispatch, and to be taxed.

The Guinea Islands were also near the African mainland, but were originally settled by Jewish exiles from Portugal. They grew sugar, and had considerable success in the sixteenth century, importing many slaves into the islands. The islanders also developed contraband trade with the mainland, smuggling goods past the royal factors who were attempting to operate a monopoly of trade with the Congo. It was São Tomé islanders who built the trading base at Luanda to exploit the shell fisheries, and it was they who supplied the first of the backwoodsmen who opened up trade with Angola.

The prosperity of the islands did not survive the sixteenth century. Madeira and Azores began to suffer from over-population. Cape Verde was exposed to raids from the Dutch and English, so that eventually Ribeira Grande was abandoned to the bush, the settlers retreated to the interior, and oceanic trade, with the exception of salt ships, by-passed the islands. By the nineteenth century, the cloth industry also was dead. São Tomé was eclipsed by the growth of the slaving port of Luanda and by the sugar plantations of Brazil. Its population was progressively weakened by tropical diseases, until it dwindled almost to vanishing point.

In their historical and cultural development, the Cape Verde and Guinea Islands resemble the West Indies rather than any African society. Like the West Indies, they were largely populated by slaves, but because these came from different ethnic groups in Africa, the society and culture they established was a hybrid one. It was naturally greatly influenced by Portugal and the Catholic church. A creole dialect is spoken in both island groups, and Catholicism, often enriched by centuries of cross-fertilisation from African religious beliefs, is the dominant cultural influence. John Harris, visiting São Tomé at the height of the labour scandals in the twentieth century, was impressed by the survival of Catholic influence:

> Along the roadsides, in the secluded corners of out of the way *roças* [estates], nestling in plantation groves, the traveller may see miniature chapels constructed from rustic forest tree branches, very similar to the fetish houses of the mainland of Africa. In most of these one also sees little prayer-stools, and in all of them a rude cross roughly cut out with the native axe and the crosspieces bound together with forest vines. Most of these crosses are surrounded by native pagan charms, and thus all that is least essential in Christianity is joined together in native religious fervour with the superstitions of paganism.[2]

Cape Verde generally has more Portuguese cultural influence than São Tomé, for the population of the latter was very small when the heavy influx of African contract workers took place at the end of the nineteenth century. The islands resemble the West Indies in other respects. They have always been heavily dependent on a few export crops, and have a tendency to suffer from over-population and from inability to produce enough food. They have, from time to time, been of considerable commercial and strategic importance as the currents of world trade have shifted direction, but this importance has seldom left behind it any permanent benefit for the inhabitants beyond the new genetic strains introduced by the sailors who visited the island brothels. Finally, in the twentieth century, emigration has become part of the expectations of the population, emigration which relieves over-crowding and offers otherwise unimagineable opportunities, but which arguably impoverishes the islands still more since they lose the enterprising and the young whose productive labour is employed elsewhere while the inhabitants who remain, and the economies of the island generally, are supported by remittances from abroad.

São Tomé and Principe

At the beginning of the nineteenth century, there were perhaps 13,000 people on the islands of São Tomé and Principe. About half of these were slaves, and the other half was made up of the coloured creole population and the *Angolares*. The latter were the descendents of ship-wrecked Angolan slaves who had settled on the east coast. Thus this tiny island community was clearly stratified socially. Some of the creoles had begun to grow coffee early in the century, and in 1827 the cocoa bean was introduced, but it took a long time

---

2. Harris, pp.270-1.

for either plant to become established, and it was coffee grown on the cooler high ground of the islands that first proved successful. By 1877 over 1,000 tonnes were being exported. Cocoa lagged far behind, only 287 tonnes being exported in the same year.[3]

However, from 1888 onwards, world prices carried cocoa to immense heights of profitability while coffee stagnated. The boom in cocoa production lasted till 1919, and presented Lisbon imperialists with dazzling and intoxicating success. Having recited the tale of São Tomé's imports from Portugal and her exports, her budgetary surpluses and her customs revenues, Oliveira Martins summed it all up by exclaiming: 'What other form of cultivation, what kind of mine can offer such profits?'[4]

The success of cocoa was indeed impressive. The rise in exports can be seen in the accompanying table:[5]

COCOA EXPORTS FROM SÃO TOMÉ AND PRINCIPE

Date	Tonnes
1888	1,518
1892	5,000
1895	7,202
1900	11,482
1908	27,187
1912	36,090
1917	29,097
1919	55,830

With the coming of the cocoa boom, all available land in the islands was bought up by Lisbon-based companies and banks or by individual entrepreneurs. By 1904, some ten major companies with capital amounting to 8,276 *contos* were operating in the islands, including the giant Companhia Agricola Colonial, which controlled almost the whole island of Principe.[6] The majority of the *roças* were thus operated as capital enterprises by outsiders, who placed managers in charge of operations in the islands. In 1914, however, companies only controlled 24 per cent of the estates and private planters 76 per cent,[7] one or two of the *roças* even being owned by enterprising natives of São Tomé.[8] Portuguese capital was over-

3. Lobo Bulhões, p.89.
4. Quoted in Tenreiro, p.84.
5. Tenreiro, p.88; Barata, p.952.
6. Castro, pp.287-9.
7. *San Thomé and Principe*, p.27.
8. Harris, p.249.

whelmingly dominant, and it is clear that investors, so reluctant to venture their funds in other colonies, were eager enough to put them into the islands. Profits from cocoa estates just before the war were said to range between 5 and 15 per cent. The capital invested made the Portuguese the most scientific cocoa producers of the early part of the twentieth century, and their product prospered at least in part because it was better produced and of higher quality. The geography of the islands, which meant that all estates consisted of land of greatly differing altitudes, and the need to employ their labour all the year, persuaded most managers of *roças* to diversify production. They generally adopted a three-tier system with oil palms grown at sea level, cocoa on the middle land and coffee in the highlands. This prevented the islands from becoming entirely given over to a monoculture.

The scramble for land in the islands had been almost entirely unregulated. Concessions were made of lengths of coastline, with the concessionaires allowed to clear and claim an unspecified area in the interior. The sea frontage was all-important, for each *roça* built its own jetty and used sea transport for bringing in supplies and taking out its cocoa. This was the obvious way to develop transport quickly for a mountainous island, but it meant that virtually nothing was done to build an infrastructure of roads and communications. Many of the *roças* also constructed their own estate railways — the *roça* Agua-Ize, for example, boasting 50 kilometres of light railway in 1898.[9] Eventually the government financed one small line into the interior from the capital, but otherwise little or nothing was spent by the authorities. In spite of the great wealth being produced by the *roças*, the main town was in a deplorable state when described by the British consul in 1915:

The existing town is in a lamentable condition. A decent house is scarcely to be found, and the tumbledown, evil-smelling huts of the natives are everywhere in close proximity to the houses inhabited by Europeans. A proper drainage system does not exist, rank grass grows in each vacant space, which are used as dumping grounds for bottles, tins and rubbish of all kinds. The woods on the outskirts of the town are the latrines of the natives, and the stench is overpowering. To all this the Portuguese inhabitants seem to be absolutely indifferent.[10]

There could scarcely be a better illustration of the phrase 'private wealth and public squalor'.

The key to the vast expansion of cocoa production was not, however, capital but labour. The *Angolares* would sometimes hire

9. Tenreiro, p.86.
10. '*Report for the year 1914 . . .*', p.5.

themselves out as workers but their numbers were small; the creoles on the other hand would never consider plantation work. To provide labour, therefore, slaves were imported, and after all slaves were freed in 1876, the plantation owners adopted the system of importing contract labourers (*serviçais*) — a system that made São Tomé notorious throughout the world in the early part of the twentieth century. The workforce of *serviçais* grew steadily from 16,000 in 1895 to 35,000 in 1909, reaching a peak of 39,000 in 1921 before declining sharply.[11]

Until 1910, the majority of these workers came from Angola, and they arrived at the rate of 3,000 — 5,000 a year. John Harris estimated that between 1888 and 1914, 67,614 had been legally imported, with many more smuggled in illegally.[12]

The labourers were obtained by slave dealers who accompanied the trading caravans from the interior, and many of them appear to have originated outside Portuguese territory. They were formally given a five-year contract (which could be renewed), and were then sent to the islands.

Once established on a *roça*, a contract labourer was unlikely ever to leave, although in 1903, in an attempt at mild regulation of the trade, 40 per cent of the workers' pay was put into a repatriation fund. Once the five-year contract was expired, the *roça* manager

sends for the Curador from San Thomé and lines up the fifty in front of him. In the presence of two witnesses and his secretary, the Curador solemnly announces to the slaves that the term of their contract is up and the contract is renewed for five years more. The slaves are then dismissed and another scene in the cruel farce of contracted labour is over.[13]

The position of contract labourers from Cape Verde appears to have been different. Most of these had no alternative but to contract themselves because of drought and famine in the islands, and were certainly not slaves. Their pay was higher and they were regularly repatriated — if they survived.

On the *roça*, the labourer lived in a barracks. There was a company store where he could spend his wages, and usually a company hospital where he would end his days, often very soon after arrival. Francisco Tenreiro, in his classic study of São Tomé, summed up the situation.

The contract worker is frequently not treated like a human but like a machine; his repatriation is difficult and many proprietors consider the children born on the *roças* (the *tongas*) as their property. It is common,

11. Barata, p.952.
12. Harris, p.191.
13. Nevinson, p.196.

though only on the fringes of the law, for them to be submitted to corporal punishment at the hands of the overseers and European administrators.[14]

The high death-rate was due principally to the prevalence of sleeping sickness, and in the first two decades of the century this disease reached epidemic proportions, particularly on the island of Principe. Henry Nevinson claimed that in 1901 the death-rate was over 20 per cent per annum[15] on the island of Principe, and in his report of 1898 the governor of São Tomé laconically recorded the arrival of 2,414 new contract labourers and the deaths of 560.[16] In 1914 the death-rate was still 8–10 per cent with a higher rate among children.

After 1908 international opinion and pressure from the rival faction of Angolan planters forced a change in the contracting system. Some workers began to be repatriated, and in 1909 the length of contracts was reduced to three years. In 1910, there was a three year moratorium on all contracting from Angola, and the planters had to seek other supplies.[17] They turned principally to Mozambique, and in 1914 set up the *Sociedade de Emigração para São Tomé e Principe*, on the model of W.N.L.A., to have a monopoly of recruitment. Mozambique was the main source of supply until 1917, after which Angola once more took first place. With shorter contracts and some repatriation, the numbers recruited annually rose steeply, averaging 7,300 a year between 1910 and 1917. Just over half this number were repatriated during the same period.[18] Foreign critics maintained that repatriation was a fraud, since only the old and sick workers were sent back to the mainland, and since they often had nowhere to go once they were 'repatriated'. It was only in 1921 that compulsory repatriation was introduced, by which time the profits from cocoa were slipping and the influence of the planters was on the wane.

The main improvement in the 1920s was the gradual eradication of the tse-tse fly. At the height of the epidemic, regulations sought to protect the workers by ordering them to 'wear trousers to the heel, blouses with sleeves to the wrist, and high collars, [and] they must wear on their backs a black cloth covered with glue.'[19] The use of human fly-papers was the bizarre solution with which the Portuguese persisted. Alexander Barns recorded in the mid-1920s that

14. Tenreiro, p.87.
15. Nevinson, p.191.
16. *Relatório, Propostos de Lei. . .:* 'Movimento de Serviçaes. . .'
17. Duffy(1967), p.211.
18. *San Thomé and Principe*, p.39.
19. Harris, p.191.

prisoners from the jails walked the bush with a sticky substance on their clothes to which the flies adhered. Whatever the reason, the mortality began to decline, and the 'native' population of the islands grew.[20] The non-*serviçal* population rose from 20,000 in 1926 to 31,000 in 1940. This population had no room to expand. It occupied some land around the town of São Tomé and around São João dos Angolares, on which subsistence agriculture took place. Some of the population supplied the local market with fish, which they caught at sea from canoes, but to a large extent they lived in a clandestine way off the plantations, organising a black market with the contract labourers in stolen food or cocoa beans which they purchased for alcohol or other goods. Henrique de Mendonça described the problem from the planter's point of view:

The freeman is a parasite on the *roça*; he lives from what he robs from it and furnishes spirits to the *serviçaes* in exchange for cocoa, coffee and bananas, and, what is worse, in exchange for the rations which the *serviçal* receives from the boss for his maintenance, for the *serviçal* gives everything he has and everything he can rob in exchange for brandy.[21]

Another group, which lived as 'parasites' on the *roças*, were escaped *serviçais*. Although the islands were very small, it proved possible for contract labourers to escape into the forests, and bands of runaways were able to maintain themselves there, evading the tracker dogs and organised manhunts of the planters. However, it was a precarious existence.

After 1920, the cocoa plantations went into decline. The bushes were attacked by disease, and the soil became increasingly depleted. By 1929 the output had fallen to 18,000 tonnes and the following year exports were dramatically halved to only 9,645 tonnes. Production never recovered, and after the Second World War it fluctuated steadily between 8,000 and 10,000 tonnes. The story can be traced in the declining productivity of the workforce. The adjoining table shows output per worker. To a certain extent, of course, this falling output was made up for by greater production of coffee and palm products, but generally it indicates a decline in the agriculture of the islands, and the penalty that was being paid for having extracted high profits by the simple application of cheap labour to virgin land.

After the Second World War, the sources from which contract workers were drawn changed somewhat. Extreme poverty in the Cape Verde Islands, coupled with a high demand for all available

20. Barns 'Through Portuguese West Africa', p.225.
21. Quoted in Vasconcellos, p.88.

Date	Tonnes of cocoa per worker
1895	0.45
1900	0.53
1909	0.89
1914	0.9
1921	0.68
1926	0.4
1940	0.2

labour in Angola, meant that increasing numbers of plantation workers now came from Cape Verde, and the government even sought to encourage this movement by making land available for Cape Verdians to purchase. This made the social stratification of the population of São Tomé even more complex, and it became divided, like so many isolated communities, by lines so fine that the casual observer could scarcely notice them. To the *Angolares*, the former slave community and *civilisado* creoles were now added the *tongas* (descendants of contract labourers), Cape Verde immigrants and Europeans. The old creole community, although of much less importance than it had been before the growth of the plantations, retained something of its dignity, and regularly provided the single deputy who represented the islands in the metropolitan parliament. It was also (barely) able to support a few newspapers. The mass of the São Tomé labourers, however, remain anonymous and silent for the historian, as the labouring class so often does. Visitors to the islands at the height of the slavery scandals, like Henry Nevinson and John Harris, record conversations with labourers and even something of their personal history. Some, we know, escaped into the forests to live the life of maroons, some even put to sea in makeshift canoes, trying to reach the mainland and freedom. The commonest response to their lot appears to have been apathy and despair, or at the best participation in black market activities with the free population. Some courageous evangelistic work was undertaken in the 1920s among the *serviçais* by African catechists from Angola, but the converts never amounted to more than a few hundred at the most.

In the Portuguese imperial plan, the islands had played their part. But after the Second World War this part was finished. There had been a time early in the century when São Tomé, with its handsome budget surpluses and favourable trade balances, had been the jewel of the empire — success achieved without the burden of pacification, and entirely by private capital. The islands continued to have a function in the neo-mercantilism of the New State, because they made Portugal self-sufficient in cocoa and helped to employ unwanted population from Cape Verde. By the 1960s, however, with the colonial economies expanding rapidly and Portugal herself near to industrial take-off, the exiguous market of the tiny islands ceased to be of any concern.

The Cape Verde Islands

Nowhere is the balance between man's needs and his environment more precarious than in the Cape Verde Islands. The ten principal islands form two groups. The northern 'Windward' group consists of

São Vicente	300.7	sq. miles
San Luzia	13.5	
São Nicolau	132.4	
Sal	83.3	
Boa Vista	239.3	

and the 'Leeward' or southern group consists of

Brava	24.7	sq. miles
Fogo	183.7	
Santiago	382.5	
Maio	103.8	

The northern group has very low rainfall, which seldom exceeds ten inches a year and is very irregular. The island of São Vicente is almost totally waterless. The southern group gets more rain, up to 20 inches a year falling among the mountains of Santiago. It is in the southern islands that agriculture is most developed and where most of the population lives, but it is this group which has suffered most from drought; the northern islands experience water shortage almost every year and their economies and populations have had to come to terms with the dry conditions.

The islands lie near to the African coast, and have always had close contacts with the ports of Upper Guinea. Slaves were brought to the islands for sale to ships or for agricultural labour, and there were some 6,000 slaves registered at the time of the emancipation in 1875. Africans have therefore made a substantial contribution to the peopling of the islands, and their influence has been strongest in the agricultural islands like Santiago. However, the islands have always been greatly influenced by their position on the shipping routes between Europe and South America, and from the fifteenth century onwards, despite their lack of water, they have been ports of call for foreign ships. This has resulted in constant infusions of 'white' blood, with the result that the population in the twentieth century is almost entirely made up of people of mixed descent. In their census returns the Portuguese tried broadly to classify the population, and concluded that between 1900 and 1950, the percentage of *mestiços* rose from 62 to 70 per cent.[22] In reality, however, almost all the population, apart from short-stay immigrants, are of mixed origin.

In 1875 the islands were still linked administratively to Guiné, and both came under a governor whose seat was at Praia on Santiago. Trade with the ports of Guiné was still important, and there was freedom of trade between the islands and the Portuguese ports on the mainland. The historic cotton textile industry, still thriving in 1800, had finally expired in the 1860s in the face of European and American competition,[23] but the islanders continued to ship salt to the African mainland, and had a flourishing salt trade also with Brazil. Two of the islands provided shipping services. American whalers used the island of Brava, and in the port of Mindelo on São Vicente there was a coaling station used chiefly by ships bound for South America. Apart from this, the islanders grew some crops for export — notably coffee, sugar and fodder crops. They also exported some cattle. The old seigneurial tenures had been finally abolished in 1863, and slavery went in 1875, leaving most of the land in the hands of peasant proprietors.

In 1864, there began a series of disastrous droughts which devastated the islands and which perhaps represent a cyclical change for the worse in the climate. Severe droughts occurred in 1864–6, 1875–6, 1883–6, 1896–8, 1899–1900 and 1903–4.[24] The first of these was accompanied by a heavy mortality and it is estimated that between 1864 and 1867 there was a 30 per cent decline in the population, which was not made up till 1878. Thereafter, although there was always a rise in the death rate during years of drought, the islanders established a pattern of emigration which was to form such a crucial part of their history in the twentieth century. The emigration was not caused only by drought, however. It was also encouraged by rapid population increase and by radical changes in the economic structure of the islands.

The cause of the population increase is not known, but it is all the more striking in that it took place throughout a period punctuated by drought. Between 1874 and 1900, the population of the islands rose

22. Barata, p.935.
23. Corry, p.26; Carreira (1968), pp.49–51.
24. Barata, p.931.

from 90,710 to 147,424 — a rise of 62.5 per cent. Then, as a result of the drought in 1903, the growth was halted and there was an overall decline of 3.3 per cent during the decade 1901-10.[25] While the interaction of drought and population might appear obvious, there is another factor that has to be considered, the crisis in the salt trade. During the years of drought, the export of salt from Maio, Boa Vista and Sal was scarcely affected — indeed it tended to benefit from the availability of cheap labour. However, in 1887 Brazil, the main buyer of Cape Verde salt, imposed tariffs to protect her own production, and in the same year the partition of Upper Guinea cut the Cape Verdians off from many of their most lucrative markets in Africa. The ports of the Casamance river fell to France and the French also took over the hinterland of the rivers of Portuguese Guinea.[26]

Until 1887, 35,000 tons of salt a year had been exported, but this fell rapidly to barely 1,000 to 2,000 tons a year. The Cape Verdians responded by seeking new markets. With the expansion of new colonies in West Africa, they were able to sell in a rapidly rising market, estimated to total 100,000 tons a year, but they faced continuous hostility from France (which finally excluded all Cape Verde salt in 1913), from customs officials who, probably rightly, accused the Cape Verdians of smuggling under cover of the salt trade, and from the generally poor reputation that the product had on the world market. This was due to the custom of using animals in the salt pans, with the consequent problem of the salt being soiled. During the First World War, salt exports climbed to 3,000 tonnes and, under the protection of the New State, to 10,000 tonnes by 1929 and 20,000 in the 1950s.

While the salt trade entered on hard times, the coaling station of Mindelo grew rapidly in importance. The first steamers called in 1838 to take on coal in the great natural harbour on the island of São Vicente, and in the following years the Portuguese built the port up as a stopping-place for ships bound for South America. Between 1887 and 1898, an average of 1,340 ships a year called at Mindelo, and a peak was probably reached in 1912 when 1,707 ships called.[27] The Cape Verde government imposed a tax on every ton of coal imported, and this proved the mainstay of the islands' finances, averaging 76 *contos* a year during those eleven years.[28] The coal was supplied by British coaling companies, and the British community became the aristocracy of Mindelo and the butt of the hostility of the

25. Brito, p.13.
26. Figueiredo de Barros, p.83.
27. Bentley Duncan, p.165.
28. *Relatórios, propostas de Lei*. . ., 'Rendimento do Imposto. . .'.

labouring population of the port, who were largely in their employ.

By 1910 Mindelo had powerful rivals in the coaling trade, and ships were calling at Tenerife, Las Palmas, Dakar or Madeira. The high price of coal was blamed, the British attributing it to the coal tax and the Portuguese to profiteering by the coaling companies. A major reason for the decline was probably the fact that São Vicente could not compete with the other islands in amenities. All its water had to be imported from Santo Antão, its coal was crudely handled from lighters by women who carried it in baskets, and the town itself could hardly rival the charms of Funchal or Las Palmas.[29] Moreover, public health was a problem. In 1921, another major drought year, the British vice-consul on São Vicente reported.

The number of vessels calling here for coal has fallen off considerably. While this may be partly due to present depression in shipping, great harm has been done to St. Vincent's coaling trade by exaggerated rumours which were current in the river Plate ports after St. Vincent had been declared plague-infected.[30]

Twenty to forty plague rats were to be found dead every morning, he went on, and the authorities had decided to round up and exterminate all the stray dogs. The port was not, however, to be closed because of the desperate need of the provincial finances. During the 1920s, only about 900 ships a year were calling, and with the onset of the great depression this fell steeply to only 583 ships in 1933.

The British coaling houses countered in the price war by holding down wages, and relations between them and the coal workers were often in a state of barely suppressed hostility. In 1911, the British consul reported

During the early days of the Republic the coaling labourers incited by agitators, struck for higher wages, but were defeated; and there was a slight recrudescence of the strike in January of this year, which was, however, soon checked by the authorities.[31]

The authorities, indeed, usually sided with the British. In 1920, all sixty-four British residents in the island signed a petition asking for a consular appointment for their protection. They wrote:

We suggest that the authorities should be made to realise that the whole life and prosperity of this island depend directly upon the activities of British

---

29. Lyall, chap. 7.
30. PRO FO 371 8368 (1922), Report of vice-consul in St Vincent, 20.12.1921.
31. PP 1911–12, vol. xcix, 'Report for the Year 1911 . . . .', p.3.

houses from whom very large taxes and customs duties are collected each year.[32]

They demanded the reorganisation of the local police and the appointment of white police officers. All these demands were met.

São Vicente was also the point at which eleven submarine telegraph cables radiated to different points of the eastern Atlantic and therefore had considerable importance in world communications.[33]

In the twentieth century the inhabitants of Cape Verde began to emigrate in large numbers in search of work. Many of them were driven by famine, leaving the agricultural islands for work in São Vicente, or crossing to Guiné, where they would squat on vacant land for a season or two, growing crops until they were able to return. Increasingly, however, the emigrants looked further afield, and small sailing boats began to make regular crossings to the United States and to South America. This emigration reached its peak during the two decades 1910–30 when 34,000 Cape Verdians left the islands. Between 1910 and 1920, the emigration rate was nearly 16 per cent of the population.[34]

In the following decade, emigration was more than balanced by those returning, driven back by the slump in the United States to their drought-prone islands. For those not lucky enough to get a passage to the United States, the last resort was to sign contracts to work in São Tomé. Between 1912 and 1943, 37.51 per cent of emigrants went to the United States, 25.52 per cent to São Tomé, 9.3 per cent to Portugal, and the rest either to West Africa or South America.[35] The experience that so many of the islanders had of the United States made English a widely-understood language in the archipelago, and led to the spread of Protestant sects and to other manifestations of American culture. It strengthens the comparison that can be made between the islands and the West Indies.

Either through inefficiency or through lack of concern, the Portuguese authorities took little action to avert famine or counter the effects of drought. The drought of 1920–2 was one of the most disastrous for the islands. In 1921, the British consul reported laconically that owing to the failure of last year's crops and the continued drought, many natives are dying of starvation. The Portuguese Government sent 200 *contos* to relieve the situation.[36] This was the equivalent of about £1,500 at that time. In 1923, the consul

32. PRO FO 371 5492 (1920), Petition, 28.8.1920.
33. *Cabo Verde* (1934), p.69.
34. Brito, pp.21–30.
35. Barata, p.939.

reported: 'Owing to drought, the crops were deficient for the third year in succession, and as the authorities failed to import the necessary foodstuffs, conditions for a long time bordered on a state of famine.'[37] The famines of the early 1920s in fact led to an overall population decline of 8.3 per cent during the decade, with the island of Santiago, whose agriculture was most severely hit, losing 17.4 per cent of its inhabitants. The New State did little to remedy the islands' basic problem, which was lack of water storage. Relief work avoided total disaster during the droughts of the 1930s, but 1941-2, 1946-8 and 1959-60 were also bad years. The first of these ranked as one of the major disasters of the islands' history and the population, which had recovered with the return of emigrants during the 1930s, fell by 18 per cent between 1940 and 1950, a large number of people simply dying of starvation.

Emigration once again was the only answer, but this time the Portuguese saw that it was channelled into the empire. Of the emigrants 58.8 per cent now found their way to São Tomé and Angola, 23.6 per cent to Portugal and only 1.8 per cent to the United States. The food famine in Cape Verde was thus manipulated by the régime to make good the labour famine in São Tomé.[38]

Not all emigrants from Cape Verde, however, went to fill vacancies as unskilled labour. The islanders generally had a much higher level of education and of literate culture than the other areas of the empire; they were Portuguese-speakers, basically Portuguese in culture and mostly of mixed race. The distinction of *indígena* and *civilisado* had never been applied to Cape Verdians. They were, in fact, the ideal employees of a régime which claimed that it was seeking to create a new Brazil in Africa. Cape Verde islanders, therefore, found increasing opportunities to enter the administration and government agencies in the other colonies. Emigration from the islands, then, formed two streams, one of the destitute willing to take unskilled labouring jobs, the other of the educated or semi-educated destined for positions somewhat higher in the social hierarchy of the empire. The position was described by Eduino Brito in his study of the islands' population:

There exists, however, a great qualitative difference between emigration directed towards Guiné and that which is destined for the province of S. Tomé and Principe and Angola. While in the latter the emigrant population finds itself among the lowest classes from the cultural point of view, destined

36. PRO FO 371 7109, 'Portugal Annual Report 1920', p.25.
37. PRO FO 371 10590, 'Portugal Annual Report 1923', p.25.
38. Brito.

for the hard tasks of agriculture, to Guiné go only those individuals with literate skills who are going to fill public or business appointments.[39]

Meanwhile, when rainfall allowed, the islanders persisted with their attempts to produce crops for the market. Their coffee acquired a good reputation, and they produced exportable quantities of hides and oil-bearing castor and *purgueira*. By the 1930s, a small amount of canned fish and, of course, salt was also being exported. Spirits were produced for sale to visiting ships, but among the imports were now to be found cotton cloth and sugar, commodities which the islands had once produced for themselves and even exported. Fifty years of intermittent drought had, however, driven most of the peasants deep into debt, and by the 1930s, land was once again owned by monopolistic, absentee landowners who allowed the indebted peasantry a precarious right to use the land.

In spite of the manifest poverty of the islands and the urgent need for drought relief measures, the New State exacted a massive budget surplus from the islands. In the financial year 1935/6, the surplus came to 9,019 *contos* out of total receipts of 30,000 *contos*, and the accumulated surplus in that year equalled 27,186 *contos* or the equivalent of a whole year's revenues. Of the budget 70 per cent went to pay the costs of the administration.[40]

A certain amount of government expenditure took place on Santiago with the building of the Tarrafal concentration camp in 1937, and with the subsequent development of stop-over facilities for aircraft. The first of these was a flying-boat station built by the French in the 1930s at Praia; this was followed by airfields on Maio and Santiago and finally by the international airport on Sal, which has become a major earner of foreign exchange for the islands.

Until the 1960s, when some economic surveys were carried out, the government paid no attention to the islands and their plight. The rigid economic formula that each territory should finance expenditure from its own income was singularly inappropriate for these islands which were so subject to climatic disasters. (The independent Cape Verde state presumably wants to try to maintain its economic independence, and the years under Portuguese rule will at least have taught it what are the problems.) The islands served the empire as an important strategic communications centre and as a prison camp, but there appeared to the Salazar régime to be no point in investing where no returns seemed possible. Instead it was claimed that Cape Verdians could profit by employment opportunities in the

39. Brito, p.30.
40. *Cabo Verde* (1938), p.12.

rest of the empire, and this policy was quite logical, given the régime's premise that the colonies and Portugal formed a single state, with a single economy and a single citizenship, and granted that the islands would never become independent and have to fend for themselves or establish economic self-sufficiency.

10
PORTUGAL AND THE WARS OF INDEPENDENCE

Was 1961 the decisive year?

A great deal has been written about the wars of independence in the Portuguese colonies. During the war itself, much of this writing was inevitably produced by the committed on both sides, who sought to influence world opinion in favour of their cause. At the time of writing, six years after the end of the war and five years after independence, the history of the war is still being written from a strongly ideological point of view. In Angola the struggle continues on the borders of South West Africa, and with it the battle of words; in Mozambique the Frelimo régime and its expatriate intellectuals are still busy with the process, no doubt essential for a new nation, of political myth-making.

One of the most commonly heard interpretations of the war is that the events of 1961 took Portugal by surprise, and that her response forced her to take seriously for the first time the need to introduce social reforms and to bring about the economic development of the country. Gerald Bender writes, for example:

Once the guerrilla forces had been repulsed. . .Lisbon turned its attention to reforms. The decrees of September 1961, intended to abolish forced labour [and] illegal land expropriation . . . were part of an overall effort to win the hearts and minds of Africans. Officials in Lisbon hoped to show Africans that they had more to gain by staying with Portugal than by supporting the liberation movements and, relative to its pre-war performance, Portugal expended considerable effort and money in an attempt to improve social and economic opportunities for Africans.[1]

The war, therefore, is seen as being responsible for the considerable increase in the pace of social and economic change that took place in the last fifteen years of colonial rule. The war is also seen as primarily responsible for the overthrow of the Salazar-Caetano regime in Lisbon in 1974. The war had created discontent through heavy military expenditure and conscription, and the officers had become politicised through their contacts with the ideologies of the guerrillas against whom they were fighting.

1. Bender, pp.158–9.

War, certainly, has always been one of the most powerful forces for change, and it is not the intention of this chapter to suggest otherwise. However, as with the French Revolution, many changes that were patently already in progress when the cataclysm occurred have in retrospect been attributed to it. Without the French Revolution in Europe, and without the wars of independence in the Portuguese colonies, history would no doubt have been different, but not perhaps so very different.

Long before the events of 1961, the Portuguese had initiated fundamental changes in their colonial economic policy, which, by radically altering the type of production, were about to alter radically the social structure of the colonies. In the late 1950s and early 1960s, the régime was also facing a political challenge, even a political crisis, which had nothing directly to do with the outbreak of revolt in Angola in 1961. Indeed, with the perverseness with which cause and effect sometimes appear to operate, the revolt in Angola, far from shaking the régime, probably helped it to overcome the challenge to its survival.

Economic change

During its first two decades, the economic policies of the New State had been characterised by strict monetary controls, a low level of borrowing, a strong currency, discouragement of foreign investment, direction of the economy by government agencies, and a neo-mercantilism which sought to make Portugal and her colonies self-sufficient in as many commodities as possible. During these decades the colonies, and to a less extent the mother-country as well, were assigned the role of increasing primary production, so that self-sufficiency could be achieved in grains, sugar, tea, coffee, vegetable oils, cotton and other commodities. These crops were produced by peasant farmers or rural labourers, and the ideology of the régime reflected its dependence on peasant labour, praising traditional peasant virtues and decrying policies which would lead to the education and urbanisation of this class.

By the 1950s the economies of Portugal and her colonies were entering a new phase. Portugal herself had begun seriously to industrialise. By the early 1960s, she was averaging a 9 per cent annual increase in industrial production, and in 1964 exports of manufactures had risen to constitute 45 per cent of all her exports.[2] At the same time, her economic relations with Europe grew much more rapidly than her relations with her overseas territories. Not only did

2. Abshire and Samuels, p.346.

trade with the countries of the EEC and EFTA increase rapidly, but her invisible earnings from tourism and from emigrant workers in Germany and France came to dominate her international exchange position, relegating her favourable trade balance with the colonies to relative unimportance.[3] As Portugal herself industrialised, the first moves were made to foster complementary industrial development in the colonies. The 1950s saw a notable expansion of mining in Angola. Iron ore mining at Cassinga began in 1956, and manganese, mica and copper were also mined and exported. In 1955, the first successful oilwells were drilled, and a refinery was built at Luanda to process the crude. Hydro-electric projects were constructed in both Angola and Mozambique to provide the industries with cheap power. Factories for textiles and for the processing of cashew were started in Mozambique, and in the early 1960s factories producing tyres, cement, fertiliser, aluminium, some steel products, petrochemicals and numerous consumer items were constructed. Much of this new industrial growth, based on mining, power and manufacturing for the local market, had barely begun by 1961. What, however, is important is that the vital changes of policy had been decided on long before the outbreak of war. Industrialisation involved other changes. The economy now required increasing numbers of literate, skilled and semi-skilled workers, and the expansion of education began accordingly. Likewise, the régime abandoned its restrictive attitude towards foreign capital, and began to allow French, German, American and South African participation in the economy. These trends intensified after the outbreak of fighting, and were stimulated by the political requirements of counterinsurgency, but they were both well established before 1961.

The crisis of the New State 1958–1962

The risings that took place in Luanda in February 1961, and in various parts of northern Angola in March, initiated the long struggle of the colonies for independence. Their full significance, however, can only be appreciated in the context of a profound crisis for Salazar's government, to which events in Angola contributed but which would undoubtedly have occurred even without the colonial risings. There are three aspects to this crisis; first, an attempt from within the ruling élite to oust Salazar from power; secondly, a daring attempt by opposition elements in Portugal to initiate change by both constitutional and unconstitutional means; and thirdly,

3. Robinson, p.152.

sustained international pressure against the régime. These three aspects are, of course, interwoven and reacted on one another, yet in a significant way they are independent phenomena, and it is easy to imagine each taking place without the other two.

The challenge from within the establishment had always been a possibility, for the monarchists, the army, big business, the church and the bureaucracy seldom saw eye to eye on the major issues of the day, and Salazar was always having to balance the factions. A major sign of discontent within the élite appeared when Salazar had Craveiro Lopes replaced by Admiral Tomás as the régime's nomination for president in the 1958 elections. In April 1961 Lopes and a number of senior officers (including Costa Gomes) unsuccessfully attempted to force Tomás to dismiss Salazar from office. Plans were laid for a military coup in which a large number of leading military figures were involved including the minister of defence, General Botelho Moniz, but it appears that no one had enlisted the support of the lower ranks.[4] The revolution of the generals failed in 1961 — in 1974 the revolution of the captains was to be more successful.

This political in-fighting took place against the back-drop of the flamboyant activities of General Delgado and Henrique Galvão,[5] and the rather more private machinations of the Communist party. Up to 1958, Salazar's police had managed to silence the public critics of the régime and to keep the activities of the Communists underground. Galvão and Delgado were, however, difficult opponents to deal with. Galvão was a senior colonial official and began his opposition from within the Portuguese parliament, where he sat as a government-sponsored deputy. He was eventually framed on a treason charge, and fled into exile in 1952. Delgado was still more senior, having held top government appointments in the diplomatic service and the air force. In 1958 he stood in opposition to Salazar's nominee in the presidential elections, and spent the six months, when campaigning was comparatively free, enlivening the Portuguese political scene with popular and populist politics. His platform amounted simply to a denunciation of the régime, and a lot of ink has been spilled to little purpose by people who have tried to decide whether Delgado was left- or right-wing, and in favour of, or against, the independence of the colonies. He attracted an astonishingly wide range of support, from the Communists to the extreme right-wing monarchists, who all united in their desire to see Salazar

4. Robinson, pp.77-8.
5. Accounts of these extremely well-known events can be found in Figueiredo; Soares; Robinson; Galvão.

go. It was significant that Delgado received strong backing from the whites in Angola and Mozambique, who sought to express their dislike of the centralised dictatorship of Lisbon through Delgado's campaign.

After Delgado's inevitable defeat at the polls and his flight into exile in 1959, his organisation turned to international intrigue and attempts to sabotage Salazar's government in various ways. The most flamboyant of these attempts was Galvão's seizure of the *Santa Maria* in January 1961 and the subsequent hijacking of a Portuguese airliner to distribute leaflets over Portugal. Part of Galvão's plan in 1961, and implicit also in Delgado's plotting, was the intention to detach the colonies from Portugal and to use them as a base for a government-in-exile from Lisbon. Galvão may have had contacts in Luanda, but it is most unlikely that he was in any way connected with the rising that took place there in February 1961.[6]

While Salazar was facing these challenges, he had also to ride an international storm. In 1960 the campaign against Portugal at the United Nations reached a climax with the resolution calling on her to accept self-determination for the colonies. There had been a long build-up towards this resolution; the confrontation had been foreseen ever since Portugal had joined the United Nations in 1955, and even from as early as 1951 when the use of the term 'colonies' was dropped. At the same time, events in India were moving to a climax.

Tension between Portugal and India had existed ever since 1951, when Nehru had formally asked for the surrender of Goa. Portugal had refused and had then had to face a sustained campaign against her Indian colonies organised both from within and from without by Indian political organisations. There were, however, more things at stake than the battle of ideologies. In the 1950s, Portugal began to open up the great iron ore deposits in Goa, making the territory potentially a very rich prize for Nehru. In addition, Goa operated as a free port through which imports poured into the Indian subcontinent, undermining the Indian drive for industrial self-sufficiency. Still closer to the realities of everyday political life was Nehru's need to hold together the Congress Party which had won India's independence and the unity of which was always most assured when a national enemy had to be faced. In 1962 Nehru faced a general election, and the attack on Goa in December 1961 was in many ways the culmination of his election campaign.

The same fateful year, 1961, saw Ghana file an official complaint against Portugal with the International Labour Office, alleging that

6. Pélissier (1978), pp.375–7.

she had not complied with the Abolition of Forced Labour Convention. An investigating commission was duly despatched to test the claims.

This multiple crisis, which came to a head in 1961, petered out early in 1962. Goa indeed was lost, but in January 1962 an army coup in Beja ended in ignominious failure. The Angolan revolts were crushed, and the International Labour Organisation (ILO) reported in April, largely exonerating Portugal of the forced labour accusations. Salazar was once more in control. What had been the nature of the crisis, and how had the régime survived?

The crisis had been brought on by poor political management of a series of difficult and delicate situations both at home and abroad, all of which had been foreseen and to a certain extent prepared for. India's campaign against Goa, Delgado's challenge, the United Nations resolution and the ILO investigation had all been anticipated. So indeed had the outbreak in Angola, though no one had had any suspicion of the level of violence that would occur. The political misjudgement, however, had come about because the régime had become too detached, too isolated from the currents of world opinion and from the forces at work in its own society. The men who had come to power with Salazar after 1926 had mostly belonged to a younger generation than the republicans they replaced.[7] Now, thirty years later, these men were ageing and out of touch. In particular there seems to have been no understanding at all of the aspirations of Indian or African nationalism, and very little realisation that the economic changes which were leading to the industrialisation of Portugal and to the new orientation of her economy and of her migrant workers towards western Europe was leading to increasing frustration at, and discontent with, the paternalist state of the 1930s with its Catholic political philosophy and its fantasies about the virtues of poverty. In other words, the men around Salazar had become too inflexible and unresponsive.

Yet Salazar survived this crisis, the very act of survival forcing the régime to modernise and to adapt to the modern world. This was done with considerable success and, in the short run at least, there can be little doubt that the African wars strengthened Salazar's government and helped it to survive. At first the wars created national unity and even patriotism, while the high military expenditure provided a boost to the economy and made of Salazar a Keynesian in spite of himself. Moreover, the rapid expansion of the colonial economies and the military establishments during the 1960s

---

7. Graham and Makler, p.14.

provided new careers and fresh employment opportunities for discontented elements among the ruling élite in Portugal.

The nationalist revolt

A large number of accounts of the nationalist risings in Portuguese Africa have been written and a reasonably coherent version of the events has been widely agreed in spite of the view, held apparently by the nationalists as much as by their Portuguese predecessors, that political man lives by myth alone. The first rising broke out suddenly, and apparently with little planning, in February 1961 in Luanda and was followed by a massive rural insurrection in the northern coffee-growing regions of Angola. These revolts were crushed by the Portuguese army and by bands of settler vigilantes, but from that time onwards, planned and organised guerrilla war was waged in the north and east of Angola. In 1963, hostilities began in Guiné and in 1964 in Mozambique.

The nationalist risings in Portuguese Africa were exceptional events in the history of decolonisation. Only in Algeria had there been any comparable series of events, for in the rest of Africa the colonising powers had collaborated willingly in the decolonisation process, and had gone out of their way to ease the hand-over of power to a respectable nationalist élite who would keep Africa safe for European trade and business. No such nationalist movement had appeared in the Portuguese colonies, partly because the sort of social change which constituted the seed-bed of nationalism in other colonies had only just begun in the Portuguese territories, but principally because Portugal adopted a rigidly repressive attitude to expressions of dissent. Groups of radicals had been forming among *mestiços* and *civilisados* of the towns. Some of these travelled abroad to Lisbon, South Africa or the United States and made contacts with the opposition in Portugal and with each other. They were few in number, and the fact that their opinions were largely formed and expressed in exile made for very close relations between the nationalist leaders — indeed the nationalist movements in the Portuguese colonies can almost be said to have had a common leadership. *Mestiços*, Goanese and Cape Verdians, because of their superior education, often played a key role. The close contacts, and even friendships, among the leaders contrasts strongly with the often deep divisions that existed within their respective movements.

The mid-1950s saw the intensification of the Indian campaign against Goa and the first black African states moving towards independence. Salazar's government took up a totally intransigent attitude not only refusing to acknowledge and establish a dialogue with the nationalists, but even refusing to accept that they existed within the colonies at all. In a sense, this was a self-fulfilling belief. In 1957 branches of the secret political police, PIDE, were established in the colonies, and from then on opposition organisations were systematically rooted out and crushed with large numbers of suspects being arrested and interned or simply disappearing. So successful were PIDE that the nationalists were not able to maintain more than the most rudimentary organisation inside the colonies and could not communicate regularly with those cells that did exist.

The activities of PIDE drove the nationalist leadership into exile and so created one of the major characteristics of Portuguese colonial nationalism, a characteristic that distinguished it from almost all other similar movements. The nationalism of Guiné, Angola and Mozambique had to develop and articulate itself almost entirely abroad. The parties were organised, financed and staffed, and had to conduct all their affairs, in friendly neighbouring states, and this situation persisted practically until the moment of independence. The fact that the movements were organised abroad and operated from foreign bases was used by the régime to discredit them, to claim that the actual inhabitants of the colonies were loyal to Portugal and that the only trouble came from foreign-inspired intriguers. This claim scarcely bore examination, but it remained true that the independence movements were deeply influenced by their foreign connections.

Foreign sponsorship helped to perpetuate, and even created, divisions in the movements. Each neighbouring independent country wanted to act as patron to a successful nationalist movement. Thus the deep split between the Angolan parties was exacerbated by rival sponsors. Zaire backed UPA, MPLA was based at Conakry and later Brazzaville, and UNITA found a home in Zambia. In eastern Africa, Frelimo was based in Tanzania, but for some time a rival, called COREMO, existed with a base in Zambia, and other even more shadowy movements found encouragement in Malawi.[8] Being based abroad, the independence movements were inevitably heavily dependent on the goodwill of their hosts and on outside funds. They had to seek alliances among the great powers, which meant that they had to become expert diplomats even before they became administrators or bush fighters. A large part of the struggle for independence, in fact, was fought at the diplomatic level.

From the beginning, the movements had a strong tribal orientation. UPA, founded by Holden Roberto in 1958, was an avowedly

8. Henriksen, p.177.

Kongo movement and derived most of its support from the BaKongo and its motivation from Kongo politics. MPLA, although politically more radical, more cosmopolitan and with a *mestiço* leadership ideologically committed to non-tribalism, was always in fact a party of the Mbundu. UNITA found its support among the Ovimbundu. In Mozambique Frelimo for a long time drew its principal support from the Makonde in the north, and even when its leadership made a decisive break with the Makonde leaders in 1968,[9] something of the old tribal animosities remained and for the Makua and other Muslims of the north Frelimo was always the party of the Makonde and therefore not a movement to which to give support. PAIGC in Guiné was possibly the most united of the movements, but even so it never rallied much support from the Muslim Fula. As Cabral regretfully remarked, 'the Fula peasants have a strong tendency to follow their chiefs', and the chiefs, he admitted, were 'tied to colonialism'.[10] PAIGC was also a movement for the liberation of Cape Verde, and Cape Verdians dominated its leadership, even in Guiné. This was another potential source of difficulty, for the Guiné Africans were bound eventually to get restive under the leadership of the *mestiço* islanders. This latent hostility does not appear to have weakened the struggle against the Portuguese, but it proved influential in post-independence politics and was the dominating factor in the coup which overthrew the government of Guiné in 1980.

Being based abroad meant, for the nationalists, being much more influenced by foreign thought and foreign revolutionary models than were their counterparts in British and French Africa. The leaders of Frelimo and PAIGC formed their movements while the Vietnam war was in progress and while Che Guevara was still a living legend. Moreover they were able to see many of the other African states ten years on from independence and they did not like what they saw. 'The liberation struggle', wrote Cabral, 'does not finish when the national flag is raised and the national anthem played.'[11] They were determined that their movements would have something of the discipline of the Vietnamese, the organisation of the Cubans, and above all that they would not become dominated by an élite which, once it had come to power, would merely occupy the shoes of the departed colonial rulers.

As a result of these factors, and of the reality of actually having to fight for their independence, the nationalist movements in the Portuguese colonies became equipped with a more coherent ideology

9. Henriksen, p.179.
10. Cabral, p.49.
11. Cabral, p.87.

and a clearer understanding of the post-colonial problems than most of their 'British' or 'French' counterparts. However, again unlike the leaders in other African countries, there was a tendency to become divorced from the ordinary wishes of ordinary people. Intellectuals like Mondlane, Cabral, Neto or dos Santos were among Africa's most distinguished writers and political thinkers but they were none of them populist politicians. This is nowhere better illustrated than in the very early days of the rising in Angola. The nationalist leaders were entirely taken by surprise when urban guerrillas began action in Luanda and when a peasant jacquerie broke out in the Baixa de Cassange cotton growing region in 1961.[12] To this day no one really knows which group, if any, had a hand in organising these risings. However the exiled nationalist leaders hastened to claim credit for the action, to claim their responsibility and to try to use the events to their advantage. But it was all very much being wise after the event. Nor did the fact that the parties had to concentrate their attention first and foremost on international diplomacy and then on military action make the task of building up contacts with the people any easier. The nationalist theoreticians attached great importance to such contacts, but found that in practice it was difficult to carry out. Among the plantation workers of Zambesia, for example, political contacts were made in the early days of the war. These, however, were soon broken up by the police, and no further politicising of this important sector of the population took place. After independence it was found that Frelimo had very little understanding of the conditions on the plantations or of the aspirations of the workers.

The Portuguese government's greatest mistake was its failure to establish any means of listening and responding to the sentiments and opinions of the African people. It may be that this is a legacy that has been passed on to its nationalist successors.[13]

The Portuguese military response

In one way the Portuguese had prepared for trouble in the colonies; in another they were totally unprepared. Throughout the 1950s, there had been growing signs of dissidence and unrest, ranging from the major political opposition campaign of Delgado and his sympathisers to remote and obscure religious movements in rural Angola and Mozambique. The régime had responded to these challenges by

12. Pélissier(1978), chap.11.
13. This is the question posed by Vail and White at the end of their study of Zambesia.

tightening its security and by adopting a totally uncompromising attitude to all who tried to open a dialogue with it. In the short term this response was successful. The nationalist organisations, which had really only shown signs of life in Angola, were forced underground or into exile and rural protest was crushed. However, the unwillingness of the régime to listen, even to sympathetic criticism, and its failure to take steps to win the loyalty of a wider section of opinion or to cultivate support among the emerging African élite were to prove highly damaging.

The PIDE action against the nationalists was coupled with more overt security precautions to coincide with the declaration of independence of the Congo in 1960. Troops and police were reinforced along the Congo frontier, for it was known that to a large extent the BaKongo of northern Angola looked upon Leopoldville as their cultural and ethnic capital. Yet, for all these precautions, the Portuguese were quite unprepared for the violence of the revolt that broke out between November 1960 and March 1961. Their unpreparedness was probably really due to these revolts being almost totally unorganised; they were uprisings by local groups which took the nationalist leaders as well as the authorities unawares.[14]

The initial response of the Portuguese was extremely violent. Settlers armed themselves and metropolitan troops were sent out to suppress the risings using an indiscriminate violence that showed the extent to which the authorities had had their nerve shaken. Once the immediate crisis had passed, however, the Portuguese proved much more flexible than their previous record would have suggested was possible. They quickly adopted a threefold approach to the rebellions.[15]

First, there was the continuation of military action, which involved for Portugal the systematic build-up of her forces in Africa and their training in the arts of bush warfare. Second was the diplomatic offensive, for just as the nationalists played the circuit of international conferences and sought to isolate Portugal, so the Portuguese responded by building alliances, seeking practical aid and trying to sabotage the efforts of her opponents. On both sides there was to be an intricate counterpoint between the war in the bush and the war of words in the conference halls. Finally came the offensive on the political front at home. Although never admitting the validity of the nationalists' case, the government moved swiftly and effectively to reform its administration and to remedy some of the

14. E.g. Pélissier(1978),pp.372,410.
15. Accounts of the massacres and counter massacres were assembled by Teixeira; Addicott.

shortcomings of which it was accused. This battle for the 'hearts and minds' was fought, as such battles generally are, by repentant ruling élites, with a considerable degree of cynicism and hypocrisy, but in many ways it was not unsuccessful.

From the start, the Portuguese realised that the nationalists would have to be, at the least, contained by the military until victory was won on the diplomatic front or through local developments. Fighting began in Angola in 1961 but not in Mozambique until 1964. During this time the Portuguese built up their armed forces from a few thousand garrison troops and police to an army of 125,000 men. Most of the troops were regulars or conscripts from Portugal, but as the war continued there was a deliberate policy of Africanisation, so that by the end of the war perhaps as many as 60 per cent of the troops fighting the nationalists were black. The air force also had to be built up. In September 1965, a year after Frelimo had launched its war in northern Mozambique, the Portuguese only had five out-of-date aircraft operational in the area.[16] Gradually the forces were equipped with modern jets and helicopters. The armed forces were divided between the three colonies, and their disposition changed little during the course of the war; 30,000 men were stationed in Guiné and 50,000 in Angola and Mozambique.

Portugal's basic military strategy was to confine the war to the frontier districts, away from the main towns, communication routes and economically sensitive areas. In this strategy they were at first aided by the nationalists themselves, who had their training areas and supply depots in neighbouring countries and who operated most securely in frontier regions. Moreover, the nationalists had adopted a plan of sapping the strength of the Portuguese by tying down their forces and gradually exhausting their patience and their resources; a plan which could be achieved on the frontier as well as in the interior. Until the 1970s, the struggle remained something of a phoney war, except in Guiné. Casualties remained low, and the war scarcely impinged on the lives of the majority of the population. Both sides had been appalled at the atrocities committed in the initial stages of the rising in Angola, and went out of their way to play down the violence and bitterness of the struggle. Each side welcomed deserters from its opponents, and made a point of treating prisoners well in order to persuade yet more to desert.

As with so many other guerrilla wars, both sides could claim to control the same part of the country. The nationalists frequently claimed to control large areas of the colonies. Except in Guiné, where such claims could in part be justified, guerrilla activity was

16. Report by Lord Kilbracken, *Rhodesia Herald*, 29.9.1965.

largely confined to areas which were thinly populated or even empty of population altogether. The Portuguese continued to hold all the towns and economically productive regions, and could move freely wherever they chose. The nationalists for their part could often move easily among the villages and at night, their tactics being to mine roads, intimidate government headmen, and keep a large military force guessing as to their whereabouts.

One factor which kept the nationalists confined to the frontier regions was the tribal nature of much of their support. UPA's forces in Angola were all made up of BaKongo, and could not easily operate outside the Kongo language area; in Mozambique most of the manpower of Frelimo were Makonde or Nyanja from the Lake region, and they too operated most effectively near to home. It was in Guiné that the Portuguese lost most ground early in the war, and that the nationalists early established a significant hold on the country. However, Guiné was so small that virtually the whole of the country was a frontier zone.

At intervals, the Portuguese army would mount large-scale sweeps through country held by the nationalist forces. These usually resulted in the destruction of bases and the loss of arms, but never in the total elimination of the guerrilla presence. The largest and most effective of these sweeps was the famous operation 'Gordian Knot', carried out in northern Mozambique by General Arriaga in August 1970. This appears to have pushed the active war zone, which had been creeping south, right back to the Tanzanian frontier and to have destroyed temporarily any hope that Frelimo had of operating further south.

The other major tactic of the Portuguese army was to re-group the population into large settlements which could be controlled and defended. The Portuguese called these *aldeamentos*, and began to build them in the Kongo area soon after the outbreak of the war. By the early 1970s, at least one million Angolans, and possibly as many Mozambicans, had been resettled in *aldeamentos*. These entities were guarded with their own militias, who were lightly armed with rifles. It was the Portuguese plan that Africans in the villages would either be won over to their side or, which was just as good, would be compromised in the nationalists' eyes by their association with Portuguese activities.[17] The *aldeamentos* also had an economic function, and were in some ways the lineal descendants of the African *colonatos* set up in the 1940s and 1950s. They allowed for co-operative marketing and production, and were centres where medical and educational facilities could be concentrated.

17. Bender, chap.6.

Although Portuguese planters had to abandon operations in northern Mozambique, nowhere else were guerrillas able to damage the economy of the colonies. Coffee planting continued throughout the war in the north of Angola, and production continued to increase. After the initial attacks on Cabinda, the territory was made safe for Gulf Oil and the nationalists largely abandoned their efforts there. The Benguela railway remained vulnerable throughout the war, and was frequently attacked after 1968. However, it was never put out of action while the Portuguese ruled in Angola. In 1968 also, the nationalists made public their intention of preventing the building of the Cabora Bassa dam on the Zambesi. 'If we do not destroy the Cabora Bassa scheme, or at least make it twice as costly, we shall have received our greatest setback,' said Mondlane in March 1968.[18] Yet the dam proceeded ahead of schedule. The most the nationalist campaign against the dam achieved was to force the Portuguese to form closer military ties with South Africa and Rhodesia to protect their vast investment. It appears that South African military and air force detachments were used in defence of the dam.

The diplomatic struggle

After the initial violence and its suppression, the war was fought as much in the field of diplomacy as on the battlefield. Indeed, much military action was undertaken by both sides for its effect on world opinion rather than for any military advantage to be obtained. The objective of the nationalists was first to try to win the support of the Organisation of African Unity (OAU) and to gain the legitimacy of being recognised as the heirs of the Portuguese. In Angola, the OAU at first backed Holden Roberto's UPA and in 1964 even recognised his government-in-exile, which went under the initials GRAE. The rival MPLA had to build its diplomatic support first among the eastern bloc states, and then with radical African régimes, before making its assault on the OAU itself. Even when its credentials had been accepted, it had to run in tandem with UPA for some years. Military action was frequently undertaken by each of the two parties simply to bolster its own claims to recognition. For instance, MPLA's front in Cabinda in 1964 and UPA's decision to open campaigning in the east of Angola in 1966 were undertaken with diplomatic rather than military objectives in mind.

In Mozambique and Guiné, the leading nationalist parties did not have serious rivals in the field, yet they had constantly to watch the

18. *The Times*, 11.3.1968.

activities of fringe organisations, like FLING or COREMO, which had little support in the country but were able to find international backers — FLING had a home in Senegal and COREMO in Zambia. Break-away nationalist leaders, indeed, always stood a chance of finding an international forum for themselves, because of the disunited state of the anti-colonial forces during the 1960s. This was the period when China and Russia were competing strongly for influence in Africa, and when Ghana and Egypt represented poles of influence in Africa which did not always pull in the same direction. Although it might be thought that Portugal would have little chance of finding allies in black Africa, this was not the case. She was frequently able to exert considerable influence in Zaire and in Zambia, both countries being heavily dependent on Portuguese railways to get their minerals to the coast. Malawi was also a friendly state and of great value in protecting Mozambique's western flank. Portugal also tried her hand, though without much long-term success, at interfering in African politics. She offered support to Biafra during the Nigerian civil war, and allowed the island of São Tomé to be used by aircraft sending supplies to the breakaway state. In general, however, her African diplomacy was successful only in that it deprived the guerrillas of the complete freedom of action in neighbouring states that they would have liked.

Apart from the struggle for recognition in Africa, the nationalists sought support in international agencies. Their success in attracting international support was due in no small part to the fact that they set up a joint organisation, CONCP, which made sure that they spoke with a common voice. CONCP brought together Frelimo, PAIGC and MPLA, and at least one of its effects was to isolate rival nationalist movements and make them appear in the eyes of the world as mere splinter groups, CONCP won immediate success at the United Nations where the Afro-Asian group of states, together with the eastern bloc, could always win a majority in the General Assembly. The United Nations duly passed a series of resolutions condemning Portugal and urging her to grant independence to her colonies. It also appointed a special commission to receive delegations and collect information on the colonies. Portugal was even expelled from some United Nations bodies and conferences. Yet, if the nationalists could always win a vote in the General Assembly, the Portuguese had enough friends in the Security Council to veto any call for action, and after the death of President Kennedy in 1963, the sympathy of the United States for the nationalist cause waned markedly.[19]

19. Abshire and Samuels, chap.16.

The diplomatic struggle was fought in other areas as well. The Vatican's condescension was a valued propaganda prize. Portugal secured a major victory when Pope Paul VI visited Fatima in 1967, but by 1970 the Vatican, always better informed than most lay intelligence agencies, had sensed the imminence of a nationalist victory and granted an audience to guerrilla leaders.[20] There was also a keenly-fought campaign in the columns of the western press. Both the Portuguese and the nationalists tried to build up a body of support among the intelligentsia of the West, and the verbal guerrilla warfare which these fought in newspapers and books was fierce.

The nationalists formed competent organisations in Britain, the Netherlands and elsewhere, which ran publicity offices and produced English-language journals. In Britain, they had a spokesman in the House of Lords, organised speaking tours for nationalist leaders, and issued a flood of news releases. Portugal for her part operated through organisations like the Anglo-Portuguese Friendship Society and through sympathisers among Conservative members of parliament and the Conservative press. Both sides used the technique of the official visit. Sympathetic journalists would be invited to undertake a tour of guerrilla-held districts, and on their return would write articles and books on their experiences with the nationalists. The articles stressed that the guerrillas controlled a large amount of territory (after a while the proportion became standardised, they held two-thirds of Guiné and one-fifth of Mozambique), and that they had established an administration in the liberated areas which was running schools and was marketing crops produced by the peasants. They ended with an account of the cost of the war to Portugal. A week or so later would come the counter-blast from some parliamentarian or journalist of the right who had been taken by the Portuguese authorities on a tour of the supposedly occupied areas. They reported that guerrilla activity was at a low ebb, that the Portuguese could move about freely, that African refugees were returning to Portuguese protection, and that the army was doing constructive work in the villages. The articles appeared under headlines like 'Portugal grapples with the problem of prosperity' and made statements such as 'There is no longer a military problem.'[21]

Portugal's main diplomatic concern was to secure the support of NATO, of her southern African neighbours, and of Western business interests. NATO needed Portuguese bases, and there was a discreet campaign to emphasise the value of the Cape Verde Islands

20. *The Times*, 3.7.1970.
21. *Daily Telegraph*, 4.4.1969.

and the Azores in global strategy. In general, NATO's behind-the-scenes support for Portugal never wavered, and the supply of arms continued to flow to the Portuguese forces. Of particular value was the access to modern strike aircraft. The southern African connection, on the other hand, was a delicate balancing act, for in 1965 Rhodesia declared independence unilaterally and Britain called on Portugal to observe sanctions. Portugal's line was one of strict international rectitude. She did not recognise the new régime, and acquiesced in the charade of the Beira blockade. By 1968, however, it was clear that Britain was turning a blind eye to sanctions-breaking, and that Portugal's co-operation with the Smith régime would not endanger her support from NATO. Thereafter contacts between the three white governments in southern Africa became more open. Regular military conversations were held, intelligence was exchanged, and increasingly there was active participation by South African and Rhodesian security forces in aid of the Portuguese.[22]

Portugal's final campaign was fought to try to attract foreign business to its colonies. This naturally had an economic purpose, but it was also a shrewd move in the diplomatic war. Portugal reasoned that if she could attract foreign investment, this would increase the commitment of the western nations to her defence. It would also prove to the world that Portugal meant to stay in the colonies — an important psychological victory to win — and that the guerrillas were harmless as they could not even endanger the investments of foreign business. The three major foreign investment schemes were the Cassinga iron mines in Angola; the Cabinda oilfields and the Cabora Bassa dam in Mozambique, although there were also many others. Two of these, the oil and the dam, were sited in regions where the guerrillas had opened war zones, so that the successful development of these projects was an impressive propaganda victory for the Portuguese. Frelimo in particular had made its international campaign against the dam a test of its strength *vis-à-vis* the régime. Its diplomacy did secure the withdrawal of some would-be participants like Italy, but the building of the dam went ahead and the point was made that Frelimo had neither the military strength nor the diplomatic muscle to halt it. It has, of course, been argued that Frelimo really wanted to see the dam built so that the independent Mozambique would start life endowed with this great asset. If this is so, the strategy behind the campaign of the 'dam-busters' remains obscure.[23]

22. *The Times*, 12.3.1968.
23. *Sunday Times*, 25.10.1970; *Guardian*, 30.4.1971.

Who won the diplomatic struggle? Ultimately the winner would be whoever won the military and political battles as well, for in international affairs, as in so many other fields of activity, recognition and legitimacy ultimately depend on success. Yet the military struggle, in its turn, depended on the outcome of the diplomatic campaign, because neither side could have fought for longer than a few weeks without the aid it received from its international backers. As the struggle continued, the psychological advantage fluctuated. Initially, the nationalists won the advantage since their revolt focused world attention on Portugal's colonies in a thoroughly unwelcome way. Then, as the internecine battles within the nationalist camp deepened and as Portugal was demonstrably able to control her colonies, the balance swung back the other way. Portugal could be credibly represented as winning, and this enabled her to launch her great investment programmes. Salazar's departure from office in 1968 marked another turning-point. Caetano proved a more durable and more conservative successor than anyone had foreseen, but from the start the question began to be asked, when would Portugal reach a settlement in Africa? When would the régime face the facts of the modern world and come to terms with the nationalists?

Acute observers were already convinced that the future of Africa lay in political events in Lisbon, not on the outcome of the smouldering war in the colonies. After 1968 the cracks in the façade of the régime were eagerly scanned by interested parties to see if they revealed in any way the outline of the future. In the early 1970s, Portugal once again appeared to regain the initiative through the successful governorship of General Spinola in Guiné — which seemed to establish the simple fact that Portugal's rule in Guiné was not going to collapse as the pundits had foretold — and through the success of Arriaga's campaign in northern Mozambique. By 1972, however, the tide had set strongly in the other direction. The church had moved near to breaking with Portugal; and the White Fathers had withdrawn their missions. Guerrilla activity had at last become effective in the Tete district of Mozambique, and in the summer of 1973, what had been intended as an important psychological boost to the régime — Caetano's state visit to London — misfired disastrously when *The Times* published Adrian Hasting's revelations about massacres carried out by Portuguese troops at Wiryamu and elsewhere.[24]

Besides being bad for Portugal's position in the world, the

24. Hastings.

Wiriyamu massacre was an all too clear indication that her political campaign to win support within the colonies had gone badly wrong.

Portuguese policies to develop the colonies during the 1960s

The Portuguese were well aware that there was no purely military solution to the nationalist revolts. One senior officer told a *Times* reporter in July 1969:

'Militarily the situation is stable. They can't overthrow us and we can't get rid of them. For us, the most important thing, more important than killing the enemy and getting their weapons, is to win the civilian population over to our side.'[25]

The policy makers of the régime must presumably have thought this was possible, for otherwise it is difficult to see how they hoped to win in the long term. Their domestic anti-insurgency policy had a number of thrusts to it. First they pressed ahead with a major programme of industrial investment structured by an Interim Plan (1965–7) and a third six-year Development Plan (1968–73).

If development plans are nothing else, they are at least a barometer of the public policy of a government. Seen in this light, the Interim Plan and the third six-year plan show the extent to which government policy had changed direction. The Interim Plan, for example, involved the expenditure of 14.4 million *contos* (approximately £180m. in 1965), and although transport and communications were still the largest item, 34 per cent was now earmarked for investment in energy and industry, and 14.5 per cent for housing and social expenditure.[26] The proposed financing of the plan also showed changes. Of the planned investment 25 per cent was to take the form of foreign credit, and 26 per cent was to be financed by central government, with only 10 per cent coming from the provincial budgets (although once again Mozambique and Angola were very different, the former generally being less well able to finance its own investment than the latter).[27]

The full investment targets of these plans were not met (the shortfall on the Interim Plan in Angola was estimated by Mario de Andrade to be 67 per cent!),[28] but the general lines of policy were certainly realised. The colonies, and in particular Angola, saw spectacular growth of their economies during the war. In Angola the growth was in part led by exports of coffee, iron ore, oil and

25. *The Times*, 12.8.1969.
26. OECD, *Portugal* (1966), pp.31–5.
27. Andrade and Ollivier, p.103; Kuder, p.313.
28. Andrade and Ollivier, p.100.

diamonds. Coffee, although grown in areas exposed to guerrilla attacks, expanded its exports from 87,000 tons in 1960 to 225,163 tons in 1967;[29] iron ore production rose from 100,000 tons in 1957 to 7 million tons in 1971; oil exports were 58,000 tons in 1958, but new investment in the 1960s led to production estimated at 15 million tons by the early 1970s. In 1968 total Angolan exports were double the value they had been at the start of the war.[30] Mozambique's exports, by contrast, were only 49 per cent up over the same period.

A rise in exports need not necessarily develop other sectors of the economy. Iron ore from Cassinga, for example, was mined in a highly automated way, and was loaded directly on to ore carriers at Moçamedes. What, however, is striking about the economic growth of the 1960s and 1970s is that it spread throughout all sectors of the economy. In typical New State fashion, local industrialisation was heralded by the formation of a *junta*. In 1962, the *Junta de Desenvolvimento Industrial* was set up to preside over the diversification of Angola's local industries, which experienced an annual growth rate of 13 per cent during the 1960s. The growth was concentrated in textiles, chemicals, food and drink, petroleum products, tobacco, paper, clothing and footwear, cement and construction.

This expansion is clearly related to increased local spending-power deriving from higher wages, white settlement and the high military budgets, but it was also the result of the relaxing of constraints on foreign investment and the willingness of the government to embark on deficit financing and to raise the level of public debt — two major departures from traditional Salazarist economic policy. A further very significant departure was the gradual decline in the importance of Portugal's trade with her colonies. This is most clearly seen in the declining proportion of Portugal's own trade with Africa, but it can also be seen in the underlying growth in importance of foreign as opposed to imperial markets for the colonies themselves.

A clear political objective of this policy was to seize the initiative from the nationalists by triggering off major social change which would offer an attractive future to the African population. There is no way of measuring how successful this policy was, but it is worth noting that it was in Angola, where the greatest economic and industrial growth took place, that the guerrillas were in the end least successful.

The second line of Portuguese colonial policy, and one closely

29. Andrade and Ollivier, p.82.
30. Andrade and Ollivier, p.88.

linked with the investment programme, was the rapid expansion of social services. Schools and clinics were built rapidly throughout the colonies, and frequently the work was done by the army or took place within the confines of a strategic village, so that the connection between this and the military effort was obvious to all. The rapidity with which the social infrastructure was built up is clearly testified in the figures. For example, in Mozambique the numbers attending primary school rose between 1964 and 1972 from 427,000 to 603,000, and secondary school attendance rose from 19,761 to 44,368.[31] What was clearly not thought out in any detail was how the régime would respond to the demands and aspirations of the generation which was receiving an education under this programme.

The war effort also brought with it a great improvement in communications. Airfields were built throughout the colonies, and the length of tarred (and mine-proof) road dramatically increased. New highways opened up areas previously remote. Mozambique, for instance, received its first north-south highway, and the first road bridge across the Zambesi was built at Tete in 1969. Before that date not only did cars have to cross the river by ferry (or by train at Sena where you could hire your own steam locomotive and truck if you wanted to cross), but the only all-weather roads linking north Mozambique with Zambesia and southern Mozambique went through Malawi and Rhodesia.

The third line of policy consisted of a major effort to win the support of certain ethnic groups. The nationalists experienced extreme difficulty in overcoming 'tribal' mistrust, and this the Portuguese were able to exploit, as they had earlier during the wars of pacification. In particular, the Portuguese realised the political potential in the hostility between Muslim and Christian. It is one of the supreme ironies of the war that, although the government looked upon the church as an ally and preached the civilising virtues of Catholic orthodoxy, it found that elements within the church were becoming increasingly hostile and that mission-educated Africans were joining the nationalists; on the other hand, the Muslims (Yao, Swahili and Makua in Mozambique and Fula in Guiné), who had traditionally been discouraged and harassed as a 'de-nationalising' force by the colonial authorities, were suddenly discovered to be allies, the conservatism of their social structure and traditional education making them poor ground for the nationalists to cultivate for support. The Portuguese army in Guiné found itself building mosques to uphold a régime that made Catholic values the basis of its ideology.

31. Kuder, p.291.

The fourth policy was to step up immigration, in the hope that eventually a large white population would be an unassailable bulwark against insurgency. The white populations of Angola and Mozambique both doubled during the war, and, according to Cabral, it was even planned that white settlers should come to Guiné. The original development plans for the area irrigated by the Cabora Bassa dam also made provision for extensive white immigration. Rather belatedly, the Caetano régime began to contemplate allowing the colonies a modicum of self-government, and in 1971 constitutional changes were introduced to devolve some powers on to the colonial governments.

Fifth, there was a major reform of the status of the African population — the first significant change since 1899. In 1961, all forms of compulsory labour, even for public works, were abolished, and the status of *indígena* disappeared for the first time since the nineteenth century. Thus the whole population was accorded equal rights before the law.

To a large extent these new policies were brought into being by the war, but most of them had their roots and their rationale in pre-war developments. The decision to promote some forms of industrialisation in the colonies had already been taken, and the great expansion of education was clearly in part a response to the new needs of industry. The end of compulsory labour and of forced growing of crops was all foreshadowed by the economic changes which required the release of the labour force for industrial purposes, although it was actually precipitated by the ILO investigations. The war, indeed, brought about more in the way of indirect changes than direct ones. High military expenditure forced the government to abandon its rigid monetarist doctrines, and to enter what it considered the immoral world of inflation and deficit finance. It did so with caution and circumspection, but the result was a very considerable stimulus to both the metropolitan and the colonial economies. As much as 80 per cent of military expenditure actually occurred in Africa, and this represented a vast injection of funds into the economies of Mozambique, Angola and Guiné.

The limits of success

Because the Portuguese régime and its counter-insurgency campaign suddenly collapsed in 1974, it may appear inappropriate to talk of the 'success' of the Portuguese campaign against the guerrillas. However, for all but the last two years of the war, the Portuguese counter-measures were remarkably effective. In Angola, the initial rising of 1961 had affected altogether six districts in Angola out of fifteen, but in spite of continued guerrilla activity by UPA and the emergence of MPLA and UNITA as active military forces, Portugal retained its control of Angola, and over most of its population and its economic resources. Most striking of all was the continued boom in coffee production in the areas most affected by the rising, and the return of the hundreds of thousands of BaKongo who had fled Angola in 1961, to settle in the protected villages and grow coffee. In Cabinda, despite its exposed nature as an enclave, guerrilla action proved very ineffective, the population apparently preferring home-grown nationalist leaders. In Mozambique, as late as 1971, the war was confined to the two northern districts, and the attempts to open fronts in Tete and Zambesia had been failures. In Guiné the nationalists had gained control of considerable stretches of the country, but had made little progress towards forcing a solution, and had to face a stalemate after 1968 when it became clear that the future of Guiné would be decided by events elsewhere.

The weakness of the guerrilla movements remained what it had been at the start. They were unable to organise on a national basis, and what internal organisation there was existed only in the territory of friendly ethnic groups. For example, Frelimo was able to hold its party congress in 1968 inside Mozambique, a significant propaganda success, but it was not able to set up an organisation among the Makua, the largest ethnic group, or establish rapport with the mine-workers of the *Sul do Save*, who tended to lend their support to rival nationalist groups. At the time, the Portuguese secret police, PIDE, were given much of the credit for fomenting internal dissension, supporting rival splinter parties, encouraging deserters and even pursuing a policy of assassination of the nationalist leaders. Both Cabral and Mondlane were indeed murdered, the former in 1972, the latter in 1969, but it has been suggested that PIDE had little to do with either crime, and that the murders were the result of internal dissensions within the nationalist parties.[32]

In the international diplomatic arena, the Portuguese recovered from the early setback when it appeared that they had lost the backing of the United States, and up to 1971 they lost scarcely any ground to the nationalists — the much-publicised support for the nationalists from Sweden not being seen as significant. Not only did Portugal hold her international position, but she clearly strengthened it through the close ties with Rhodesia and South Africa and through the involvement of foreign capital.

Further evidence of success was the steady Africanisation of the armed forces. As had been the case during the wars of pacification,

32. *Sunday Times*, 8.4.1973; Henriksen, p.180; Vail and White.

there were always more Africans fighting for the Portuguese than against them in the field.

In general, therefore, Portugal's counter-insurgency had proved remarkably successful — successful, that is, as long as nobody questioned the long-term future. How the régime ever hoped to bring the war to an end is not clear. Nor is it clear that they had any coherent ideas about the constitutional future of the colonies when their immigration and education policies should finally bear fruit. There was talk of various types of federal association with Portugal, but the implications of such a solution in an Africa made up of independent states and in a world polarised by rival ideologies were never thought through. With hindsight it is clear that already by 1971 the colonies were living on borrowed time. The military had achieved as much success as was possible, but the politicians had not responded in kind. The régime was bankrupt of ideas and was trapped by the intransigence of its own rhetoric. The irony is that no one appreciated this more than the prime minister himself.

Like a house eaten away by termites, the colonial government appeared whole and intact until the moment of its collapse. The collapse was totally unforeseen by the nationalists. In 1961 they had been taken by surprise by the outbreak of violence in Luanda and Cassange; in 1974 they were equally unready for the collapse of their opponents. It was a tragedy for Mozambique and Angola — particularly for Angola — that independence came before the nationalists had been able to resolve their own differences, before they had formulated clearly what they would do with victory, and before they had been able to organise cadres throughout the country and politicise more than a fraction of the inhabitants.

The collapse of the régime

It has been quite obvious to all commentators that the collapse of Caetano's government in April 1974 was in some way the result of the wars in Africa, but it is far from easy to pinpoint exactly how the war brought down the régime. One version of events has it that the war in Mozambique began to go badly for Portugal in 1972. The guerrillas at last successfully established themselves in Tete province and began raids south of the Zambesi. The Portuguese response showed how disturbed the military had become. Indiscriminate raids on villages in the Tete district led to the Wiriyamu massacre and to the catastrophically bad publicity which this event brought on the régime. As morale worsened among the armed forces, so a group of middle-ranking officers became increasingly politicised and prepared themselves for a coup in which a political solution of

African problems featured high on the agenda.

This version of events is important but it underestimates the purely domestic origins of the coup. Since 1968 Portugal had been changing rapidly. Caetano was anxious to modernise Portugal, and introduced new and younger men into the government ministries and corporations. This new generation talked less in the outdated language of Salazarian nationalism, and openly espoused the liberal capitalism of the European Economic Community. Initial feelers were made towards associating Portugal in some way with the EEC in 1970, and in March of that year Richard Gott of *The Guardian* recorded an interview with Rogerio Martins, the young minister for industries, who spelled out some new ideas:

'What we have to do now is to awaken the political consciousness of the managerial class. . . We want to create an economic environment that will enable them to make themselves rich here. In a more liberal atmosphere this should be possible. The younger generation will acquire the new spirit required.'[33]

Caetano's young men were clearly oriented towards Europe and began to look upon Africa as a burden. Yet Caetano himself was excessively cautious in introducing change; rather, he was inconsistent, at one moment apparently liberalising the régime and then clamping down with purges and repression. It was a dangerous policy, for it raised expectations that were then not fulfilled.

The war was also having economic repercussions. These were not, as some left-wing journalists seemed to imply, the impoverishment of Portugal. The contrary was, in fact, the case. Richard Gott wrote in 1970:

The country is far from being ruined by war. . . [It] does not lack millionaires. Lisbon is booming as money pours into the construction industry. Portugal, in fact, does not give the impression of a country obsessed or even particularly preoccupied by its overseas wars.[34]

Wars seldom do impoverish a country, but rather by creating full employment and by raising the level of government expenditure they usually create prosperity. Under the impact of war spending, Portugal's economy rapidly modernised. Shipbuilding and the oil industry grew, and the industrial workforce increased. Wages rose, and inflation, held at bay for so long by monetary policies, began to take a grip on the country, having the usual stimulating effect on manufacturing industry and on trade union activity. Shortage of capital at home was indeed accentuated by the high level of expendi-

33. *Guardian*, 25.3.1970.
34. *Guardian*, 23.3.1970.

ture in the colonies, and foreign capital began to enter the country in considerable quantities. With these economic changes, the old institutions of Salazar's corporate state atrophied — in particular the *gremios* and workers' syndicates which had been the régime's attempt to organise representation in industry. While these economic trends were overturning the sacred pillars of Salazarist orthodoxy one by one, the ties between colonies and mother-country were beginning to loosen. There was a steady but significant decline in the importance of colonial trade to Portugal's industries.

It is arguable that Portugal had already begun to 'decolonise' long before such an idea had been articulated by the political élite or even formulated in their minds. Caetano may have privately initiated moves towards a solution in Africa. There were rumours in 1970, for example, that he was thinking of abandoning Guiné in exchange for the nationalists leaving Portugal the Cape Verde Islands.[35] Eventually, pressure from the old guard of Salazar's supporters forced him to shelve such heretical notions, but increasingly a tone of doubt could be detected in ministerial speeches, as though Portugal was opening the door a crack to some negotiated solution. Between 1968 and 1974, what was clearly happening was a gradual shift of opinion among the ruling élite of Portugal, a shift away from the colonial fundamentalism of Salazar towards a willingness to examine the void that lay beyond the immediate military necessities of counterinsurgency.

As in the period 1958–62, a crisis built up for the régime in a number of directions at once in 1973–4. Some notable set-backs occurred in Africa, though nothing to cause any military crisis; at the same time, the régime became embroiled in the absurdities of the trial of the 'Three Marias', and with the Vatican over its African policies. It faced industrial trouble at home and the effects of the world depression brought on by the 1973 war in the Middle East. To this was added growing dissent among junior conscript officers, many of whom were of left-wing persuasion. As in 1961, however, the most immediate threat came from revolt within the establishment — but this time with mortal consequences. The most overt sign was the publication in February 1974 of General Spinola's book *Portugal and the Future*, but this was only a symptom of the loss by the ruling élite in Portugal of the will to govern. As with almost every Revolution, this was the decisive factor, and skilled revolutionaries know that however well they organise militarily and however well they mobilise popular support, their ultimate victory is only won when the rulers lose the ability and the will to run the government.

35. *Guardian*, 23.3.1970.

As the details of the coup become clearer,[36] it is remarkable how many high-ranking officers seem to have known of its imminence and, instead of organising resistance to it, sought to find the position they would occupy in the new order. Those privy to the conspiracies included not only Costa Gomes, the left-wing chief of staff, and Spinola himself, but even Kaulza de Arriaga, the generalissimo from Mozambique who had frequently been tipped as the possible leader of a right-wing coup. Caetano himself seems to have known something of what was afoot, and to have offered to hand over the government to one of the generals.

As so often, it was something comparatively trivial that precipitated events. A grievance over pay and promotion within the armed forces polarised opinion between regular and conscript officers, and politicised many men who had not previously been politically aroused by their African experiences. A grievance over pay and conditions of service has always counted for more than volumes of political theory in creating a political consciousness. The coup itself took place on 25 April 1974, but the actual events of that day were the least important part of the overthrow of Salazar's system. The dictatorship had already been deserted by its generals, had lost its ideology, had abandoned its economic policies, and at the end was headed by a man who no longer wished to continue to rule.[37]

Although Portugal's position in the 1970s cannot be isolated from its African wars, it is possible to analyse the revolt of 1974 in such a way that, as has been shown, Africa plays only a peripheral role. What is incontestable, however, is that the revolution in Lisbon had the most profound effect on Africa.

The end in Africa

The Revolution of the Flowers in April 1974 brought General Spinola to the head of affairs in Portugal, although not exactly to power. His government initially had no intention of leaving Africa — it was committed only to finding a political solution to the problem of the colonies. Events, however, did not wait for a political solution. When Caetano's régime collapsed, the whole colonial administration fell with it. Soldiers retreated to barracks and would no longer risk their lives defending a defunct ideology. Still more strikingly, the authority structure of the régime shrivelled up. Officials and their regulations were simply no longer obeyed as

36. Robinson.
37. Robinson.

people waited to see where the new focus of authority would be. There was some talk of a coup by the white settlers, but in spite of the politicking of men like Jorge Jardim in Mozambique, no UDI was ever remotely likely. The white settlers, unlike their Rhodesian counterparts, had never controlled the administration or the armed forces; they had never had political parties and had no leaders.

The nationalists moved quickly into the political vacuum. For the first time, they began to penetrate south of the Zambesi, and in Angola all three movements hurried to establish their presence in the centre and south of the country and to stake their claims to control the capital. Within six months, Spinola had gone and Portugal had named the day when she would withdraw from Africa. The withdrawal was hasty and chaotic, and accompanied by a mass exodus of white settlers who left offices unmanned, business incomplete and all the complex affairs of a modern state with no one at the helm. It is wrong to blame either side or any individual for this exodus and the collapse which followed. A slower hand-over was politically impossible, particularly in Angola where the nationalists had already begun to fight among themselves over the inheritance. In Mozambique, where Frelimo was the only possible claimant to power, little attempt was made to persuade the whites to stay on, and many decisions were made which can only be interpreted as deliberate attempts to speed their departure. Once again, Frelimo probably had no alternative but to establish its own cadres swiftly and decisively. Its own weakness in the south of the country was such that a transitional period, with the capital in the hands of white settlers and with a hostile Rhodesia and a barely neutral South Africa just across the frontier, was too dangerous to contemplate.

Although some would claim that a violent and cathartic break with the old order was not only inevitable but also beneficial, it is difficult not to conclude that, in the short term at least, decolonisation led to severe problems. The exodus of white settlers, officials and military personnel deprived the colonies of almost the whole of their managerial and technical class. These could, to a certain extent, be replaced by importing a whole new class of expatriate technocrats — the Cubans in Angola and an assorted 'international brigade' of helpers in Mozambique. More difficult to replace were the petty bourgeoisie, the shopkeepers, artisans, market gardeners, mechanics, *et al*. The absence of this class has tended to paralyse the economies of the new states.

The nationalist takeover severed most of the arteries of the economic life of the former colonies. The links with Portugal were cut, the technocrats left, and the petty bourgeoisie with their vital role in the economy were expelled and replaced by political cadres whose task was to create a planned economy from units designed and fashioned essentially for capitalist enterprise. How successfully this can be done still remains to be seen, but it may not be wholly irrelevant that Portugal's colonial legacy includes the mechanisms by which the Salazar régime at its height succeeded in imposing a unique degree of central planning on the economies of Angola, Mozambique and Guiné.

GLOSSARY

Aldea	A village. Fiscal unit in Portuguese India.
Aldeamento	Protected village settlements.
Ambaquista	*Mestiço* population of the interior of Angola. After the town of Ambaca.
Angolar	Descendant of shipwrecked Angolan slaves living on São Tomé.
Aringa	Large fortified stockade in Zambesia.
Assimilado	African granted full legal status as a Portuguese citizen.
Caderneta	Pass-book.
Capitão-mor	A man holding a military or judicial commission, usually in areas where no regular administration existed.
Chefe do posto	District commissioner. The lowest rank of Portuguese administrator.
Chicunda	Name given to the slaves and slave soldiers of the Zambesi warlords.
Cipai	African soldier in government service.
Circunscrição	The basic rural administrative division
Civilisado	The same as *assimilado* but more generally used.
Colonato	Government sponsored agricultural settlements
Concelho	The basic urban or semi-urban administrative unit.
Conto	1,000 *escudos* or 1,000,000 *reis*. The *real* was replaced in Portugal by the *Escudo* in 1911.
Estado Novo	The New State. The name given to Salazar's régime.
Grêmio	Employers' association sponsored by the government.
Indígena	Native. The status of all Africans not specifically granted Portuguese 'civilised' status.
Junta	Board or council. Usually a government-appointed board.
Machamba	An African cultivation plot in Mozambique
Mestiço	Person of mixed African and European descent.
Morador	Portuguese settler.
Mossambaze	African trader in Portuguese service in Mozambique.
Mussoco	Head tax collected in Zambesia.
Muzungo	Name given to a member of the Portuguese community (not necessarily white) in Zambesia.
Palhota	Hut tax.
Prazo	Land grant in Zambesia.
Presídio	Fortified military post in Angola.
Regedor	Government-appointed headman.
Roça	Plantation in São Tomé and Principe.
Senhor	Feudal lord. Used to describe Portuguese land-owning class, particularly in Zambesia.
Sertanejo	Backwoodsman.

Sertão	Backlands.
Serviçal	Contract labourer.
Sul do Save	The part of Mozambique south of the Sabi river.
Tonga	Term used on São Tomé for the children of contract labourers.

BIBLIOGRAPHICAL GUIDE FOR ENGLISH READERS

General Reading

Easily the best general study of the Portuguese empire in Africa is still Duffy's *Portuguese Africa*, originally published in 1959. This is primarily a study of colonial policy and institutions, and as such it has not been bettered by any publication in English. Duffy's achievement is all the more remarkable since he had virtually no detailed monographs from which to work. Hammond's *Portugal and Africa* is an admirable survey of the empire up to the end of the Monarchy, and treats economic issues in greater depth than Duffy. There have been two attempts to produce general histories of the principal colonies — Henriksen's *Mozambique* and Wheeler and Pélissier's *Angola*. Both are very valuable as accounts of the origin and progress of the wars of liberation, but they are less satisfactory in dealing with the earlier history of the territories. Abshire and Samuels' *Portuguese Africa* is particularly valuable for the period 1945-65.

Portuguese Africa before 1875

There are invaluable histories of Mozambique in the sixteenth and seventeenth centuries by Axelson. These are based on detailed archival research, and have a strictly narrative format. More interpretative is Alpers' *Ivory and Slaves in East Central Africa*, which is a commercial history of northern Mozambique. This is closely paralleled by Hafkins' thesis, which covers the same region but from a more political standpoint. Zambesia has been the subject of studies by Isaacman, Newitt and Rea and of a number of theses of which Mudenge's is the most important. The most up-to-date study of southern Mozambique is that by Hedges.

Birmingham's *Trade and Conflict in Angola* is still the best introduction to the history of Angola. The west central African kingdoms and their relations with the Portuguese can be studied in Vansina, Miller and Martin.

Rodney's *History of the Upper Guinea Coast* is indispensable for the history of Guiné, and Bentley Duncan for the Azores and Cape Verde Islands.

Diplomacy of the Partition Period

Graham is vital for the background to the partition in east Africa. Axelson has provided a very detailed general study of the partition itself, and there are monographs on different regions by Anstey, Hanna and Warhurst. Wheeler has described the death-throes of the Gaza monarchy in southern Mozambique, and articles by Drechsler, Willequet and Vincent Smith deal with the relations of Portugal with Britain and Germany before the First World War. Two writers have made the railway diplomacy of the period their speciality; Katzenellenbogen, whose books are detailed and specialised, and Vail, who has written of the Trans-Zambesia railway with admirable brevity. Duffy's *A Question of Slavery* is a survey of pre-war diplomacy on labour questions.

Angola

The works of two writers are indispensable for the study of Angola. Pélissier's massive three-volume work is at present only available in French, but is a highly intelligent interpretative work as well as being an inexhaustible quarry of information. Equally distinguished is the work of Clarence-Smith. His thesis has led to a number of articles and to *Slaves, Peasants and Capitalists in Southern Angola*, which, in spite of its limited geographical coverage, is one of the best introductions to Portuguese colonialism. Other important studies of Angola are Jill Dias and Birmingham on the origins of settlement in Cazengo; Heimer's important collection of essays entitled *Social Change in Angola*, which contains articles by Wheeler and Christensen on the Bailundu revolt and Pössinger's invaluable study of the Ovimbundu. Bender's *Angola under the Portuguese* has useful chapters on the convict settlements, white colonisation and the war-time *aldeamentos*. Finally there is a good, new study called *Angola: Five Centuries of Conflict* by Henderson. Of the works dealing with the missionary impact, those by Edwards and Childs are the most significant.

Mozambique

The outstanding work on modern Mozambique is without doubt Vail and White's detailed but interpretative and highly readable *Capitalism and Colonialism in Mozambique*. Isaacman and Ranger have written about the Barue rising in 1917, and there are three important anthropological studies of the peoples of southern Mozambique by Junod, Fuller and Helgesson all of which are concerned with the impact of Christianity and mine labour. Vail has written an article surveying the history of the chartered companies, and Neil Tomlinson has published some of his research into the labour history of the Mozambique Company in a collection of papers, given at a conference in Edinburgh in 1978, in which a number of other research reports on the modern history of Mozambique are included.

The Nationalist Risings

An immense amount has been written about the nationalist parties, the wars of liberation and the post-independence prospects of the territories. John Marcum's exhaustive study of the movements in Angola can be supplemented with somewhat more digestible accounts by Wheeler and Pélissier and Henderson, while Andrade and Ollivier have produced a tight economic analysis on Angola in the 1960s. Henriksen's *Mozambique* contains a good account of the war in east Africa, and there is a valuable short account at the end of Vail and White. Of the writings of the nationalists, Mondlane's *The*

Struggle for Mozambique and Cabral's *Revolution in Guiné* are basic texts. Of personal accounts of the war, Basil Davidson's books on Angola and Guiné are distinguished by their excellent writing; John Paul's *Mozambique* is perhaps the most personal and politically unpretentious account of the war. Hastings'· *Wiriyamu*, following his press articles in 1973, undoubtedly made the greatest impact. Keith Middlemass's *Cabora Bassa* is a study of the economics and politics of the Zambesi dam.

Guiné and the Islands

The writings of Nevinson and Harris made São Tomé widely known at the beginning of this century; since then the most significant book has been Lyall's account of his travels in Cape Verde and Guiné.

Portugal

For English readers wanting to find out about modern Portugal two books are indispensable: Oliveira Marques' history of Portugal and Robinson's *Contemporary Portugal*, which manages to impart more information per square inch of print than one would have thought possible. Wheeler's *Republican Portugal* is a detailed political history, while Graham and Makler's book, also confusingly entitled *Contemporary Portugal*, is a collection of essays by political and social scientists aimed evidently at an academic readership. Other writings on modern Portugal have a more obvious political intent. On the political right there are biographies of Salazar by Derrick and Egerton and a brilliant journalistic portrait by Ferro. The most responsible and recent study of this kind is *Salazar and Modern Portugal* by Hugh Kay. Nogueira, Portugal's foreign minister for many years, explains the régime's diplomatic position in *The United Nations and Portugal*. On the political left there have been personal memoirs by Galvão and Soares and an excellent and occasionally profound study of modern Portugal by Figueiredo. The interesting work *Oldest Ally* by Fryer and Pinheiro presents the rare combination of a traveller's portrait of Portugal with Marxist social and political analysis. Highly entertaining also is Bloom's account of Alves Reis and the great currency fraud of the 1920s.

British Government Publications

British Government publications form an important source for the history of the Portuguese colonies in the twentieth century. Up to 1916, regular reports by British consuls were presented to parliament, and can be consulted in the annual series of Parliamentary Papers. After 1916, occasional consular reports were published by the Department of Overseas Trade. During the war, handbooks were prepared by the Foreign Office, largely from consular reports, and there is one for each of the Portuguese colonies. The naval intelligence division of the Admiralty also produced detailed handbooks for Portuguese East Africa and the Niassa Company's territory. During the Second World War they produced a volume on Portugal itself.

Bibliographies

Costa's bibliography of Mozambique, published in 1946, is now very much out of date. Rita Ferreira's ethnographical bibliography is still useful. There is an important bibliography of Mozambique since 1920 by Allen, and Isaacman's *Tradition of Resistance*. . . contains a full and valuable bibliography.

Angola lacks a good general bibliography, but works listed in Pélissier, Bender and Clarence Smith form a comprehensive list.

McCarthy has produced a bibliography for Cape Verde and Guiné.

Ronald Chilcote has published a list for the nationalist movements, now somewhat out of date, and there was a further list published by Flores in *Current African Bibliography*, 1974.

SELECT BIBLIOGRAPHY

This bibliography only includes items referred to in the text.

MANUSCRIPTS

Dr A.J.Board to family, Balovale, 26.9.1935.
(Copies of Dr Board's letters are in the author's possession)

Public Record Office, London (FO 371)

5491 (1920)	Encloses G.Lardner Burke to CO,17.11.1920.
5492 (1920)	Petition signed by British residents of St Vincent, 28.8.1920.
7109 (1921)	Portugal Annual Report, 1920.
7110 (1921)	Consul-General Bringes to FO, Luanda, 16.4.1921.
7211 (1922)	Consul-General Hutcheon to FO, Luanda, 12.8.1922.
8368 (1922)	Report of Vice-Consul, St Vincent, 20.12.1921.
8374 (1922)	Consul-General Hutcheon to FO, Luanda, 28.9.1922.
8374 (1922)	Ambassador Carnegie to FO, Lisbon, 13.12.1922.
8375 (1922)	Coded telegram Smuts to FO, 31.1.1922.
8377 (1922)	Enclosing Acting Governor of Tanganyika to CO, Dar es Salaam, 27.5.1922 and 4.10.1922.
9480 (1923)	Acting Consul-General Long to FO, Lourenço Marques, 13.12.1922.
9485 (1923)	BSA Co to FO, 'Memorandum on the Port of Beira', 5.12.1923.
10590 (1924)	Portugal Annual Report, 1923.
11086 (1925)	Consul-General Long to FO, Lourenço Marques, 24.2.1925.
11094 (1925)	Minute by Villiers on *Diário de Notícias* to Austen Chamberlain, 16.11.1925.
11934 (1926)	Minute by T.S.Shone 10.3.1926.
11934 (1926)	'Portuguese Misfeances', 10.3.1926.

PRESS REPORTS, ARTICLES, ETC.

The Guardian, *London*

'The past threatens Portugal's future' by Richard Gott, 23.3.1970.
'A new era in Portugal' by Richard Gott, 25.3.1970.
'Cabora Bassa — symbol of white rule', 30.4.1971.

Rhodesia Herald, *Salisbury*

'Portuguese and rebels locked in combat' by Lord Kilbracken, 22.9.1965.

The Sunday Times, *London*
'Dynamite on the Zambesi', 25.10.1970.
'The men who killed black Africa's top guerrilla' by Basil Davidson, 8.4.1973.

Daily Telegraph, *London*
'Portugal goes her own way' by Sir Colin Coote, 4.4.1969.

The Times, *London*
'Black man in search of power, 1', 11.3.1968.
'Black man in search of power, 2', 12.3.1968.
'Weary hide and seek war in Angola', 12.8.1969.
Letter from Sir Dingle Foot, 18.5.1970.
'African guerrillas meet the Pope', 3.7.1970.

BRITISH GOVERNMENT PUBLICATIONS

Admiralty (Naval Intelligence Division)

A Manual of Portuguese East Africa (London, 1920).
A Manual of Portuguese Nyasaland (London, 1920).
Spain and Portugal, vol.2:*Portugal* (London, 1942).

Department of Overseas Trade

Report on the Economic Situation in Angola, 1925.
Report on the Commercial, Economic and Financial Condition of Portuguese East Africa, 1927.
Economic Conditions in Portuguese East Africa, 1929.
Economic Conditions in Portuguese East Africa, 1935.
Report on Economic and Commercial Conditions in Angola, 1937.
Report on Economic and Commercial Conditions in Portuguese East Africa, 1938.
Portuguese West Africa: Angola, 1949.

Parliamentary Papers

1908,cxv, 'Report for the Year 1906 on the Trade and Commerce of Angola'.
1908,cxv, 'Report for the Years 1906-7 on the Trade of Angola'.
1910, ci, 'Report for the Year 1908 on the Trade of the Province of Angola'.
1911-12,xcix, 'Report for the Year 1911 on the Trade of the Cape Verde Islands'.
1912-13,xcix, Report for the Year 1911. Trade of the Portuguese Possessions in East Africa'.
1914, 'Report on the Trade, Agriculture etc. of Portuguese Guinea'.
1914-16,lxxiv, 'Report for the Year 1914 on the Trade of San Thomé and Principe'.

Foreign Office

Portuguese Guinea (London, 1920),Handbook no.118.
San Thomé and Principe (London, 1920),Handbook no.119.

PORTUGUESE OFFICIAL PUBLICATIONS

Anuário da Guiné Portuguêsa (Lisbon, 1948),edited by Fausto Dias.
Anuário de Moçambique (Lourenço Marques, 1917), edited by Sousa Ribeiro.
Cabo Verde, vol. 1 of *Informação Econômica sobre o Império*. Edições da Exposição Colonial Portuguêsa (Oporto, 1934).
Cabo Verde na Exposição-Feira de Angola (Praia, 1938).
Distrito de Tete: Relatório do Governador 1911-1912 (Lourenço Marques, 1913).
Providencias tomadas pelo General J.M.R. Norton de Matos, como Alto Commissário da Republica e Governador Geral (Lisbon, 1922).
——, Decreto no. 1, mandando por em vigor 'Estatuto do Alto Commissário da Republica em Angola'.
——, Decreto no. 4, promulgando a Carta Orgânica da Provincia de Angola.
——, Decreto no. 40, revogando todas as providencias sobre trabalho indigena, posteriores a 18 de Abril de 1918.
——, Decreto no. 77, regulamentando a existencia e funcionamento das missões religiosas.
Provincia de Moçambique: Relatórios annexo ao Boletim Official (Lourenço Marques, 1909).
Recenseamento Geral da População em 1950 (Lourenço Marques, 1953).
Relatório, Propostas de Lei e Documentos . . . apresentados na Camara dos Senhores Deputados . . . em Sessão de 20 de Março de 1899 by António Eduardo Villaça (Lisbon, 1899).
Rendimento do Imposto do Carvão de Pedra na Ilha de S.Vicente.
Movimento de Serviçaes e Colonos na Provincia de S.Thomé.

O.E.C.D.

Portugal (Paris,1966).

UNITED NATIONS

Economic Survey of Africa since 1950 (New York, 1959).

BOOKS AND ARTICLES

Abshire, D.M. and Samuels, M.A.,*Portuguese Africa: a Handbook* (London, 1969).
Addicott, L., *Cry Angola!* (London, 1962).
Allen, C., 'Mozambique since 1920: a Select Bibliography', *Mozambique* (cyclostyled, University of Edinburgh, 1979).
Almeida, A.A. de, *Monografia Agricola de Massinga* (Lisbon, 1959).
Almeida de Eça, F.G. de, *História das Guerras no Zambeze: Chicoa e Massangano (1807-1888)*, 2 vols. (Lisbon, 1953-4).
Alpers, E.A., 'The French Slave Trade in East Africa (1721-1810)', *Cahiers d'Etudes Africaines*, vol. 10, pp. 80-124.
——, *Ivory and Slaves in East Central Africa* (London, 1975).
Andrade, M. de and Ollivier, M., *The War in Angola* (Dar es Salaam, 1975).
Anstey, R.T., *Britain and the Congo in the Nineteenth Century* (Oxford, 1962).
Axelson, E., *Portuguese in South-East Africa 1600-1700* (Johannesburg, 1960).
——, *Portugal and the Scramble for Africa* (Johannesburg, 1967).
——, *Portuguese in South-East Africa 1488-1600* (Johannesburg, 1973).
Barata, O., 'O Povoamento de Cabo Verde, Guiné e S.Thomé', *Cabo Verde, Guiné, São Tomé e Principe*, Curso de Extensão Universitária, ano lectivo de 1965-66.
Barns, T.A., *Angolan Sketches* (London, 1928).
——, 'Through Portuguese West Africa', *Journal of the African Society*, vol. 28, 1928-9, pp. 224-34.
Bender, G.J. *Angola under the Portuguese* (London, 1978).
Bentley Duncan, T., *Atlantic Islands* (Chicago, 1972).
Bhila, H.H.K., 'The Manyika and the Portuguese, 1575-1863' (unpublished Ph.D. thesis, London University, 1971).
Birmingham, D., *Trade and Conflict in Angola* (Oxford, 1966).
——, 'Early African Trade in Angola and its Hinterland', in Birmingham and Gray (ed.), *Pre-Colonial African Trade* (Oxford, 1970).
——, 'The Coffee Barons of Cazengo', *Journal of African History*, vol. 24, 1978, pp. 523-38.
Bloom, M.T., *The Man who stole Portugal* (New York, 1966).
Boleo, O., *Moçambique* (Lisbon, 1951).
Boserup, E., *The Conditions of Agricultural Growth* (London, 1965).
Bravo, N.S., *A Cultura Algodoeira na Economia do Norte de Moçambique* (Lisbon, 1963).
Brito, E., *A População de Cabo Verde no Século XX* (Lisbon, 1963).
Brito Camacho, M., *Moçambique: Problemas Coloniais* (Lisbon, 1926).
Cabral, A., *Revolution in Guinea* (London, 1969).
Cameron, V.L., *Across Africa* (London, 5th edn, 1877).
Capela, J., *O Imposto de Palhota e a Introdução do Modo de Produção capitalista nas Colónias* (Oporto, 1977).
Carreira, A., *Panaria Cabo-Verdiano-Guineense* (Lisbon, 1968).

——, *Angola: da Escravatura ão Trabalho Livre* (Lisbon, 1977).
Carson Graham, R.H., *Under Seven Congo Kings* (London, 1930).
Castro, A., *A Economia Portuguêsa do Século XX* (Lisbon, 1973).
Cech, D., *Inhambane* (Wiesbaden, 1974).
Chilcote, R., *Emerging Nationalism in Portuguese Africa* (Stanford, 1969).
Childs, G.M., *Umbundu Kinship and Character* (Oxford, 1949).
Clarence-Smith, G., 'Mossamedes and its Hinterland, 1875–1915' (unpublished Ph.D. thesis, London University, 1975).
——, *Slaves, Peasants and Capitalists in Southern Angola 1840–1926* (Cambridge, 1979).
Coissoro, N., 'O Regime das Terras em Moçambique', *Moçambique*, Curso de Extensão Universitária ano lectivo 1964-5 (Lisbon).
Cole, G.D.H., *The Common People* (London, 1938; 2nd Edn, 1946).
——, *Companhia de Diamantes de Angola* (Lisbon, 1963).
Corry, J., *Observations upon the Windward Coast of Africa* (London, 1807; reprint, 1968).
Costa, M., *Bibliográfia Geral de Moçambique* (Lisbon, 1946).
Costa, R. da, *O Desenvolvimento do Capitalismo em Portugal* (Lisbon, 1975).
Crone, G.R. (ed.), *The Voyages of Cadamosto* (London, 1937).
Curtin, P., *The Atlantic Slave Trade: a Census* (Madison, Wisconsin, 1969).
Davidson, B., *The Liberation of Guiné* (London, 1969).
——, *In the Eye of the Storm* (London, 1972).
Derrick, M., *The Portugal of Salazar* (London, 1938).
Dias, Jill, 'Black Chiefs, White Traders and Colonial Policy near the Kwanza: Kabuku Ambilo and the Portuguese 1873–1896', *Journal of African History*, vol. 17, 1976, pp. 245-65.
Dias, Jorge, 'Estruturas Socio-economicas em Moçambique', *Moçambique*. Curso de Extensão Universitária, ano lectivo 1964-5, pp. 77–96.
Diffie, B. and Winius, G., *Foundations of the Portuguese Empire 1415–1580* (Oxford, 1977).
Drechsler, H., 'Germany and South Angola 1898–1903', *Présence Africaine*, vol. 14/15, 1962, pp. 7-23.
Dubins, B., 'Political History of the Comoro Islands 1795–1886 (unpublished Ph.D. thesis, Boston University, 1972).
Duffy, J., *Portuguese Africa* (Cambridge, Mass., 1959).
——, *A Question of Slavery* (Oxford, 1967).
Edwards, A., *The Ovimbundu under two Sovereignties* (Oxford, 1962).
Egerton, F.C.C., *Salazar* (London, 1943).
Faria, D., *Portugal do Capricorno* (Lisbon, 1965).
Felgas, H.E., *História do Congo Português* (Carmona, 1958).
Ferro, A., *Salazar: Portugal and her Leader* (London, 1935).
Figueiredo, A. de, *Portugal: Fifty Years of Dictatorship* (London, 1975).
Figueiredo de Barros, A.F. *Provincia de Cabo Verde: Relatório e Subsidios no Inquerito determinado pelo Governo desta Provincia* (Praia, 1917).
Flores, M., 'A Bibliographic Contribution to the Study of Portuguese Africa (1965–1972)', *A Current Bibliography of African Affairs*, vol. 7, 1974, pp. 116-37.

Select Bibliography

Freire de Andrade, A., *Rapport presenté au Ministre des Colonies à propos du Livre 'Portuguese Slavery' du Missionaire John Harris* (Lisbon, 1914).
Fryer, P. and Pinheiro, P.M., *Oldest Ally* (London, 1961).
Fuller, C., 'An Ethnohistoric Study of Continuity and Change in Gwambe' (unpublished Ph.D. thesis Northwestern Univ., Evanston, Ill., 1955).
Galvão H., *The Santa Maria: My Crusade for Portugal* (London, 1961).
—— and Selvagem, C., *Império Ultramarino Português* (Lisbon, 1952): vol. iii, *Angola*; vol. iv, *Moçambique*.
Gaspar, J.M., 'A Colonisação branca em Angola e Moçambique', *Estudos de Ciencias Políticas e Sociais*, vol. 7, pp. 31-54.
Gavicho de Lacerda, F., *Cartas da Zambezia* (2nd edn, Lisbon, 1923).
Gomes da Costa, General, *A Guerra nas Colônias* (Lisbon, 1925).
Graham, G.S., *Great Britain in the Indian Ocean* (Oxford, 1967).
Graham, L.S., and Makler, H.M., *Contemporary Portugal* (Austin, Texas, 1979).
Gregory, T., *Ernest Oppenheimer* (Oxford, 1962).
Hafkin, N.J., 'Trade, Society and Politics in Northern Mozambique, c. 1753–1913' (unpublished Ph.D.thesis, Boston University, 1973).
Hammond, R.J., *Portugal and Africa 1815-1910* (Stanford, 1966).
Hanna, A.J., *The Beginnings of Nyasaland and North-Eastern Rhodesia* (Oxford, 1956).
Harris, J.H., *Dawn in Darkest Africa* (London, 1914).
Hastings, A., *Wiryamu* (London, 1974).
Hedges, D., 'Trade and Politics in Southern Mozambique', unpublished Ph.D. thesis, (London University, 1977).
Helgesson, A., 'The Tshwa Response to Christianity', unpublished MA thesis, Witwatersrand University, 1971).
Henderson, L.W., *Angola: Five Centuries of Conflict* (London, 1979).
Henriksen, T., *Mozambique* (London, 1978).
Herrick, A.B., *Area Handbook for Mozambique* (Washington D.C., 1969).
Hutchinson, R. and Martelli, G., *Robert's People* (London, 1971).
Isaacman, A., 'The Origin, Formation and Early History of the Chikunda of South Central Africa', *Journal of African History*, vol. 13, 1972, pp. 443–62.
——, *Mozambique: the Africanization of a European Institution, the Zambesi Prazos 1750-1902* (Madison, Wisconsin, 1972).
——, *The Tradition of Resistance in Mozambique* (London, 1976).
Junod, H., 'Le Mouvement de Mourimi', *Journal de Psychologie Normale et Pathologique*, Vol. 21, 1924, pp. 865–82.
——, *The Life of a South African Tribe*, 2 vols. (2nd edn, London, 1927).
Katzenellenbogen, S., *Railways and the Copper Mines of Katanga* (Oxford, 1973).
——, *South Africa and Southern Mozambique: Labour, Railways and Trade in the Making of a Relationship* (Manchester, 1981).
Kay, H., *Salazar and Modern Portugal* (London, 1970).
Kimble, G.T., *Tropical Africa*, 2 vols. (New York, 1960).
Kuder, M., *Moçambique* (Darmstadt, 1975).
Lanning, G. with Mueller, M., *Africa Undermined* (London, 1979).

Lavradio, Marquês do, *Portugal em África depois de 1851* (Lisbon, 1936).
Liesegang, G., *Beiträge zur Geschichte des Reiches der Gaza Nguni im Südlichen Moçambique* (Cologne, 1967).
Lima, M.H.F., *Nação Ovambo* (Lisbon, 1977).
Lima, J.B.F., *Distrito de Moçambique: Circunscrição de Erate* (Lisbon, 1962).
Livingstone, D., *Missionary Travels and Researches in South Africa* (London, 1857; new edition, 1905).
Lobo Bulhões, M.E., *Les Colonies Portugaises* (Lisbon, 1878).
Lupi. E. do C., *Angoche* (Lisbon, 1907).
Lyall, A., *Black and White make Brown* (London, 1938).
Lyne, R.N., *Mozambique: its Agricultural Development* (London, 1913).
─── , 'The Agriculture of Mozambique Province, Portuguese East Africa', *Bulletin of the Imperial Institute*, vol. 9, 1913, pp. 102-10.
McCarthy J.M., *Guinea-Bissau and Cape Verde Islands: a Comprehensive Bibliography* (New York, 1977).
Mackay, W., *The Prisoner of Chiloane* (London, 1890).
Marcum, J., *The Angolan Revolution*, vol. 1, *1950-62* (Boston, Mass., 1969).
Marques, J.M., *Esboço para um Monografia Agricola do Posto Sede dos Muchopes* (Lisbon, 1961).
Martin, P., *The External Trade of the Loango Coast* (Oxford, 1972).
Marwick, M.G., 'Another Modern Anti-Witchcraft Movement in East Central Africa', *Africa*, vol. 20, 1950, pp. 100-12.
Maugham, R.C.F., *Zambezia* (London, 1910).
Maxwell, K., 'Pombal and the Nationalisation of the Luso-Brazilian Economy', *Hispanic American Historical Review*, vol. 48, 1968, pp. 608-31.
Medeiros, C.A., *A Colonização das Terras Altas da Huila* (Lisbon, 1976).
Mello Machado, A.J. de, *Entre os Macuas de Angoche* (Lisbon, 1968).
Mendes, A., *O Trabalho Assalariado em Angola* (Lisbon, 1966).
Middlemass, K., *Cabora Bassa: Engineering and Politics in Southern Africa* (London, 1975).
Miller, J.C., 'Slaves, Slavers and Social Change in Nineteenth Century Kasanje', in Heimer (ed.), *Social Change in Angola* (Munich, 1973).
─── , *Kings and Kinsmen* (Oxford, 1976).
Mitchell, H.F., *Aspects of Urbanisation and Age Structure in Lourenço Marques, 1957* (Lusaka, 1975).
Mondlane, E., *The Struggle for Mozambique* (London, 1969).
Mouser, B.L., 'Trade, Coasters and conflict in the Rio Pongo from 1790-1808', *Journal of African History*, vol. 14, 1973, pp. 45-64.
Mouzinho de Albuquerque, J., *Moçambique 1896-1898* (Lisbon, 1899).
Mudenge, S.I., 'The Roswi Empire and the Feira of Zumbo' (unpublished Ph.D. thesis, London University, 1972).
Muralha, P., *Terras de Africa* (Lisbon, 1925).
Naylon, J., 'An Appraisement of Spanish Irrigation and Land Settlement Policies since 1939', *Iberian Studies*, vol. 2, 1973, pp. 12-17.
Neil Tomlinson, B., 'The Nyassa Chartered Company: 1891-1929', *Journal of African History*, vol. 18, 1977, pp. 109-28.

——, 'The Growth of a Colonial Economy and the Development of African Labour: Manica and Sofala and the Mozambique Chartered Company, 1892-1942' in *Mozambique* (cyclostyled, University of Edinburgh, 1979).
Neto, J.P., *Angola: Meio Século de Integração* (Lisbon, 1964).
——, *Comercio Externo de Cabo Verde, Guiné e São Tomé e Principe* (Lisbon, 1966).
Nevinson, H., *A Modern Slavery* (London, 1906; reprinted, 1968).
Newitt, M.D.D., 'Angoche, the Slave Trade and the Portuguese, c. 1844-1910', *Journal of African History*, vol. 13, 1972, pp. 659-72.
——, *Portuguese Settlement on the Zambesi* (London, 1973).
——, 'Portuguese Conquistadores in Eastern Africa', *History Today*, vol. 30, 1980, pp. 19-24.
Nogueira, F., *United Nations and Portugal* (London, 1963).
Norton de Matos, J.M.R., *A Situação Financeira e Econômica da Provincia de Angola* (Lisbon, 1914).
Nunes, H., 'Território de Manica e Sofala', *Boletim da Agencia Geral das Colonias*, no. 50, 1929, pp. 202-43.
Oliveira Marques, A.H., *History of Portugal*, 2 vols. (New York, 1972).
Orde Browne, G.St.J., *The African Labourer* (Oxford, 1933; reprint 1967).
Paiva Couceiro, H.de, *Angola: Dois Annos de Governo,* Edição Commemorativa (Lisbon, 1948).
Paul, J., *Mozambique: Memoirs of a Revolution* (London, 1975).
——, 'Revolution and Quietism: the Anglican Experience in Mozambique', *Mozambique* (cyclostyled, University of Edinburgh, 1979).
Pélissier, R., *Les Guerres Grises* (Orgeval, 1977).
——, *La Colonie du Minotaure* (Orgeval, 1978).
——, *Le Naufrage des Caravelles* (Orgeval, 1979).
Pires, E.A., *Evolução do Ensino em Moçambique* (Lourenço Marques, 1966).
Pössinger, H., *Landwirtschaftliche Entwicklung in Angola und Moçambique* (Munich, 1968).
——, 'Interrelations between Economic and Social Change in Rural Africa: the Case of the Ovimbundu of Angola' in Heimer (ed.), *Social Change in Angola* (Munich, 1973).
Ranger, T.O., 'Revolt in Portuguese East Africa', *St Antony's Papers*, no. 15, 1963, pp. 54-80.
Rea, W.F., *The Economics of the Zambesi Missions 1580-1759* (Rome, 1976).
Ribeiro, E., 'A Zambezia Agricola', *Boletim da Agencia Geral das Colônias*, no. 50, 1929, pp. 59-73.
Richards, A., 'A Modern Movement of Witch-finders', *Africa*, vol. 8, 1935, pp. 448-61.
Rita Ferreira, A., *Bibliógrafia Etnológica de Moçambique* (Lisbon, 1962).
——, *O Movimento Migratório de Trabalhadores entre Moçambique e a Africa do Sul* (Lisbon, 1963).
Robinson, R., *Contemporary Portugal* (London, 1979).
Rodney, W., *History of the Upper Guinea Coast 1545-1800* (Oxford, 1970).
Rodrigues Júnior, A., *Colonizacão* (Lourenço Marques, 1958).

Ross, E.A., *Report on Employment of Native Labour in Portuguese Africa* (New York, 1925).
Salgado, F.R., *Le Brésil et les Colonies Portugaises* (Lisbon, 1930).
Samuels, M.A., *Education in Angola 1878–1914* (New York, 1970).
Santos, E. dos, *Religiões de Angola* (Lisbon, 1969).
Santos, F.M.O., 'Moçambique: Aspectos Demográficos e Econômicos', *Boletim da Agencia Geral das Colônias*, no 50, 1929, pp. 3–10.
Shepherd, W.C.A., 'Recruiting in Portuguese East Africa of Natives for the Mines', *Journal of the African Sociaty*, vol. 33, 1934, pp. 253–60.
Silva Cunha, J.M.da, *O Trabalho Indígena* (Lisbon, 1955).
Silva Rego, A. da, *O Ultramar Português no Século XIX* (Lisbon, 1969).
Soares, M., *Portugal's Struggle for Liberty* (London, 1975).
Soremekun, F., 'Religion and Politics in Angola', *Cahiers d'Etudes Africaines*, vol. 11, 1971, pp. 341–77.
Teixeira, B., *The Fabric of Terror* (New York, 1965).
Teixeira da Mota, A., *Guiné Portuguesa*, 2 vols. (Lisbon, 1954).
Teixeira Pinto, J., *A Ocupação Militar da Guiné* (Lisbon, 1936).
Tenreiro, F., *A Ilha de São Tomé* (Lisbon, 1961).
Thomas, R.G., 'Forced Labour in British West Africa: the Case of the Northern Territories of the Gold Coast 1906–1927', *Journal of African History*, vol. 14, 1973, pp. 79–103.
Tucker, J.T., *Angola: the Land of the Blacksmith Prince* (London, 1933).
Vail, L., 'The Making of an Imperial Slum: Nyasaland and its Railways, 1895–1935', *Journal of African History*, vol. 16, 1975, pp. 89–112.
——, 'Mozambique's Chartered Companies: the Rule of the Feeble', *Journal of African History*, vol. 17, 1976, pp. 389–416.
—— and White, L., *Capitalism and Colonialism in Mozambique: a Study of the Quelimane District* (London, 1980).
Van Onselen, C., 'Randlords and Rotgut 1886–1903', *History Workshop*, Autumn 1976, pp. 33–89.
Vansina, J., *The Kingdoms of the Savanna* (Madison, Wisconsin, 1966).
Vasconcellos, E.J. de C., *S. Tomé e Principe* (Lisbon, 1918).
Verger, P., *Bahia and West African Trade 1549–1851* (Ibadan, 1964).
Vincent Smith, J., 'Britain, Portugal and the First World War, 1914–1916', *European Studies Review* vol. 4, 1974, pp. 207–38.
——, 'The Portuguese Republic and Britain 1910–1914', *Journal of Contemporary History*, vol. 10, 1975, pp. 707–27.
Vintras, R.E., *The Portugal Connection* (London, 1974).
Warhurst, P., *Anglo-Portuguese Relations in South-Central Africa 1890–1900* (London, 1962).
Wheeler, D., 'Gungunyane the Negotiator: a Study in African Diplomacy', *Journal of African History*, vol. 9, 1968, pp. 585–602.
—— and Pélissier, R., *Angola* (London, 1971).
—— and Christensen, C.D., 'To Rise with one Mind: the Bailundu War of 1902', in Heimer (ed.), *Social Change in Angola* (Munich, 1973).
——, *Republican Portugal* (London, 1978).
White, C.B., 'New England Merchants and Missionaries in Coastal Nineteenth Century Portuguese East Africa' (unpublished Ph.D. thesis,

Select Bibliography

Boston University, 1974).
Wield, D., 'Mine Labour and Peasant Production in Southern Mozambique', *Mozambique* (cyclostyled, University of Edinburgh, 1979).
Wiese, C., 'Expedição Portuguesa a M'Pesene', *Boletim da Sociedade de Geografia de Lisboa*, 1891, pp. 235-73, 297-321, 331-412, 415-30, 465-97; 1892, pp. 373-431, 435-516.
——, 'Zambezia', *Boletim da Sociedade de Geografia de Lisboa*, 1907, pp. 241-7.
Wilensky, A.H., *Trends in Portuguese Overseas Legislation for Africa* (Braga, 1971).
Willequet, J., 'Anglo-German Rivalry in Belgian and Portuguese Africa', in Gifford and Louis (ed.), *Britain and Germany in Africa* (London, 1967).
Young, S., 'Fertility and Famine. Women's Agricultural History in Southern Mozambique', in Palmer and Parsons (ed.), *The Roots of Rural Poverty in Central and Southern Africa* (London, 1977).

INDEX

Abdul Injai, 69
Accão Nacional de Moçambique, 173
Act of Union, 35
Acto Colonial, 185, 186
Administration, colonial, 139, 147, 169, 199, 245; in Angola, 92, 105, 110-1, 119, 187-8; of Concession Companies, 93; development of, 160-3, 175-7, 184-6, 188; of empire prior to 1850, 3; of empire under the New State, 43, 88; in Guiné, 188; inefficiency of, 115, 119, 163, 176, 188; *mestiços* in, 143, 163, 216; in Mozambique, 160, 175; *see also* Chartered Companies, *chefe do posto*, Concession Companies, *palhota*, *prazos*, *regedor*
Administrative Overseas Reform Act, 185
Admiralty, British, 85, 252, 255
Afrikaner Nationalists, 48, 198
Afro-Portuguese; in East Africa, 8, 9, 10, 11, 13, 14, 20, 21, 24, 28, 29, 57, 60, 62, 86, 103, 148; in West Africa, 2, 3, 4, 5, 6, 13, 14, 15, 17, 20, 24, 54, 148, 203; *see also mestiços, muzungos*
agriculture, 106, 194-5, 199, 201; African in Angola, 94-5, 102-3, 109, 134-5, 180; African in Mozambique, 18, 34, 83, 94-5, 98, 99-100, 103-4, 114; in Cape Verde, 211, 212, 216; compulsory crop growing, 121-4, 136; in Guiné, 103-4, 188; in São Tomé, 209-10; white in Angola, 109, 134-5, 156-8, 178; white in Mozambique, 34, 81, 88, 159, 180, 196; and underdevelopment, 12-13
Agua-Ize, São Tomé, 206
Aguiar, Alfredo de, 145
Ajuda, Dahomey, 4, 5
Albasini family, 145
Albuquerque, Afonso de, 50
aldea, 78, 248
aldeamentos, 124, 231, 239, 248
Algeria, 225
Almeida, Francisco de, 50
Almeida, João de, 65-6
Alves Reis, 178
Alves Roçadas, J.A., 162
Ambaca, Angola, 178
ambaquista, 6, 248
Amboim, Angola, 178
Ambriz, Angola, 22, 65
American Board Commissioners, 125
Amerindians, 142
Andrade, José do Rosario, 28
Andrade, Mario de, 237, 257
Angoche, Mozambique, 16, 18, 22, 60, 62, 63
Angolares, 204, 207, 209, 210, 248
Anno Bom, 201
anti-clericalism, 44
Anti-slavery Society, British and Foreign, 39
António Enes, town of, Mozambique, 126
Arabs, 8, 15, 52
aringa, 59, 103, 248
armed forces; *see* Portuguese
Arriaga, General Kaulza de, 231, 236, 245
assimilado, 101, 105, 138-147, 248; *see also civilisado*, integration, *mestiços*

264

Index

Assis Júnior, A. de, 144, 146
Atlantic, 25, 38, 45, 201
Australia, 151
Austria, 9, 188
Axis powers, 45, 46
Azores, 1, 153, 201, 203, 235; base in Second World War, 45

backwoodsmen; *see also* Afro-Portuguese
Bahia, Brazil, 4
Bailundu kingdom, Angola, 17; rebellion in, 126, 251
Baixa de Cassange, Angola, 124, 228, 240, 242
BaKongo people, Angola, 51, 70, 104, 138, 170, 227, 229, 230, 241; *see also* Belgian Congo, Congo Free State, Kongo, São Salvador, Zaire
Balanta people, Guiné, 69, 104
balance of payments; of colonies, 112, 190, 191, 195, 210, 217; of Portugal, 73, 189, 195, 221
Balfour, A.J., 41
Balovale, 119
bananas, 194
Banco de Angola e Metropole, 178
Banco Nacional Ultramarino, 76, 175, 176, 178, 179, 191; *see also* currency
Baptist Missions, 65–6, 124, 125, 131, 132
barkcloth trade, 2
Barns, T.A., 105, 159, 208–9, 257
Barotseland, 24, 30
Barue, Mozambique, 55, 59, 60, 79, 81, 87, 129–30; rebellion of 1917, 41, 61, 70, 88, 119
Basas Orgânicas da Administração Colonial, 185
beans, 194
Beira, Mozambique, 83, 137, 173, 254; blockade, 235; port of, 79, 198; railway to Umtali, 34, 79, 198; Trans-Zambesia railway from, 36, 83, 179, 198; *see also* railways

Beit, Alfred, 37
Beja Coup, 224
Belgian Congo, 131, 133, 229; *see also* Congo Free State, Zaire
Belgium, 86, 90, 92, 121; *see also* Leopold II
Belo, João, 184, 185
Bender, Gerald, 154, 219, 251, 257
Bengo river, Angola, 157
Benguela, Angola, 3, 6, 17, 172; description by Cameron, 149, 151–2
Benguela highlands, 154
Benguela Railway, 37–8, 76, 77, 89, 90, 118, 154, 178, 198, 232; *see also* Williams
Benin, 2
Berlin Congress, 27, 30, 65, 73, 124
Biafada people, Guiné, 104
Biafra, 233
Bible, 132, 133
Bihé, Angola, 17, 125, 135
Bismarck, Otto von, 27, 32
Bissagos Islands, Guiné, 70
Bissau, Guiné, 5, 51, 69
Blantyre, 36
Boa Vista Island, Cape Verde, 211, 213
Board, A.J., 119, 254
Boers, 26, 34; in Angola, 53, 67, 102, 155, 156; *see also* Transvaal
Bolama, Guiné, 4, 5, 26, 68
Bonjisi, 130
Boroma Mission, Mozambique, 125
Boror Company, 87, 88, 116
Botelho, General Moniz, 222
Brava Island, Cape Verde, 211, 212
Bravo, N., 122, 123, 257
Brazil, 78, 150, 155, 203, 216; emigration to and from Portugal, 153, 154, 164; independence of, 18, 25; salt trade with, 212, 213; slave trade with 3, 4, 5, 7, 10, 13, 157
Brazzaville, 225
British consuls; in Luanda, 73, 108, 111, 178, 206, 254, 255; Lourenço Marques, 131, 254, 255; São Vicente, 214–5, 254

Brito, Eduino, 216, 257
Brito Camacho, M., 159, 161, 163, 177, 192, 257
Brussels Conference, 75
Buba river, Guiné, 4
budgets: Angola, 178-9, 186; colonial, 73, 106, 175, 186, 188-9, 240; Mozambique, 112,; Portugal, 181; São Tome, 210; *see also* balance of payments
Buta, Alvaro Tulante, 66

Cabinda, 4, 5, 27, 65, 132; nationalist movement in, 232, 241; oilfields, 235
Cabora Bassa dam, 232, 235, 240
Cabral, Amilcar, 227, 228, 240, 257; assassination of, 241
Cacheu, Guiné: river, 4; Companies, 3
Caderneta, 108, 248
Caetano, Marcello, 185, 219, 236, 240, 242, 243, 244, 245
Caia, Mozambique, 116
Cameron, V.L., 149, 151-2, 257
Canary Islands, 201, 214
Cape Colony, 26, 34
Cape Delgado, Mozambique, 8
Cape Verde Islands; 15th- 16th centuries, 1, 2, 3, 201-3; 17th-19th centuries, 4, 211; coaling station at, 191, 213-5; economy of, 190, 217; emigration from, 207, 210, 215, 216; *mestiços* in, 142, 143-4, 163, 225; population of, 213; Portuguese influence in, 204; relations with Guiné, 68; salt trade from, 202, 212-3, 216; Tarrafal concentration camp, 152, 217
Capelo, H., 30
capital investment; in Angolan plantations, 19, 157, 180; in caravan trade, 17, 18; in charter companies, 79-89; in coffee, 135; in diamonds, 92-3; foreign, 169, 221, 235, 236; in Portugal, 29, 72-3, 183, 190, 243-4; Portuguese investment in colonies, 75-6, 180, 205-6, 220, 237-8, 239; in railways, 34, 90; and the scramble for Africa, 24-5, 79; in the slave trade, 3, 4, 16, 17; in sugar, 92, 158, 192-3; *see also* development plans
Capitão-mor, 55, 160
captaincy, 78, 201
caravan trade, 6, 9, 11, 12, 13, 14, 16, 17, 22, 62, 63, 70, 74, 84, 95-7, 103, 104, 125
Carmona, Oscar, 181
carrier service, 6, 13, 21, 56, 98, 102, 105, 107, 108
Carta Orgânica, 185
Carvalho, Henrique de, 30
Casamance river, Guiné, 4, 28, 69, 213
cashew, 20, 83, 159, 188, 221
Cassava, 13
Cassinga, Angola, 89, 221, 235, 238
Castile, 1, 7, 201; *see also* Spain
Castro, João de, deputy from São Tomé, 145
Catholicism, 100, 102, 132, 139, 149, 182, 203-4, 239; Catholic Missions, 64, 65, 67, 106, 124-5
Catumbela river, Angola, 157
Cazengo, Angola, 18, 22, 102, 109, 156, 157
Cela, Angola, 165; *see also colonatos*, white settlement
cement, 221, 238
censorship, 44
Central Africa; Portuguese trade with, 2-11, 23; partition of, 24-33; *see also* Rhodesia
Central America, 142
Chá Oriental, 136
Chaimite, battle of, 53, 58
Chamberlain, Austen, 41, 254
Charles et Georges, affair of the, 25
charter companies, 42, 73, 76, 79-85, 86, 89, 107, 141; *see also* British South African Company, Moçamedes Company, Mozambique Company, Niassa Company

Index

Châtelain, Héli, 125, 133
chefe do posto, 55, 100, 105, 108, 134, 161, 187, 188, 248
chicunda, 10, 11, 23, 52, 60, 61, 64, 79, 97, 248; see also slaves
chiefs, 14, 16, 18, 20, 22, 31, 38, 58, 59, 60, 62, 63, 64, 66, 68, 71, 84, 94, 97, 98, 99, 147, 160, 227; *regedores*, 100, 104-6, 108; indirect rule, 53-4
Childs, G.M., 127, 251, 258
Chimoio, Mozambique, 159
China, 233
Chinde, Mozambique, 36
Chopi people, Mozambique, 56, 59, 98, 138
Christianity, 12, 64, 124-34, 146, 210, 239; see also Catholicism, Missions, Protestantism
Chuabo people, Mozambique, 104
Church of England Missions, 35, 125-6, 133, 170
Churchill, W.S., 45
(cipais, 55, 56, 98, 248; see also Portuguese Armed Forces
(circunscrição, 161, 248; see also administration
civet, 2
civilisado, 101, 138-47, 161, 186, 210, 216, 248; see also *assimilado*, *mestiço*
Clarence-Smith, G., 155, 251, 258
climate, 148, 201, 211, 212, 216; see also drought
cloth trade, 2, 9, 11, 72, 217; see also textile industry
coal; Cape Verde coaling station, 191, 213-5; Moatize coalfields, 36, 179, 189; see also Mindelo, São Vicente
cocoa; in Angola, 18, 19; in São Tomé, 18, 19, 38, 40, 74, 76, 141, 170, 204-5, 206, 209-10
Codigo do Trabalho Indígena, 185
coffee; in Angola in the 19th century, 18, 19, 102, 157; in Angola pre-1940, 103, 135, 158, 220; in Angola post-war, 135, 170, 193, 194, 225, 232, 237, 238, 241; in Cape Verde, 212, 216; in Mozambique, 87; in São Tomé, 204-5, 206, 209
Coimbra University, 181
Cokwe people, Angola, 16, 17, 103, 125
colonatos, 103, 111, 164-7, 189, 196, 231, 248
Communism, 222, 227
Comoro Islands, 8, 9, 26, 62
Companhia Agricola Colonial, 205
Companhia Colonial de Buzi, 81
Companhia de Diamantes de Angola; see Diamang
Companhia União Fabril, 72
Company of Para e Maranhão, 3, 4
Compulsory Crop Growing, 95, 121-4, 136, 147, 185, 192
Concelho, 126, 161, 248; see also administration
Concession Companies, 44, 56, 72-93, 115, 121-4, 136, 159, 171, 175, 205-6; see also capital investment, Chartered Companies, Diamang, Sena Sugar
CONCP, 233
Congo Free State, 30, 37, 39, 40, 65, 85, 90, 196, 199; see also Belgian Congo, Zaire
Congo river, 2, 3, 5, 6, 22, 26, 27, 28, 29, 30, 34, 65, 73
Congregational Church, 128
Congress Party, 223
Conselho do Governo, 161, 171
Conselho Legislativo, 144, 171-2, 199
contract labour, 15, 51, 74, 88, 91, 93, 98, 101, 105, 106-20, 138, 141, 146, 157; in Mozambique Company territory, 82, 116; Scandals, 74-5, 158, 207-11; see also labour laws, migrant labour, South Africa
convicts, 51, 148, 150-2, 160-1
Cooléla, battle of, 58
co-operatives, 137
copper: Copperbelt, 38, 39, 90;

mines, 90, 221; trade in, 2, 37
copra, 18, 19, 87, 88, 94, 116, 194
Cordeiro, Luciano, 30
Cordon, Victor, 29
COREMO, 226, 233
Costa, Afonso, 44
Costa, Eduardo da, 176
Costa Gomes, F. de, 222, 245
Cotonang, 124
cotton, 183, 191, 220; in Angola, 18, 89, 106, 124, 155, 156, 157, 158, 194, 228; in Cape Verde, 1, 203; in Mozambique, 81, 106, 121-4, 136, 163, 191-2, 194; *see also* compulsory crop growing
Coutinho, João de Azevedo, 81
Craveiro Lopes, President, 222
Cruz, family of, 22, 28, 60
Cuamato, battle of, 67, 68
Cuango river, Angola, 6, 149
Cuanza river, Angola, 6, 13
Cuanza Norte, Angola, 135
Cuba: revolutionary influence of, 227, 246; slave trade with, 7, 10, 16
Cunen river, Angola, 27, 64, 67, 125, 155, 165, 197
currency, colonial, 76, 83, 87, 175, 176, 178, 179, 195, 220
Curzon, Lord, 41
Customs, 63, 73, 74, 84, 89, 97, 178, 189, 205; *see also* tariffs

Dahomey, 4
Dakar, 214
Damão, 46; *see also* Goa
Damaraland, 125
Dande river, Angola, 157
De Brazza, Count Savorgnan, 26
Delagoa Bay, Mozambique, 8, 25, 26, 98, 113; *see also* Lourenço Marques
Delgado, General Humberto, 173, 181, 222-3, 224, 228
Dembos, Angola, 64, 65, 66
Department of Native Affairs, Angola, 110
development plans, 189, 194, 195-7, 237-8

Diamang, 77, 92-3, 118, 121, 135, 141-2, 186
diamonds; in Angola, 92-3, 179, 190, 238; in South Africa, 19, 38
Diamond Corporation, 92
Diu, 48; *see also* Goa
drought, 68, 70, 99, 100, 103, 110, 155, 207, 211, 212-3, 215, 216, 217
Dutch; *see* Netherlands
Dutch East India Company, 78
Dutch Reformed Church, 126

East India Company, 78
education: for Africans, 101, 109, 139-41, 145, 146, 168, 196, 197, 221, 231, 239, 242; among Cape Verdians, 216, 225
Edwards, Adrian, 128, 134, 251, 258
EEC, 164, 221, 243
EFTA, 221
Egypt, 32, 163, 233
Elizabethville, 178
emigration, 119-20, 142, 147, 164, 197; to Brazil, 153, 164, 190; from Cape Verde, 204, 215, 216; to EEC, 164, 190, 221; to Nyasaland, 64, 73, 87, 117; from southern Mozambique, 19, 113; whites to South Africa, 136; to Zambia, 119; *see also* migrant labour, white settlers
Empresa Nacional de Navigação, 76
encomienda, 78
Enes, António, 58, 59, 86, 176, 177
English language, 215; press, 34, 83, 234; teaching, 125
epidemics, 114, 141, 142, 154, 208, 214
Escola Colonial, 162
Estado Novo (New State), 43-8, 101, 102, 111, 119, 121, 127, 161, 162, 164, 172, 180-200, 213, 216, 217, 220; *see also* Portugal, Salazar

fairs, 160; in Angola, 3, 6, 149-50; in Mozambique, 9
Falupe people, Guiné, 104
family, 98, 103, 128; white, 148, 151, 168

Farelay, 63
Farim, Guiné, 4
Fascism, 43, 46, 180-4, 198
Fatima, 233
Fernando Po, 201
feudalism, 13, 20-1, 76-9, 88, 89, 93
firearms, 5, 6, 7, 16, 17, 36, 51, 59, 61, 62, 63, 67, 68, 70, 74, 96, 99, 174
fishing, 209, 217; in Angola, 155, 156
FLING, 233
Fogo Island, Cape Verde, 201
Fontes Pereira, 144
forced labour, 107-8, 109-10, 117-8, 119, 136, 142, 186, 219, 223, 224, 240; *see also* compulsory crop growing
Foreign Office, British, 33, 39, 40, 41, 42, 85, 87, 111; *see also* British Consuls, Great Britain
Fort Jameson, 29
France, in Cape Verde, 217; colonies in Africa, 39, 49, 76, 147, 213; emigration to, 221; investment, 19, 79, 86, 89, 221; islands in Indian Ocean, 9, 10, 15, 26; Revolution, 220; and scramble for Africa, 27, 28, 32, 68, 213; trade with, 3, 4, 5, 6, 7, 10, 16, 25
Franco, General, 44, 45, 181
Freire de Andrade, A.A., 145, 161, 259
Frelimo, 219, 226, 227, 228, 231, 233, 235, 241, 246
frontiers, 27, 28, 29, 30, 68
Fula people, Guiné, 5, 21, 52, 54, 70, 104, 227, 239
Funchal, Madeira, 214

Gabon, 25
Galvão, Henrique de, 105, 118, 119, 162, 187, 222-3, 259
Garvey, Marcus, 132, 145
Gaza kingdom, Mozambique, 57-9, 130, 175
Geba river, Guiné, 4
Germany; colonies in Africa, 49, 56, 79, 121, 147, 169; emigration to, 221; influence in Angola, 37, 40, 41, 67, 68, 89; investment, 86, 221; and Niassa Company, 42, 84; partition agreements with Britain, 33, 35, 36; relations with Portugal in Second World War, 45; and the scramble for Africa, 27, 28, 30, 32, 67; trade, 32, 33, 68; World War I, 40, 41, 61, 63, 68, 70, 108; *see also* South West Africa
Ghana, 223, 233
Gladstone, W.E., 32
Goa, 10, 46, 48, 50, 150, 190, 225; independence of, 223, 224; *see also* India
gold; mines in Cassinga, 89; mines in Manica, 81; trade in, 1, 2, 7, 8, 11; *see also* Rand
Gott, Richard, 243, 254
governors, colonial, 171, 173, 186, 199; of Angola, 3, 4, 18, 24, 151, 154; of Mozambique, 8, 24, 145, 160-2, 175; *see also* high commissioners
GRAE, 232
Great Britain, 32, 49, 75, 114, 147, 168, 184, 213, 234, 235; capital investment, 72, 82-3, 169; and Germany, 33, 35, 40, 63, 89; and Salazar, 45; and slave trade, 14, 15, 25; trade with, 3, 4, 5, 6, 7, 13, 19, 203; Ultimatum from, 25, 28, 29, 30, 31, 33, 34, 77; 1920s, 42, 43, 44, 84, 85; *see also* British consuls, Foreign Office
grémios, 173, 183, 195, 244, 248
Grémio Africana; in Angola, 144; in Mozambique, 145
groundnuts, 18, 69, 94, 188, 192
Guevara, Che, 227
Guiné: 15th-18th centuries, 1-3, 4, 5, 148, 203; 19th century, 20, 21, 26, 28, 97, 212, 213; 20th century, 49, 51, 52, 53, 54, 95, 103, 138, 140, 142, 143, 170, 188, 190, 215, 216-7; *mestiços* in, 142, 143; pacification of, 49, 68-70; war of

independence in, 225, 226, 230, 232, 234, 236, 239, 241, 244, 247; whites in, 148, 152, 240; see also Upper Guinea
Gujerat, 10
Gulf Oil, 232
Gungunhana, 53, 57-8, 130
Gwambe people, Mozambique, 114, 130

Harpers Magazine, 39
Harris, John, 102, 203, 207, 210, 252, 259
Hartley, 8
Hastings, Adrian, 236, 259
health, 114, 141-2, 239; see also epidemics
Helgesson, A., 128, 251, 259
high commissioners, 53, 110-1, 161, 177-80, 186, 191; see also Brito Camacho, António Enes, Mouzinho de Albuquerque, Norton de Matos
Hitler, Adolf, 45, 131
Holy Ghost Fathers, 67, 125, 127
Hornung, James, 43, 91-2, 116, 117; Hornung contract, 91-2, 173, 192; see also Sena Sugar Estates
horse trade, 2
hospitals, 125, 141, 149, 151
House of Lords, 234
Huambo, Angola, 135, 178
Hudsons Bay Company, 78
Huila, Angola, 22, 67, 102, 104, 109, 153, 155
Humbe, 37
Humpata, Angola, 53, 156
Hutcheon, A.B., 108, 111, 254
hydro-electric power, 197, 221, 232, 235, 240

Ibo, Mozambique, 10, 18, 83, 84, 148-9
illiteracy, 152, 154, 166, 170
ILO, 199, 223-4, 240
Imbangala people, Angola, 6
Imperial British East Africa Company, 79

independent churches, 129-34, 228; see also messianism
India, state of, 46, 48, 176, 194, 223, 224, 225; trade with, 8, 94
Indian Ocean, 9, 25, 26
Indians, 10, 13, 17-8, 20, 28, 57, 62, 83, 84, 94, 97, 138, 150, 156, 160, 170
Indígena, status of, 101, 116, 143, 146, 185, 186, 216, 225, 240, 248
industrialisation, 220, 223, 235, 237, 238
Inhambane, Mozambique, 8, 10, 57, 98, 114, 115, 116, 125, 133, 136
Instituto Superior de Estudos Ultramarinos, 162
Integration, 47, 100, 105, 111, 138-42, 166, 167-71, 184, 185
Iron Ore; in Angola 221, 235, 237, 238; in Goa, 223
irrigation, 165-7, 189, 196-7, 240
Islam, 141, 239; in Guiné, 5, 21, 70, 227; in Mozambique, 59, 62-4, 126, 129, 131, 227
Italy, 43, 181, 235
ivory trade, 7, 8, 9, 10, 11, 12, 14, 16, 17, 59, 62, 94, 155

Jardim, Jorge, 246
Jesuits, 125, 148
Jews, 153, 203
Johannesburg, 113, 130; see also Rand
Joseph II of Austria, 188
Junod, Henri, 128, 251, 259
Junta da Exportação de Algodão, 122, 124, 163, 192
Junta de Defesa dos Direitos de Africa, 145
Junta de Desenvolvimento Industrial, 238
Junta Geral, 172

Kafue river, 28
Karanga people, Rhodesia, 8, 52
Kariba, 28
Kasai river, Angola, 6; province of, 30

Kasanje, Angola, 5, 6, 7, 149–50
Katanga, 37, 89, 178
Kazembe, 9
Kazonzola, 132
Kennedy, President J.F., 233
Kenya, 196
Kilwa, 9
Kimbangu, Simon, 132
Kimberley, 19, 38
Kionga, Mozambique, 41
Kongo, kingdom of, 1, 5, 7, 22, 24, 49, 54, 64–6, 124, 131, 203; region, 64–6, 73, 119, 124, 126, 131, 132, 144, 227, 231; *see also* BaKongo people
Koran schools, 141
Kruger, Paul, 34
Kwanyama people, Angola, 67
Kylsant, Lord; *see* Philipps

labour laws, 92, 98, 101, 106–112, 177, 199
labour supply, 12–13, 19, 33, 35, 38, 39, 56, 84, 90, 95, 101, 106–24, 165, 195, 213; in Angola, 39, 66, 110–12, 118, 128, 134; to Mozambique Company, 82, 116; to the Rand, 39, 40, 42, 58, 84, 197; to São Tomé, 207–11; in Zambesia, 87, 91–2, 116; *see also* migrant labour
Lago province, Mozambique, 120
land; African rights, 95, 102–4, 139; in Angola, 18, 19, 49, 102–4, 157, 168; grants to concessionaires, 89–90, 179; grants to immigrants, 153, 164–7; law, 101, 102–4; in São Tomé, 206
Las Palmas, 214
Lassy, Simon, 132
League of Nations, 118, 181
Lebanese, 138
Lebobmbo diocese, Mozambique, 125, 170
Leopold II, 37, 39, 40, 85; *see also* Congo Free State
Leopoldville, 229

Lettow Vorbeck, General Paul von, 41
Lewis and Marks, 84
liberalism, 46
Licungo river, Mozambique, 59
Liga Africana, 145
Liga Angolana, 144, 145, 146
Liga Filafricana, 125, 133
Limpopo river, Mozambique, 57, 58; barrage, 153; settlement scheme, 165, 189, 197
liquor trade, 19, 20, 67, 74, 75, 151, 157, 158, 159, 217
Lisbon, 2, 19, 29, 37, 43, 65, 73, 74, 75, 81, 144, 145, 150, 162, 166, 169, 171, 173, 174, 175, 176, 177, 179, 186, 205, 219, 223, 225, 236, 243, 245
Lisbon Geographical Society, 30, 162
Livingstone, David, 24, 149–50, 260
Loango, 5, 6, 7
Lobito, Angola, 137, 178
Lobo, José de Araujo, 28
Lolo people, Mozambique, 104
London, 30, 37, 177, 236
Long, British Consul General in Lourenço Marques, 131, 254
Lourenço Marques, 113, 131, 159; African population of, 109, 114, 116, 137, 138, 170, 199; government in, 57, 58; *mestiços* of, 144, 145; missions near, 125; railway to Transvaal from, 26, 34, 38, 90, 197, 198; South African plans to control, 35, 40, 42, 43, 179; trade at, 8, 9, 96; whites of, 166, 170
Luabo, Mozambique, 91
Luanda, 18, 22, 64, 65, 108, 111, 125, 132, 148, 178, 221, 223; African population of, 109, 137, 138; *mestiços* in, 143, 144; prize court at, 15; railway from, 30, 178; risings in, 170, 221, 225, 228, 240, 242; trade at, 1, 2, 5, 6, 7, 73; whites of, 150, 151, 166, 170, 172
Luangwa river, 9, 28
Luenha river, Mozambique, 79

Index

Lunda, district of Angola, 93, 125, 132, 135, 141; states, 6, 7, 9, 16
Lurio river, Mozambique, 62, 63, 83, 189
Lyne, R.N., 114, 116, 260

Macanga, Mozambique, 60, 87
Macequece, Mozambique, 159
Machado, J.J., 162
Machado, Vieira, 153
machambas, 122-4, 248; see also compulsory crop growing
Mackay, Wallis, 160, 260
Macmahon, Marshal, 26
Madagascar, 8, 9, 15, 62
Madeira, 1, 102, 155, 201, 214
Madrid, 44
Mafulo, 131
Mafura, 18
Magalhães, José de, 145, 146
Maganja da Costa, Mozambique, 60
Maio Island, Cape Verde, 211, 213, 217
maize, 13, 18, 81, 103, 135, 159, 160, 173, 220
Makonde people, Mozambique, 62, 63, 84, 97, 104, 137, 227, 231
Makua people, Mozambique, 9, 10, 22, 51, 59, 61, 62-4, 70, 84, 112, 119, 120, 227, 239, 241
Malange, Angola, 163
Malawi; see Nyasaland
Mandinga people, Guiné, 5, 104
Manganese, 221
Manganja people, Mozambique, 104
Manica, Mozambique, 8, 9, 28, 31, 34, 60, 79, 156, 159-60, 173; see also Mozambique Company
Manicongo, 54; see also Kongo
Manjacasse, Mozambique, 58; see also Gaza
Marave, chief, 63
marriage, 49, 98, 129, 143, 167-8
Martins, J.P. Oliveira, 205
Martins, Rogerio, 243
Mashonaland, 28, 52, 60; see also, Rhodesia,
Massangano, Mozambique, 22, 60

Massano de Amorim, Pedro, 162
Massingire, Mozambique, 60
Matabele, 29, 59
Matala, Angola, 165
Matamba, Angola, 6, 7
Maugham, R.C.F., 93, 260
Mauritius, 26
Mayotte Island, 26
Mazoe river, Mozambique, 79
Mbundu people, Angola, 6, 22, 51, 128, 132, 138, 227
Mcapi, 130
McMurdo, Colonel, 34, 90
Mello Machado, A.J., 126, 260
Mendonça, Henrique de, 209
Messianism, 129-34
mestiços, 8, 55, 60, 137, 138-47, 148, 149-50, 156, 160, 163, 167-8, 170, 199, 207, 210, 225; numbers of, 142, 212; in war of independence, 225, 227; see also Afro-Portuguese
Methodist Church, 125, 128, 133
migrant labour, 49, 104, 121, 129, 180; in Angola, 134-5; mortality of, 114, 141; to Natal, 19, 98; to Rand, 19, 20, 74, 75, 84, 98-9, 112-5, 145, 191, 197; to South West Africa, 99; see also contract labour, emigration, forced labour
Miranda, A.J., 144
Missions, 27, 32, 49, 50, 54, 71, 106, 133-4, 139, 140, 152; Church of England, 35, 125-6, 133, 170; in Kongo, 24, 49, 64-6, 124-5, 132; in Mozambique, 125-6, 129, 133; among Ovimbundu, 127-8; in Shire highlands, 24, 26, 29, 35; in southern Angola, 49, 67, 125; see also Catholicism, Christianity, Protestantism
Moatize coalfields, Mozambique, 36, 179, 189
Moçamedes Company, 37, 76, 88-9
Mocidade Portuguesa, 184
modus vivendi, 38, 75
Mohamed Musa Sahib (Musa Quanto), 16

Index

Moise Noir movement, 132
Mombasa, 8
monarchism, 161, 182, 222
Mondlane, Eduardo, 228, 232, 252, 260; assassination of, 241
Monomotapa, 54; *see also* Karanga
Mossambazes, 9
Moçamedes, Angola, 22, 67, 96, 110, 153, 155–6, 172, 238
Mourimi movement, 130
Mouzinho de Albuquerque, J., 53n, 62, 84, 126, 153, 154, 162–3, 168, 176, 177, 260
Mouzinho de Silveira, 21
Moxico, Angola, 125
Mozambique Company, 34, 36, 42, 76, 79–83, 86, 91, 116, 156, 159, 176, 179, 186, 192; *see also* charter companies
Mozambique District, 110, 113
Mozambique Island, 7, 8, 9, 36, 85, 148, 150
Mozambique Sugar Company, 76, 91
Mozambique-Transvaal Conventions, 35, 38, 112–15, 179
Mpadi, 131
Mpeseni, 29
MPLA, 226, 227, 232, 241; and Luanda rising, 170, 225
Msiri, 16
Mtoko, 28, 60
muceques, 166, 170
Muchope, Mozambique, 122–3
Muralha, Pedro, 91, 260
Muslim coastal states, Mozambique, 9, 10, 11, 18–20, 21, 22, 51, 59, 60, 61, 62–4; *see also* Angoche, Makua
Mussoco, 55, 86, 88, 106, 248; *see also palhota*, taxation
Mussolini, 43, 181
Muzungos, 21, 57, 60, 62, 86, 103, 248; *see also* Afro Portuguese, chicunda

Nacala, Mozambique, 36, 189
Nalu people, Guiné, 104

Namarral people, Mozambique, 62, 63
Namib Desert, 25
Nampula, Mozambique, 119
Napoleonic wars, 25
Natal, 19, 34, 38, 57, 96, 98
Nationalist movements, 143, 145, 147, 169, 170, 194, 224, 225–6, 229, 231, 234, 241, 246; ideology of, 227–8, 242
NATO, 46, 48, 198, 234–5
Naulila, battle of, 41
Nazis, 43
Nehru, J., 223
Netherlands, 234; trade with Portuguese, 3, 4, 5, 6, 7, 9; wars with Portuguese, 3, 203
Netherlands Railway Company, 34
Neto, Agostinho, 228
Nevinson, Henry, 39, 208, 210, 252, 261
New State; *see* Estado Novo
Ngoni people; diaspora, 21, 57, 103; Mpeseni's, 29; of Natal, 57, 96; of northern Mozambique, 52, 60, 61, 130; *see also* Gaza kingdom
Ngwila, 131
Niassa Company, 39, 41, 42, 62, 76, 83–5, 160, 179, 186; *see also* Charter Companies
Niassa province, Mozambique, 120, 122
Nigeria, 233
Norton de Matos, J.M.R., 110–1, 153–4, 161, 177–9, 180, 195
Nossi Bé, 26
Nova Lisboa, 137
Nyaneka people, Angola 67, 104, 155, 156
Nyanja people, Mozambique, 231
Nyasa, Lake, 29, 35, 36, 59, 62, 133
Nyasaland, 26, 35, 36, 42, 64, 117, 119, 120, 130, 197; Malawi, 226, 233, 239

oil, 90, 179, 221, 232, 235, 237, 243
Okavango river, Angola, 27, 67, 156
Oman, 8

opium, 19; Company, 91
Oporto, 72, 166
Oppenheimer, Ernest, 92
Organisation of African Unity, 232
Ovambo people, Angola, 27, 39, 51, 54, 56, 64, 67-8, 70, 96, 99, 132
Ovimbundu people, Angola, 6, 17, 96-7, 103, 104, 126, 127, 128, 132, 133, 134

PAIGC, 227, 233
Paiva Couceiro, Henrique de, 50, 65, 66, 90, 151, 154, 161, 177, 261
Paiva de Andrada, J., 28, 79
Palestine, 131
palhota, 55, 65, 66, 69, 70, 74, 101, 106, 112, 115, 118, 160, 178, 188, 248
palm oil, 18, 94, 193, 194, 206, 209
Pan-African Congress, 145
Papel people, Guiné, 51, 69
Partido Nacional Africana, 145
Partido Republicano Colonial, 173
Paul, John, 133, 252, 261
Paul VI, Pope, 233
Pélissier, René, 101, 118, 130, 132, 133, 139, 145, 146, 251, 261
Pemba Bay, Mozambique, 153
pepper trade, 2
Pereira, family of, 22, 87
Persian Gulf, 8
Peru, 7, 78
petroleum; see oil
Philipps, Owen, 42, 84
Phoenicians, 50
PIDE, 226, 229, 241; see also police
Pizarro, Francisco, 7
plantations, 150, 194, 200; in Angola, 18, 109, 118, 156-9, 170, 232; in Mozambique, 81, 87, 104, 116, 123, 136, 159-60, 179, 180, 228, 232
Plymouth Brethren, 125
police, 89, 101, 108, 115, 145, 181-2, 198, 199, 228, 230
Pombal, Marques de, 4
population, 98, 122, 136, 138, 142-3, 152, 203; of Cape Verde, 204, 211, 212-3, 215; *mestiços*, 142-3; on Mozambique, 119-120; of São Tomé, 204, 208-9; whites, 152-3, 154, 164
Portugal; 15th-19th century, 2, 7, 10, 12, 13, 14, 18, 20, 21, 25, 49, 57, 69, 96, 98, 150, 155, 175, 210; 19th-century economy, 72-3; colonial trade of, 72-5, 84, 121, 188, 238; exports, 72-3; investment in colonies, 89; manufacturing, 72, 244; under the monarchy, 31, 50, 144, 173, 175-7, 186; under the Republic, 31, 40, 43, 63, 76, 87, 121, 127, 139, 144, 158, 161, 173, 177, 180, 184, 186, 189, 214; under the New State, 43-8, 85, 121, 127, 134, 169, 196, 211; in the 20th century, 37, 41, 42, 100, 101, 146, 152, 166, 169, 216, 219; and the United Nations, 46-8, 223-4; and the wars of independence, 219-47; and the scramble for Africa, 24-33, 76, 77
Portuguese armed forces, 51-2, 53, 58, 61, 67, 69, 98, 150, 151-2, 156, 160, 177, 182, 183, 222, 224, 225, 228-32, 235, 239, 242; Africanisation of, 230, 241-2; and the coup of 1974, 242-3, 244-6
Portuguese language, 2, 127, 188, 203, 216
Portuguese Legion, 184
Portuguese Opposition, 181-2, 221, 222, 225, 228
Praia, Cape Verde, 212, 217
prazos, 10, 21, 22, 23, 55, 56, 59, 60, 61, 77, 78, 85-8, 91-2, 108, 116, 117, 122, 159, 160, 175, 179
press, 144-6, 173, 210, 234, 243
Principe Island; see São Tomé
Protestantism, 64-6, 101, 125-9, 132; 139, 215; see also Missions

Quelimane, Mozambique, 16, 26, 36, 59, 87, 119, 131, 137
Querimba Islands, Mozambique, 9; see also Ibo

Index

railways, 56, 67, 71, 75, 89, 91, 97, 109, 137, 177, 178, 180, 233; Beira-Umtali, 34, 79, 198; Benguela, 37–8, 89, 90, 118, 154, 178, 232; Lourenço Marques-Transvaal, 26, 34, 35, 38, 42, 43, 90, 112, 113, 175, 197; Moçamedes, 37, 89, 99; Mozambique, 189; Nyasaland, 35–6, 42, 83; Quelimane, 36–7; São Tomé, 206; Trans-African, 30, 37, 75, 178; Trans-Zambesia, 179, 189; Zambesi bridge, 83, 198
Rand, 19, 20, 34, 35, 38, 39, 40, 59, 74, 75, 112–5, 116, 126, 145, 180, 197, 198
Red Sea, 9
regedor, 100, 104–6, 108, 248; *see also* chiefs
Representative Institutions, 172–4, 198, 240; in Portugal, 46, 173, 181, 222–3, 224, 228
Ressano Garcia, Mozambique, 113
Réunion, 15, 26
Rhodes, Cecil, 28, 30, 31, 37, 79, 89, 176
Rhodesia; Southern, 8, 30–1, 34, 38, 47–8, 49, 56, 57, 58, 60, 87, 90, 97, 116, 136, 138, 159, 166, 197, 198, 232, 235, 239, 241, 246; Northern, 37, 87, 97, 119, 130, 132, 138, 197; *see also* Zambia
Ribeira Grande, Cape Verde, 203
rice, 104, 136, 191, 193; *see also* compulsory crop growing
rinderpest, 99, 103
roads, 55, 56, 71, 108, 109, 178, 188, 239
Roberto, Holden, 226, 232; *see also* UPA
Robinson, Richard, 182, 252, 261
roças, 204, 205–11, 248; *see also* plantations
Romans, 50
Royal Niger Company, 79
rubber, 17, 49, 65, 66, 69, 70, 74, 81, 84, 85, 95, 96, 97,
Ruo river, Mozambique, 29

Sá da Bandeira, Marques de, 21
Sá da Bandeira town, Angola, 137
Sabi river, Mozambique, 19, 34, 58, 59, 112, 114, 116
Sal Island, Cape Verde, 211, 213, 217
Salazar, António, prime minister of Portugal. 79, 88, 152, 163, 175–200, 217, 222, 244, 245; founding of the New State, 180–184; international affairs, 43–48, 183–4, 224; wars of independence, 219, 221, 236
Salisbury, Lord, 29
salt trade, 2; from Cape Verde, 203, 212–3, 216
Salvation Army, 131
San Luzia Island, Cape Verde, 211
Santa Maria, 223; *see also* Galvão, Henrique
Santiago Island, Cape Verde, 3, 211, 212, 216, 217
Santo Antão Island, Cape Verde, 211, 214
Santos, M. dos, 228
São João dos Angolares, São Tomé, 209
São Miguel fort, Luanda, 148
São Nicolau Island, Cape Verde, 211
São Salvador, Angola, 65, 66
São Sebastião fort, Mozambique Island, 148, 151
São Tomé (and Principe); 15th–18th centuries, 1, 2, 201, 203; 19th century, 5, 19; 20th century, 38, 39, 74, 109, 118, 141, 145, 146, 152, 156, 170, 177, 190, 204–11, 215, 216, 233; investment in, 76; *mestiços* in, 142, 204; labour scandals, 39, 40, 74, 85, 158, 203, 207–11
São Tomé town, 206, 209
São Vicente Island, Cape Verde, 211, 212, 213–4, 215
Schacht, H., 45
schools, 125, 128, 139–41; *see also* education
Sena, Mozambique, 22, 36, 57, 239
Sena Sugar Estates, 43, 76, 77, 81, 91–2, 93, 116, 121, 122, 192

Senegal, 53, 69, 233
Serpa Pinto, A.A. de R., 29, 30
serviçal labour; see contract labour
sesame, 18, 97
Shangaan people, Mozambique, 56, 57, 59, 138
Shire Highlands, Nyasaland, 24, 26, 29, 35, 36
Shire river, 16, 28, 29, 36, 60
Shona people, 60
Sierra Leone, 196
Silva, João Bonifacio Alves da, 60, 62
Silva Cunha, J.M.da, 185
silver, 2
sisal, 87, 116, 194, 195
skilled labour, 109, 137, 143, 195, 197, 221, 246
slave trade, 1, 2, 3, 11, 12, 13, 14, 17, 22, 96, 175, 203; 18th century, 4, 5, 6, 7; 20th century, 109, 207; abolition of, 14, 15, 16, 17, 18, 20, 24, 25, 64, 69, 94, 95, 112, 157; in East Africa, 8, 10, 11, 12, 13, 16, 18, 19, 23, 52, 59, 62, 63, 64
slavery, 14–15, 18, 19, 39, 52, 59, 65, 71, 98, 109, 201, 204; see also *chicunda*
sleeping sickness, 141, 208–9
Smuts, J.C., 35, 42, 43, 68
soap, 191
Soares, Mario, 152
Sociedade de Emigração para São Tomé e Principe, 208
Sofala, Mozambique, 10
Soshangane, 57
Sousa, Manuel Antonio de, 28, 57, 60, 61
Sousa Coutinho, F., 4
South Africa, 15, 19, 35, 37, 38, 40, 41, 43, 47–8, 49, 58, 59, 63, 73, 90, 98, 116, 132, 136, 138, 154, 156, 166, 176, 179, 180, 185, 197, 198, 221, 225, 232, 235, 241, 246; labour agreements with, 35, 38, 42, 56, 74, 75, 82, 84, 112–115, 176, 179
South America, 211, 212, 215

South West Africa, 27, 32, 37, 39, 68, 89, 99, 156, 219
Soviet Union, 46, 47, 183, 233
Spain, 40, 43, 44, 45, 78, 165–6, 181, 198; civil war, 43, 44–5
Spanish America, 78
Spinola, Antonio da, 236, 244–5, 246
Spirit mediums, 129–30, 131
Stalin, 183
Stanley, H.M. 26
steel, 221
Sterling, 34, 35, 74, 83, 112, 176
strikes, 137, 199
sugar, 75, 98, 110, 191, 194, 201, 203, 212, 216, 220; in Angola, 18, 73, 155, 157, 158, 192–3; in Mozambique, 19, 36, 42, 81, 87, 91–2, 116, 159, 179, 192–3; in São Tomé, 1, 203
Sul do Save, Mozambique, 38, 59, 112–113, 115, 125, 138, 241
Swahili, 8, 9, 21, 22, 239
Swakopmund, 37
Swan C.A., 126
Sweden, 241
Switzerland, 86, 125

Tagus river, 42, 102
Tanganyika, 32, 63, 84, 119, 133, 196, 197; Tanzania, 226, 231
tariffs, 10, 27, 34, 36, 73, 74, 75, 83, 94, 121, 158, 175, 213
Tarrafal, Cape Verde, 152, 217
taxation, 7, 9, 22, 55, 59, 63, 65, 81, 82, 83, 86, 87, 105, 114, 118–9, 120, 122, 128, 157, 176, 178
tea, 87, 116, 193, 194, 220
Teixeira de Sousa, Antonio, 37
Teixeira Pinto, J., 69, 262
telegraph 215
Tenerife, 214
Tenreiro, F., 207
Tete, Mozambique, 22, 28, 36, 55, 60, 85, 126, 179, 236, 239, 241, 242
textile industry, 73; in Angola, 191, 192, 238; in Cape Verde, 203, 212; in Mozambique, 221; in Portugal, 191, 192

Thonga people, Mozambique, 56, 59, 98, 128, 129, 138
Three Marias trial, 244
timber, 73, 81, 193
Times, The, 236, 237
Tippu Tib, 16
tobacco, 4, 238
Toco, Simon, 132, 199
Tomás, Admiral, 173, 222
Tonga people, Mozambique, 8, 9, 11, 52, 70
Tongas of São Tomé, 207, 210
towns, 71, 137–8, 146, 148–50; population of, 137
trade monopoly, royal, 1, 2, 3, 8
Trans-African railway, 30, 37, 75, 178
transport, 19, 83, 154, 157, 158, 179, 189, 206, 237; riding, 53, 156
Transvaal, 25, 26, 34, 35, 38, 73, 90, 112, 145; *see also* Rand, South Africa
tribute, 57, 58, 59, 65, 67, 98, 99
Trigo de Morais, 165
Turkey, 131

Uganda 196
Uige, Angola, 135
Umbeluzi, Mozambique, 189
UMCA, 35
Umtasa, 60
Umzila, 57
União Nacional, 184
Union Castle Steamship Co., 42
Union Minière, 37
UNITA, 226, 227, 241
United Nations, 46–8, 198, 199, 223, 224, 233; charter, 46; Committee on Non-self-governing territories, 46; Committee of Six, 47; General Assembly, 47, 233
United States of America, 90, 102, 153, 184, 215, 216, 221, 225; civil war, 155; slave trade with, 7, 10, 15, 16, 26; and wars of independence, 233, 241; and Second World War, 45, 47
UPA, 226, 231, 232, 241; and March

rising, 170, 225
Upper Guinea Coast, 1, 2, 3, 203, 211

Vas dos Anjos, Paul Marianno, 22
Vatican, 233, 244
Versailles treaty, 41
Vietnam, 227
Vili people, 5, 6
Voz d'Africa, 145

wages, 20, 98–9, 119, 166, 168, 189, 214, 243
Walvis Bay, 27
war of independence, 127, 163, 166, 170–1, 174, 219–47; in northern Angola, 225, 228, 229, 231, 232, 240–1
Watchtower, 132
wax trade, 17, 49, 69, 81, 96
West Indies, 203, 215
wheat, 191, 193, 201
Wheeler, Douglas, 144, 250, 251, 262
White Fathers, 125, 236
white settlers, 50, 67, 74, 75, 98, 102, 106, 137, 138, 142, 143, 148–74, 180, 199, 201, 206, 222, 242, 246; convicts, 148, 150–2; in islands, 201–3; immigration schemes, 152–5, 163–7, 178, 197; officials, 50, 148, 160–3; population size, 148, 152, 164; poverty of, 152, 154, 170; in south Angola, 102, 104, 157–8, 168, 173; in Manica, 34, 81, 156, 159–60, 173
Wiese, Carlos, 52, 263
Williams, Robert, 37–8, 39, 42, 43, 89, 90, 118, 154; *see also* railways, Benguela
wine trade, 72, 73, 74, 189, 201
Wiryamu, 236, 237, 242
witchcraft, 130, 132
WNLA, 38, 39, 112–13, 179, 208; *see also* Rand, South Africa, Mozambique-Transvaal Conventions
wolfram, 45
World War, First, 31, 33, 37, 39, 40,

41, 51, 56, 63, 68, 69, 70, 84, 85, 97, 99, 108, 110, 118, 160, 176, 177, 194, 195, 213
World War, Second, 43, 44, 45, 102, 112, 128, 137, 140, 164, 170, 189, 193, 198, 209, 210

Xavier, Ignacio de Jesus, 60
Xhosa people, 132

Yao people, Mozambique, 9, 10, 59, 61-2, 70, 97, 239

Zaire, 226, 233; *see also* Belgian Congo, Congo Free State
Zambesi river, Mozambique, 9, 11, 13, 16, 19, 21, 22, 25, 26, 27, 28, 31, 34, 36, 41, 51, 52, 57, 59, 61, 62, 79, 85-8, 91, 97, 103, 108, 125, 126, 136, 179, 232, 239, 242, 246
Zambesia, 8, 9, 10, 11, 16, 52, 55, 56, 60, 63, 73, 77, 79, 85-6, 93, 103, 106, 109, 112, 116, 123, 130, 156, 191, 192, 228, 239, 241
Zambesia Company, 76, 86-7, 122
Zambia, 28, 29, 125, 226, 233
Zanzibar, 10, 15, 26, 62
Zulu: land, 9; people, 59; *see also* Ngoni
Zumbo, Mozambique, 9, 29, 31, 59